INTRODUCING

JOURNALISM AND MEDIA STUDIES

Editor
Graham Greer

JUTA

Introducing Journalism and Media Studies
Previously published as *New Introduction to Journalism* in

First published 2008

© Juta & Co Ltd, 2008
PO Box 24309, Lansdowne, 7779, Cape Town

ISBN: 978 07021 76678

Project Manager: Sharon Steyn/Seshni Moodley
Editor: Chistina Scott
Proofreader: Bronnwyn Schmidt
Typesetting: Unwembi Communications
Cartoons: Brandon Reynolds
Cover Design: Marius Roux
Indexer: Bronwyn Schmidt
Printed by: CTP Book Printers, Cape

Contents

Preface   v

Introduction   vii

The writing team   xi

Chapter 1   Critical thinking for journalists   1

Chapter 2   The virtues of journalism   18

Chapter 3   Media literacy   34

Chapter 4   Media ideology   44

Chapter 5   Media representation   52

Chapter 6   Narrative   72

Chapter 7   Genre   81

Chapter 8   Media audiences   88

Chapter 9   Ethics and the code of conduct   101

Chapter 10   What is news?   116

Chapter 11   Sources of news   128

Chapter 12   Interviewing   149

Chapter 13   News writing   163

Chapter 14   Newspaper language   182

Chapter 15   Feature writing   190

Chapter 16   Editing – getting it right!   219

Chapter 17   Development journalism   227

Chapter 18   Investigative journalism   235

Chapter 19   Online journalism   243

Sources and reading list   252

Index   256

Preface

This is a book for all who seek stories and want to communicate them to an audience. Journalism is an exciting and rewarding profession, but it is an unforgiving profession for those who do not master the basics. Becoming a good journalist requires constant practice of the craft by continual writing and re-writing, reading and interviewing and obsessively watching how other media organisations present the news on radio, television, print and on the world wide web.

But a great journalist is also sensitive to how the various facets of the media function, almost always as a profit-seeking company seeking to retain specific audiences on a regular basis in order to make the advertisers happy. If your first job is not at a company which has to make a profit in order to survive, then it may well be at a public broadcaster which relies on state-administered licence fees or subsidies to exist. You may find governments and owners and advertisers as demanding as any lobby group – more demanding, sometimes, than the readers or audiences you are meant to serve.

Journalists seek the truth. But journalists should be intensely aware that in a world of powerful economic, military and political interests, there may be no neutral narrative, or accidental audience. Ideologies shape our viewpoints, even when they are presented as common sense or the inevitable nature of life.

Journalists in the developing world, as well as journalists in immigrant communities in the industrialised economies, seem to have a particular passion for listening to the voices of the poor and the powerless. The time seems ripe for a new book that incorporates lessons learned and changes in approach. This book has been written to make journalism especially accessible to many young people interested in journalism and media studies who do not have English as their mother tongue. Yet many journalism textbooks are either from the USA or the United Kingdom and not easily understood by English second language learners.

To this end I have included contributions from some of the finest thinkers, academics and media professionals I know, including Marc Caldwell from the University of KwaZulu-Natal in Durban and Tara Turkington, a senior lecturer in online journalism at the University of the Witwatersrand in Johannesburg who also runs her own content and design company, Flow Communications. Other contributors include Renitha Rampersad, who obtained a doctorate in philosophy and literature at the University of Zululand and currently heads the public relations department at the Durban University of Technology; Richard Frank, a news website designer and online journalism trainer and researcher, currently working in the private sector in Gauteng, and freelance journalist Richard Pithouse, who has worked as a philosophy lecturer and researcher at the University of KwaZulu-Natal for 11 years and has published widely in various academic disciplines. They made writing this new book so much easier and far more fun. And it was all done while living on different continents, as Marc, Richard, Tara and Renitha are all based in South Africa, as I was until recently.

Ensuring that the text was accessible to all was the task of the editor (and my wife), Hajira Vahed and also the responsibility of author, journalist and editor Christina Scott in Cape Town. Lastly, special thanks to the 2004 Sixth Form Media Studies students of the Royal Russell School in Surrey in England who under difficult circumstances test-drove the relevant chapters. Their help was invaluable.

I hope this book plays some part in helping aspiring journalists the world over to achieve their goals.

Graham Greer
Director of the Centre for Journalism,
Trinity & All Saints College, Leeds, United Kingdom

Introduction

Why write a new textbook on journalism when there are numerous adequate ones available?

Well, the answer is simple. I believe the time is ripe for a book that will attempt to bridge the divide that has grown between media studies and journalism. I will nail my colours to the mast (an idiom meaning "I will make my opinion public") immediately by declaring that all journalists and media workers should be critical thinkers, schooled in media ethics, with a working knowledge of key concepts in media studies.

I am often asked by lecturers and students how they can go about teaching and learning all they need to know about journalism and the media. As with other sectors in education, schools of journalism and media studies worldwide are facing severe budget cuts. In order to generate funding, many are offering "popular" courses often taught by lecturers who are not qualified or experienced enough to teach them. In the English-speaking world, we are finding that more and more students in our classes no longer speak English as their first language or even as their second language. Many lecturers are primarily content specialists and have not been taught how to promote learning at tertiary level. The problems facing both teacher and student become clear.

In a report to the South African National Editors' Forum annual general meeting in 1999, I leaned heavily on former British journalist, financier and educator Patrick Coldstream's speech to the fifth United Nations Educational, Scientific and Cultural Organisation (UNESCO) consultation on higher education. I emphasised that graduates must not be seen as products shaped and constructed by educators to the specification of a demanding consumer, the employer. Good educators cannot subscribe to a partnership on these terms. The educator's calling is do with critical reflection, not conformity to existing norms. Coldstream, now a visiting professor at the University of London, said that education "is about widening the range of people's choices in life, not about narrowing them down." (Coldstream, 1997).

Business, government and educators are going to have to make every effort to promote lifelong learning as a part of our natural lifestyle. According to the British government's policy-shaping White Paper on higher education, "Lifelong learning implies a fundamental shift from a 'once in a lifetime' approach to higher education to one of educational progression linked to a process of continuous personal and professional development."

Change today is rapid. Often what we learn is already obsolete (out of date). Educated people are no longer just those with a certain level of achievement, knowledge, understanding and skill. Educated people are those who have learnt to go through life in a spirit of critical but humble questioning and learning. Students must at the end of their tertiary education be less impressed with what they have achieved. But they must be able to take advantage of limitless opportunities ahead. They must be inspired with a passionate inquisitiveness to continue learning through life.

What does it mean when we say we want to become lifelong learners? Australian and British academic Paul Ramsden, (Ramsden, 1992) outlines the following:

To analyse ideas or issues critically

To develop intellectual and thinking skills

To comprehend principles or generalisations

I subscribe to Paul Ramsden's theory of "teaching as making learning possible". I see my role as a teacher as one of producing excellent entry-level journalists and media workers.

I see the lecturer as a facilitator of learning, a source of encouragement and a guide when the road for individual students gets tough. More time should be spent with those learners who need the teacher's expertise in helping them to help themselves. This new journalism textbook has been shaped into more of an experience where learners are constantly challenged.

What lecturers will discover is that as a guide to students, your expertise will be stretched far more than ever before. Students left to explore the discipline in a structured way are far more demanding and their queries far more challenging. Some of their questions you will find very difficult to answer. Although initially slightly embarrassing, students will no longer see you as all-knowing but as someone who can direct them in their learning. The essential thing is that the students will be learning.

From the feedback I have received, the students enjoy and prefer the experience. They seemed more relaxed with their writing and more prepared to attempt difficult concepts and tasks. You, the lecturer, will notice that students start to do unsolicited work to improve their knowledge and skills. Students begin to grow in maturity and this, you will notice, is reflected in their participation in the classroom because they feel more empowered to explore the discipline.

Constantly remind yourself that what may have worked with one group of students may not work with another group. Student groups are dynamic; they change in personality from class to class. We have to be responsive to the abilities and needs of our learners and be sensitive to their current learning environment.

From my observations and discussions with other journalism lecturers from journalism schools worldwide, I formed the opinion that insufficient work was being done to encourage the students to become active, reflective and critical thinkers and learners. Most of the effort revolved around getting the learners to know the content of their subjects. I am also of the opinion that journalism courses in general are not learner-centred because their focus generally is only on what industry wants and not the learner's development.

During 2000, some learner-centred teaching methods were introduced to the first year practice of journalism course at M.L. Sultan Technikon, now the Durban University of Technology, in the province of KwaZulu-Natal. These teaching methods were extended in 2001 and presented in a far more structured and disciplined manner. The focus was on the promotion of active and reflective learning to facilitate and enhance the central skills needed to become a journalist - the ability to systematically gather, analyse and communicate information - skills that are central to higher education.

Entry level journalists are expected to think and reflect critically from day one. According to American journalism professor Betty Medsger,

> the question, What's the story? remarkably concentrates the mind. It is where the journalist begins. Learning how to answer that question involves the development and application of agile perceptions as well as continuous intellectual examination and growth. It also involves asking many questions, What? Where? When? Why? Who? How? These are habitual questions that lead to stories. Whether executed masterfully or superficially or badly, it is, nevertheless, an intellectual process of critical thinking and decision-making. To be a journalist demands both critical and reflective thinking in order to function effectively. Teaching journalism involves teaching a multifaceted concentration of the mind. Students entering the journalism classroom are asked to think - carefully, critically, reflectively and precisely - and to do so beyond their own interests, to think of the public's interest and needs. (Medsger, 1996).

The public demands that journalists have a mastery of the topics they write about so that they can interrogate experts in that topic with regard to any current events that occur and relay that information to their readers. Active learning demands that the learner analyse and reflect upon a topic. It is not sufficient for journalists to simply know something, for they must be able to absorb and communicate new understanding about it. It is important that trainee journalists learn from the beginning of their training to learn on their own and to be able to teach themselves. They cannot rely on learning only from their teachers. Once they are qualified, they will not be spoon-fed.

My research concluded that:

Learner-centred teaching methods proved successful in promoting the active and reflective learning that is required of a trainee journalist.

Group work, used effectively, does promote active and reflective learning.

The introduction of learning portfolios promotes active and reflective learning.

The writing team

Graham Greer is director of the Centre for Journalism at Trinity and All Saints College, part of Leeds University. He is the author of *A New Introduction to Journalism*, a Juta publication. His research interest is journalism education, particularly in emerging democracies. He was a senior lecturer in journalism in South Africa. Graham represented the South African National Editors' Forum on the inaugural national body dealing with language and communication for the South African Qualifications Authority. He has published, written and edited business, industrial, sport and social awareness publications. He is a former theatre critic for the Sunday Tribune newspaper in Durban and a feature writer for what is now The Witness newspaper in Pietermaritzburg.

Hajira Vahed directs Loxley Projects, a UK-based education consultancy in London. She has extensive lecturing and teacher training experience in academic development, English, Teaching English to Speakers of Other Languages (TESOL) and art. She has published widely in her field and is a co-author of *Investigating Arts and Culture*, a Juta publication. Hajira was vice-president of the non-profit KwaZulu-Natal Society of Arts or KZNSA art gallery in Durban as well as deputy gender convenor for the South African Democratic Teachers Union. She was also vice-president of the University of Durban-Westville Convocation.

Richard Pithouse is an independent writer and researcher and a former research fellow at the Centre for Civil Society at the University of KwaZulu-Natal. He also taught philosophy for 7 years at what was then the University of Durban-Westville and taught politics and economics at the Workers' College in Durban. He has published widely in both journalistic and academic fields. His work has been translated into French, German, Spanish, Italian, Japanese, Turkish and Zulu.

Marc Caldwell is a lecturer in Culture, Communication and Media Studies at the University of KwaZulu-Natal, South Africa, where he teaches undergraduate and postgraduate courses. After working as a reporter and sub-editor on the Daily Dispatch newspaper in the Eastern Cape, Marc lectured in the Department of Journalism and Public Relations at Natal Technikon (now the Durban University of Technology). He is completing a Ph.D. on journalism practice and ethics.

Tara Turkington is a freelance journalist and journalism lecturer at the University of the Witwatersrand in Johannesburg who has worked as a sub-editor, journalist and freelancer and has written and photographed for a wide variety of newspapers and magazines. She now runs her own company, Flow Communications.

Renitha Rampersad heads the department of public relations management at the Durban University of Technology. She chairs the KwaZulu-Natal region of

Public Relations Institute of Southern Africa and has completed a Ph.D on corporate social investment and HIV/Aids in South Africa.

Richard Frank was the founding editor of *DITonline*, a student news website at the Durban University of Technology. Richard Frank is a news website designer and online journalism trainer and researcher, currently working in the private sector in Johannesburg.

1 Critical thinking for journalists

chapter ◀──────────────────────────────────────

Outcomes

By the end of this chapter, you will able to:

▶ Explain the difference between journalists and public relations officers.

▶ Identify the structure of an argument.

▶ Analyse and evaluate premises, claims and conclusions.

▶ Explain three ways in which the premises of an argument can support a conclusion.

▶ Explain the different types of false ideas or errors (fallacies).

▶ Consider the link between powerful forces in society and the media.

▶ List strategies used to influence the media.

Introduction

It is important to make a clear distinction between journalism and public relations. Journalism is the struggle to tell the truth. Good journalists are loyal to the truth and seek to discover and report the truth even when this makes them unpopular with powerful forces in society or with ordinary people. Public relations aims to persuade people to accept a particular point of view. Good public relations practitioners are loyal to whoever has paid them to take on a particular project – be it persuading people to buy a particular product or to vote for a particular political party. Because readers, listeners and viewers place more trust in journalism than in public relations, people who seek to influence the public increasingly seek to present their public relations projects as journalism or to influence journalists to reproduce public relations material as journalism. For example, just as a company launching a new product will hire a public relations firm to market that product, a government launching a new policy, be it a war or a new economic strategy, will often hire a public relations firm to market the new policy.

Public relations practitioners need to think strategically. This means that the key question that they need to ask themselves is 'How can I be most effective in persuading people to believe what I have been paid to persuade them to believe?' In order to answer this question well, they need to have a good knowledge of what people already believe, why they believe those things and what they are likely to accept as true.

Journalists need to think critically. Critical thinking does not mean thinking that is always in opposition or always negative. Critical thinking means that the key question is, 'Is this true?'. Journalists have to ask themselves a range of questions:

Is this issue of interest to my readers?
Do I have the time and resources to pursue a particular story?
How can I best present my story to my readers?

Journalism emphasises critical thinking, always motivated by a fundamental commitment to discover the truth and this requires asking all kinds of questions about things like the accuracy of claims, the logic of arguments and the ways in which prejudice and power can limit our vision.

Thinking critically requires us to identify and evaluate arguments.

Identifying arguments

Claims and conclusions

An argument does not necessarily refer to a verbal fight. It is a claim with reasons given to persuade us of the truth of the claim. The *Conceptual Dictionary*, edited by AP Craig, H. Griesel and LD Witz, says, "A good argument involves building a case around something. It involves developing an argument for or against something by using evidence [*proof*] to backup or support your claims." (Craig et al, 1994).

The reasons given to support a claim will also be claims. So an argument is usually made up of a series of claims offered in order to persuade us of the truth of a main claim. The main claim is referred to as the argument's conclusion. The statements given to support the conclusion are referred to as the argument's

Definitions

Argument

Claim

Premise

premises or reasons. A series of statements is only an argument when there are premises aimed at persuading us of the truth of a conclusion.

Here is an example of a series of statements with premises that seek to persuade us to accept the truth of a conclusion:

The rates of cancer and respiratory illness are 47 times higher in Wentworth, Durban than in the rest of South Africa.

Sulphur dioxide pollution is known to cause unusually high rates of cancer and respiratory illness.

The only major sulphur dioxide polluter in the area is the oil refinery.

Therefore we can conclude that ...

Here, on the other hand, is an example of a set of statements that is linked to a common theme but does not contain premises designed to persuade us of the truth of a conclusion.

A lot of people in Wentworth are sick.
My mother lives in Wentworth.
The oil refinery is the biggest employer in Wentworth.
My brother worked there for years before he got a job in Johannesburg.

structure of an argument

First statement [premise]

Premise(s). [thematic statements, claims, reasons]

Sub-conclusions (optional)

Main conclusion / therefore

⑩ MINUTE TASK

In small groups consider the following example:
- I have lived in Wentworth all my life.
- I am proud to be from Wentworth.
- My father lived there his whole life.
- I work at the refinery.
- Without that job I wouldn't be able to look after my family.
- It is true that some people are sick.
- If the refinery was closed down I'd lose my job.
- Hundreds of other people would lose their jobs too.
- Being unemployed is worse than being sick.
- I hope that the refinery isn't closed down.
- Most of my friends live in Wentworth.

Can you identify which of these statements is the conclusion to the argument? Which premises support that conclusion? Write down the premises and conclusion.

Finding the argument

Most of the time, arguments are not set out very clearly in an interview. At times, someone will make some statements that are the premises of his conclusion and other statements that are not a direct part of his or her argument. Often people will use words like 'because' or 'therefore' to indicate that a conclusion is about to follow a premise. When people are speaking or writing less formally or using English when it is not their mother tongue or when they are unaccustomed to being interviewed, you will have to work out which of their statements conclude their argument and which of their statements support that conclusion.

When you encounter a list of statements that include an argument, perhaps in a press release or a press conference, the first step is to extract the premises and conclusion from the rest of the statements. Remember that the conclusion is only the statement or statements which the person is seeking to persuade you to accept as true; the premises are only offered to persuade you of the truth of the conclusion.

In the case above, the argument would be as follows:

Without jobs people can't look after their families.
If the refinery was closed down a lot of people would lose their jobs.
Being unemployed is worse than being sick.
Therefore ...

Sub-conclusions

It is important to note that there will often be sub-conclusions on the way to the main conclusion. Pick out two sub-conclusions in the argument below and complete the final conclusion:

Our football team is doing really badly.
Our players are very good though.
Therefore the problem is not with the players.
The problem is that our coach is suffering from depression.
Therefore we need a new coach.
Lu Wen is an excellent coach and he is looking for a job.
Therefore ...

Decoding indirect arguments

The arguments put forward to support a claim can be explicit, which means they are very clear and obvious. But arguments can also be implicit, relying on assumptions and implications which can be hidden. For example, if someone says that it is true that the country's economy is improving because evidence from the tax office shows that many new jobs have been created, they are providing an explicit argument. The growth in employment as demonstrated by the records in the tax office supports their claim that the economy is improving. But if someone says that the national economy is improving because the president or prime minister says so, then they are providing an implicit argument that the political head of the country knows what is happening with the economy and that he or she tells the truth, in order to support their claim that the economy is improving.

It often happens that people don't state their premises or conclusions directly. In these cases we have to make what is implicit, explicit. Consider the following two examples:

> Privatisation will be good for the poor.
> I know this because the president said this on television last night.
> Therefore ...

> Rich people know what is good for the economy
> Rich people support privatisation

In the first argument on privatisation, there are at least two implications or hidden premises. The first assumption is that the president really does know what the impact of privatisation will be on the poor. The second premise is that the president is telling the truth. So if we write out the full argument it might look like this:

> The president knows how privatisation will affect the poor – implied premise
> The president told the truth on TV last night – implied premise
> The president said that privatisation will be good for the poor.
> Therefore ...

Answer

I support privatisation.

Here is a second example of implicit reasons being buried in an argument on the same topic, privatisation.

> Rich people know what is good for the economy.
> Rich people support privatisation.

The second argument may look like this when we take the implied statements into account:

> Rich people know what is good for the economy.
> Everybody benefits from a good economy – implied premise
> Rich people support privatisation.
> Therefore I am for privatisation – implied conclusion

We put the implied statements in brackets to indicate that while they were not stated directly, they still need to be taken into account when we analyse the argument. Note that in the first example there are two implied premises and in the second example there is an implied premise and an implied conclusion.

Read the business section of a local newspaper, or a financial weekly news magazine. Can you detect any examples of implied statements?

Establishing clarity

Sometimes establishing clarity in an interview is quite straightforward. It is just a matter of making sure that we, as journalists, understand what is being said by the person being interviewed. The easiest way to do this is to put the premises and conclusions into your own words and then to check with the person or people making the claim that you have understood it correctly. However it is often the case that people purposefully seek to make things so complex that they are unclear to the journalist (and sometimes to the person making the statement!). This is done in order to sound so incredibly intelligent that the interviewee thus prevents criticism, or to disguise the fact that the person in question actually has nothing new to say. This represents an opportunity for the baffled journalist to insist on clarity (rather than assuming that there's something wrong with himself or herself) and to say: 'I'm sorry, I don't understand. Please repeat in clearer language.'

Answer

"As I said before, our acceptance of certain ideas about economic policies means that we don't have any more money to spend on education."

⑤ MINUTE TASK

In pairs, translate this statement into plain English.
A government minister said "I still subscribe to my previously articulated position that macro-economic fundamentals and our commitment to good governance in line with international norms poses a serious challenges to expanding social investment in pedagogy."

We can translate his or her sentence into simple English without losing any of its meaning. The plain version is a lot less intimidating [*frightening*] and a lot clearer and makes it much easier for us and our readers to ask questions about the minister's claim. And once things have been made much clearer we will often find that we no longer feel intimidated. For example, if the government is about to spend a huge amount of money on weapons, it will be easier for journalists to challenge the minister's claim that there is no tax money to spend on education. This also raises the value of follow-up questioning for clarity, bearing in mind that the inevitable response from government ministers is: 'well, that's another department, go ask them, this is my budget.' We have to challenge the idea that budgets are handed down from on high, like the Ten Commandments to Moses on Mount Sinai.

What are the relevant facts?

Removing emotion

Often the emotion with which the statement is made will be a newsworthy fact. However, the feeling accompanying the statement has no bearing on the statement's validity [*soundness, authority*]. So when we extract an argument from a statement in order to assess its validity, we must just extract the claims and not the emotions that surround them.

Consider the following series of statements by a police officer.

> I am outraged at this accusation!
> I will fight to defend my good name no matter how long it takes!

> All the police officers who put their lives at risk for this nation will be deeply offended by this unfounded accusation!

> I've never met the man who accuses me of taking the bribe!

> My family have suffered terribly through this attack on my good name by this dishonest man!

The argument made here is simply as follows:

> I have never met the man who accused me of taking a bribe.
> Therefore ...

Answer

I am innocent of the accusation.

The police officer's emotional protestations of innocence may make us want to believe it to be true, without examining the facts. But if we want a rational [*based on reason, realistic*] assessment of the claims, we need to focus on the relevant facts.

Evaluating arguments

Once we have recognised that an argument has been made and have extracted the premises and conclusion from the rest of the statements, we are ready to evaluate the argument. There are two basic questions that a journalist must ask when evaluating [*assessing*] an argument:

> Can I accept the premises as true?
> Do the premises support the conclusion?

Is it obvious?

The first test of acceptability of premises is whether or not they are clear. If they are vague or ambiguous [*unclear*] then they cannot lead to a valid conclusion. Consider the following examples:

> The government is very concerned about poverty.
>
> Therefore, they would never make an agreement with the World Bank that would harm the poor.
>
> Therefore the government's agreement to charge school fees for primary education won't harm the poor.

In this case the first premise is far too vague to be of any use. It does not lead on to the sub-conclusion because we just don't know what the government's 'concern about poverty' involves in practice.

> It is not safe to drink and drive.
> Michael drinks.
> Therefore Michael should not be allowed to drive the school bus.

In this case the second premise is not sufficiently clear. It could mean anything from 'Michael likes to have a few drinks after work with his friends on Fridays' to 'Michael is an alcoholic and is regularly drunk during working hours'. In the first case, Michael's social drinking after hours would not ordinarily bar him from driving the school bus. But if Michael was an alcoholic of any kind, then it wouldn't be safe for him to drive the school bus. So the second premise is just too vague to be useful.

Where's the evidence?

Powerful forces in society – whether political, economic, religious or cultural – seek to influence the media all the time. Often, they will make claims, involving impressive-sounding numbers or big words, that are presented as statements of fact. Often we are told that there is some sort of expertise behind the claim.

Most people feel intimidated when a claim by powerful people, organisations or countries is presented as a fact. They feel that they are not experts. They retreat, feeling that they have no ability or right to question the claim and that it must just be accepted as the truth. But while it is true that there is such a thing as specialist knowledge, it is also true that scientists, academics and other people with specialist knowledge:

> often disagree with each other;
> have often been proved to be wrong;

are often far more loyal to powerful forces in society than to the independent pursuit of truth;

often have biases;

may be unaware of their biases; and

sometimes just make silly mistakes.

This does not mean that journalists should always reject the claims of scientists, researchers and other experts with years of experience in their fields. But journalists should understand that science and other forms of expertise progress through debate and discussion within a community of experts and that many errors are made along the way.

Claims

Does the claim make sense?

If journalists are presented with a claim that is presented as a fact, the first thing that they should do is to adopt a critical attitude to the claim in order to see if it makes sense to them. You should always ask yourself the following questions:

Who is making this claim?

How did they arrive at this claim?

Who benefits from this claim?

Should I accept this claim?

Are there any other questions that a journalist should ask of himself or herself before conducting an interview?

Who is making this claim?

This question is important because we need to know if the individual or organisation making the claim is working for a powerful force in society or if they are attempting to pursue truth independently. It can happen that powerful organisations, governments or big companies can produce research that is designed to be part of public relations campaigns (such as oil companies which fund institutes whose research rubbishes claims of global warming, or tobacco companies whose medical doctors hide evidence of nicotine addiction). Research is not always a contribution to the development of knowledge. For example, if a research report has been issued which claims that casinos help to reduce poverty, we should certainly seek an independent assessment of the report. Particularly if we discover that the economist who produced the report was funded by a company that wants to build casinos, we should be wary of simply repeating the report's conclusions. Moreover we should also draw our reader's attention to the fact that the report was funded by people with a vested [*having an unquestionable right to the possession of property or a privilege*] interest. However, if the report has been produced by an economist who is working in a university department without external funding, it is more likely to be an honest attempt to establish the truth. But we will still need to engage with it critically.

We also need to know if the individual or organisation making the claim has a record of generating accurate claims. A past record of making accurate claims is not a guarantee that all future claims will be accurate but it does mean that we should at least take them seriously. On the other hand, if a person or organisation has a record of making inaccurate claims, it is possible that they may make an accurate claim one day. Their past record should make us proceed with healthy suspicion.

How did they arrive at this claim?

This question is very important because it often happens that research is just done badly. For example in South Africa's first democratic elections in 1994, an opinion poll indicated that the well-known liberation movement, the African National Congress, had far more support than their far more conservative rivals, the Inkatha Freedom Party, in the Indian Ocean province of KwaZulu-Natal. The poll turned out to be inaccurate when election day came. The Inkatha Freedom Party won control of the province. Although the research for this opinion poll was done by a well-respected company, it was done badly. The research was based on telephone interviews. Most people in the poor rural regions could not afford telephones prior to the widespread use of cellphones, and so the poll had a bias to people living in the urban areas. Because the Inkatha Freedom Party's support is traditionally strongest in rural areas, the opinion poll badly underestimated their support levels. Any journalist who was thinking critically would have realised this if he or she had asked the company how they arrived at their claim.

Similarly, had if a survey into the rate of HIV infection in a particular area was based on interviews, it might well underestimate the rate of infection. Why? Because most people will not tell a stranger that they are HIV positive. However, a survey based on blood tests is likely to give a far more accurate result as long as the samples were generated randomly and ethically and people knew that their individual results would not be made public.

Often a journalist will be able to make important observations about the value of the method used to generate the evidence simply by reading the report. But it is always useful to get the views of other people working in the particular field. A one-off survey will not be as reliable as part of a longitudinal or long-term survey, in which researchers go back to the same people over and over again, building up a relationship of trust. A medical survey based on 34 people filling in a questionnaire about their eating habits or sex life cannot be used to judge large numbers of people – too few people participated, and the risk of inaccuracy is very high. On the other hand, a well-constructed survey of fewer than 5 000 people, if it is representative of the demographics of the country, can sometimes provide important insights into national health, politics or labour issues.

Should I accept this claim?

If it seems that a claim is being made by an expert (or team of experts) without vested interests and that appropriate methods have been used to arrive at the conclusions, we should take it seriously. But that does not mean that we should assume that it is correct. We should still get a least one independent assessment of the claim: we should seek the opinion of at least one expert who is not connected to the people or project that generated the claim.

Once we have done all this we can use the claim in our reporting. Where there are questions of vested interests, questions about the methodology used to generate the claim or doubts about the claim from independent experts or other forces in society, these should be drawn to the attention of readers. Having said that, journalists need to be cautious about people with pseudo-expertise, who often claim that there is a conspiracy underway. There are many examples of how AIDS denialists, some of them highly educated, have manipulated the media by sounding so utterly convincing. But none of their claims have been substantiated in rigorously peer-reviewed academic journals. They only quote very selectively from the reliable evidence to advance their own agenda – something a journalist might only pick up on if the information is checked with at least two other sources. And people with pseudo-expertise are often self-employed, claiming that traditional educational and research institutions are too restrictive – another possible warning signal. Similar issues come up often in hot debates such as genetic engineering, genetically modified crops, stem cells, abortion, global warming, biofuels, creationism versus evolution and so on.

The conclusion of an argument

Are the premises relevant to the conclusion?

People often make arguments in which all the premises are correct but all or some of the premises are not directly relevant to the conclusion. Sometimes that is accidental. Sometimes people purposefully make an argument with accurate but irrelevant premises in order to strengthen their argument.

Consider the following examples:

> My father really doesn't like cricket.
> My mother doesn't like cricket either.
> Therefore, my brother won't want to go to the cricket match.

The fact that my father and mother don't like cricket doesn't have anything to do with whether or not my brother likes cricket. Perhaps my brother would go to a cricket match even if he doesn't like cricket – maybe to work there or to meet someone there.

> The blues is a great American music tradition.
> Robert Johnson and John Lee Hooker were both American.
> Robert Johnson and John Lee Hooker were both great blues musicians.
> Ali Farka Touré was from Mali.
> Therefore, Ali Farka Touré was not a blues musician.

The premises in this argument are all true and have some connection to the broad themes of blues music and Ali Farka Touré. But none of them have anything to do with the actual claim in the conclusion, which is that Ali Farka Touré (1939 - 2006) was not a blues musician.

What would you do in an interview if the person being interviewed made such claims?

Do the premises support the conclusion?

There are three different ways in which the premises of an argument can offer support to a conclusion. They are deduction, induction and analogy.

Deduction

Definitions

Deductions

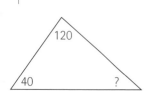

Deduction is the kind of logic [*ability to reason*] used in mathematics. In an argument worked out by reasoning, the premises, if they are true, make the conclusion certain beyond any doubt. For example:

> The angles of a triangle add up to 180 degrees.
> Triangles always have three angles.
>
> In triangle X the first angle is 120 degrees and the second angle is 40 degrees.
>
> Therefore the third angle in triangle X must be ... (fill in the blank) degrees.

Here is a non-mathematical example of a deductive argument:

> A bachelor is an unmarried man.

Sanjeev is an unmarried man.

Therefore …

Answer

Sanjeev is a bachelor.

The truth of deductive argument stems from the definitions of the words and concepts that we are using. Deductive reasoning can give us certain conclusions. But it can only make explicit the meaning that is implicit in the definitions of the words and concepts that we are using. Some people only want to use deductive reasoning because of its accuracy. However, because it cannot be applied in many situations, we have to also use less accurate forms of reasoning in order to make sense of our world.

Induction

Inductive arguments, which reach a conclusion based on close observation, are not absolutely certain. They are based on the principle that past experiences can give us a reasonable expectation of how things will work out in the future. For a long time philosophers in Europe argued that if something had happened often enough, we could be reasonably certain that it would always happen. Less than a century after the death of Jesus Christ, the Roman writer Juvenal wrote in Latin that something which could not be proven was 'a rare bird in the lands, and very like a black swan'. For 1 500 years, European writers used the example of swans, arguing that all the swans that they and everyone they knew had seen, had been white. Therefore inductive reason should lead us to conclude with certainty that all swans are white. But when Dutch explorer Willem de Vlamingh became the first European to sight a black swan in 1697 in Australia, he saw what the Ab-original peoples already knew: the swans there were black!

Definitions

Induction

Probable

Political leaders in Uganda, Zimbabwe and Namibia have told the media that homosexuality is un-African because they don't know any homosexuals. Is this an example of inductive reasoning?

Although inductive reason can't give us absolute certainty, it can tell us that something is probable [*likely to happen*] or highly probable. For example, the fact that no cases of smallpox have been reported anywhere in the world for decades means that it is highly likely that there will never be another smallpox epidemic. But it is possible that smallpox could return if the existing virus samples were mishandled in a laboratory or even through evolution.

Here are some examples of inductive arguments:

My university classes begin at 08H00.

Whenever I have left for university after 07H00, I have been late.

This morning I left at 07H15.

Therefore …

Answer

I will (probably) be late.

People in this village have voted against the government in every election since independence.

Therefore ...

Analogy

Arguments from analogy [*comparison*] are based on the assumption [*acceptance without proof*] that what has been true in one case is likely to be true in other, similar, cases. These arguments do not generate absolutely certain conclusions but they can give us a reasonable possibility of accuracy.

Consider the following examples and fill in the blanks:

My friends Kwame and Kwesi found the London Underground easy to use. Therefore when I visit London, I will probably ...

Countries that have started HIV/AIDS medication programmes have reduced the rate of new infections because people on antiretroviral drugs are less infectious.

Therefore an effective HIV/AIDS treatment programme in Bangladesh will probably ...

Fallacies

Does the link between the premises and the conclusion avoid the most common fallacies [*a false idea, error*]?

We have to use our capacity to reason, our logic, to evaluate the extent to which premises offer support to a conclusion. We have to consider each case on its own merits. There are some very common errors that people make when they are trying to think logically. It is useful to familiarise yourself with them and to make sure that you aren't making any of these errors when you are trying to see if a conclusion follows logically from the premises that are offered to support it. There are many different types of fallacies. Some are explained in the following table.

Type of Fallacy	Explanation	Your Examples
Prejudice fallacy	People often believe that they have a right to project their fears and anxieties on to groups of people who they think are different to them because of their race, culture, religion, language or sexual orientation. This always leads to illogical thinking because people make their own choices and must be judged by their own choices.	
Slippery Slope fallacy	It is often claimed that if we tolerate or allow one thing, it will lead to a whole lot of other things with much more extreme consequences. This can never be assumed and must, like all other claims, be supported with evidence.	
Straw Man fallacy	When there is a debate or disagreement, people often misrepresent their opponents' view. They then attack the misrepresentation rather than the actual view of their opponents. For example, someone is against the death penalty as a tool of effective law enforcement and feels that better policing resulting in higher rates of arrest and conviction would achieve more. You would be guilty of the straw man fallacy if you said that this means we should be soft on crime.	

20 MINUTE TASK

In pairs, suggest your own examples based on your experiences or observations to illustrate each type of fallacy. Write your answers in the table.

Power relations

Questions of power will be dealt with later in this book. It is vital for journalists to be aware of power relationships because in general, it is the powerful forces in society that have the capacity to seek to influence the media. The most powerful forces in society are usually powerful organisations or individuals in the realm of politics, business or institutionalised religion and culture. They often seek to influence the media by coercion, persuasion or seduction.

Common coercive strategies

Common coercive [*enforced or by force*] strategies for influencing media include:

The withdrawal or threatened withdrawal of advertising (often used by cosmetic companies against women's magazines).

Taking costly legal action against the publication.

Presenting the publication or journalist as an enemy of the people or an agent of a foreign power.

Bombarding a newsroom with faxes, emails and letters to the editor and constantly demanding coverage.

Outright repression.

Can you think of other coercive strategies that are used? Are there useful ways to counteract, prevent or expose coercive strategies?

Common persuasive strategies

Common persuasive strategies for influencing the media include:

The production of press releases and research reports that seek to persuade journalists to a point of view.

Inviting journalists to meetings or conferences, where experts with impressive qualifications and titles present a particular point of view.

Making a journalist's life so easy by producing what is asked for – whether it's sound bites or good photographs or press releases which don't need to be altered – that reporters grow reliant on this instead of digging up their own material.

Can you think of other persuasive strategies that are used?

Common seductive strategies

Common seductive strategies for influencing the media include:

Rewarding pliant journalists with gifts, travel and accommodation, food and drink.

Invitations to important events.

The chance to meet and spend time with important people.

Can you think of other seductive strategies that are used?

Journalists have to continually seek to balance their reporting and analysis by making an effort to:

Speak to less powerful people.
Spend time with less powerful people.
Understand how events affect their lives.
Visit the places that tend to be ignored.

Always ask one simple question of every claim: 'Whose interests does this claim serve?'

Critical thinking is not just a technical exercise in identifying and evaluating arguments. It is also a social and political practice that requires journalists to resist coercion, refuse seduction and retain their autonomy.

2 The virtues of journalism

Outcomes

By the end of this chapter you will be able to:

▶ Explain the tensions between journalism as a business and journalism as a profession.

▶ Suggest the training requirements for journalists in terms of knowledge, skills and values.

▶ Differentiate between ethics and morality, between 'being good' and 'doing good'.

▶ Explain the concepts of conscience, the moral imperative to behave well, the autonomous being and virtue.

▶ Explain ethics in relation to journalism.

▶ Consider the importance of protecting your sources.

▶ Note the limitations of a code of conduct.

Journalism ethics – an oxymoron?

Definitions

Ethics

As a reporter, I once mentioned to my news editor the title of a book I was reading: *The Virtuous Journalist*. He burst out laughing and said: "It's a very thin book, isn't it?" I shared the joke, but began to appreciate a remark made by the American authors of the book, Stephen Klaidman and Tom Beauchamp, that "it is difficult to write about 'journalism ethics' without sounding like a jerk". (Klaidman and Beauchamp, 1987:45).

We do not mean to imply that journalists are a morally defective lot ....
They are sometimes criticized indiscriminately, perhaps as a result of in-
flated expectations, and many of their failures are understandable in context.

An ethical journalist
– how is this
possible?

But whenever the words 'ethics' and 'journalism' are uttered in the same sentence, it is not unusual to hear someone joke that journalism ethics is an oxymoron [*contradictory*]. This situation should not be blamed on some imagined moral
flaw in journalists themselves, but on the conditions in which they work, where
most newsrooms prioritise 'getting the story' and the demands of the deadline
above all else. Ethical concerns are usually of secondary consideration.

However cynical we may be, journalistic ethics may today be at the heart of
journalism education. Large media organisations such as the British Broadcasting
Corporation (BBC), which has its headquarters in London in the United Kingdom,
have put the study of ethics at the centre of their staff training, from the most
junior reporter to the most senior manager.

Journalists are not, as popular belief would have it, an immoral lot. The conditions they work in are often not conducive [not very encouraging] to spending time considering all the implications of their work. British moral philosopher
Matthew Kieran, poses the issue this way:

> Many professional journalists in Britain, for example, often greet the sug-
> gestion that they ought to be ethically sensitive with sneers of disdain.
> After all, how could journalists possibly hope to get at stories that matter,
> or ones the public want to know about, if they have to be wholly honest
> in their investigations or straightforwardly respect the feelings, wishes,
> and privacy of the subjects of their reports? Moreover, the public at large
> tends to take for granted the commonsense presumption that journalists
> are ultimately concerned with one thing: what sells.

Work pressure derives not only from the difficulties of meeting deadlines, interviewing uncooperative sources and dealing with demanding editors, but also from the
fact that most journalists operate within the confines of a market-driven industry.
And when accusations of wrong-doing are made against individual journalists, the
contexts in which they work are almost never taken into account. (Kieran, 1997).

The work context

It is difficult practicing journalism as a public service, in a business that has increasingly come under the direction of accountants rather than editors. Can journalism and ethics co-exist?

Journalism is an industry, a major player in the profit-seeking market economy, and journalists are workers driven by a need to make a living in that industry. However, journalism is also a profession, a vocation founded on principles which control and regulate the behaviour of the practitioner.

Journalists therefore face twin pressures: working to keep their newspaper in business, but also (and more importantly) maintaining professional standards based on the idea of virtuous conduct and serving the public interest. This is all practised in a corporate world. If one considers the overwhelming pressures of competition in the corporate world, it becomes clear that journalists will more or less conform to producing news that sells rather than the kind of news that people need to know about their world. It is therefore easier for individual journalists to embrace the corporate ideology of their employers.

The ethical difficulties that readers complain about do not revolve exclusively around news content. Complaints also cover celebrity news, sleaze and sensationalism. Consider incidents such as when journalists get their stories wrong, allow inaccuracies to creep in or treat their sources and subjects unfairly. None of these should happen. But sometimes error follows misjudgements honestly construed on incomplete or misleading evidence available at the time of going to press. It may be unfair to make journalists morally culpable. But journalists do remain nonetheless responsible for what eventually gets into print.

Journalism and public life

A more serious matter stems from the implications journalism has for public life. The news media are responsible for providing an accurate record of events so that people, as citizens, can act in a public capacity. If the media provide incomplete accounts of public issues or allow public servants (like government ministers) to manipulate [spin] the media, this treats readers with contempt and prevents readers from full participation in society. It fails to honour that mandate.

(5) MINUTE TASK

In groups, discuss what you think the role of the media should be.

Whenever the news media embrace the profit motive as their main interest, their social responsibility ought to be called into question. For this reason, Edmund Lambeth begins his treatment of journalism ethics with a warning about news media that have developed an all-too-cosy relationship with its corporate customers. "If a storm alarm is not sounding within the halls of American journalism, one should be," He warns. (Lambeth 1992). He continues:

Introducing Journalism and Media Studies

Accumulated distrust of the news media, scepticism of journalists' ethics, and a resentment of media power are very nearly permanent features of the contemporary American scene. While the media themselves are not alone responsible for this state of affairs, it is past time for journalists and owners of newspapers and radio and television stations to articulate principles of performance that are publicly visible, ethically defensible, and rooted clearly in a philosophic tradition that continues to justify a free press. (Lamberth, 1992).

In 2004, the United Kingdom government appointed an investigation into the mysterious death of Dr David Kelly, a former United Nations weapons inspector who spoke to a *Today* programme journalist about the British government's dossier on whether weapons of mass destruction existed in Iraq under the rule of dictator Saddam Hussein. After all, the claim that weapons of mass destruction existed were the main reason for the invasion of Iraq (and such weapons, biological, chemical or nuclear, have never been found). The investigators were highly critical of the role of the press in 'outing' or revealing Dr Kelly as the source of the information that the government under then Prime Minister Tony Blair had tried to cover up the lack of evidence of weapons of mass destruction. The media pressure was so great that Dr Kelly committed suicide. As a result, the BBC began such an exercise to improve the quality of its news reporting and thereby create public trust.

Is there a public broadcaster in your area which has been criticised for making public the identity of a whistle-blower, a minor, or someone who does not want the fact that they were raped or contracted HIV/AIDS made public?

🔟 MINUTE TASK

In groups, debate whether any other news organisations should be considering improving the ethical quality of their news reporting. Substantiate your answer.

Journalism in context

Journalism does not operate in a vacuum. It is part of a world that affects editorial policy. Newspapers need to make a profit to survive in the market. That means they must attract, hold and grow a significant readership. Television needs viewers and radio needs listeners or the advertisers won't pay. There's nothing wrong with that. But when management interests impinge on editorial interests – like cutting newsroom staff in order to save money on salaries, when other reasonable options are available – it becomes more difficult for news media to serve the public interest.

Consider a newsroom as a system. A change in any part of that system will have an effect on how the newsroom functions as a whole. If a newsroom has a below-optimum number of reporters, even if the volume of output is maintained, its quality is likely to suffer. The depth of reporting (as in time-consuming investigative reporting) is often sacrificed in favour of easier (and cheaper) reporting practices, like relying on press releases. The impact in the longer term is more worrying. For instance, the South African National Editors' Forum (SANEF) surveyed reporters with less than five year's experience in 2002. The authors of the audit, Arrie (Arnold) de Beer and Elanie Steyn, found that a worrying proportion were woefully ignorant of ethical criteria in their day-to-day practice. (De Beer and Steyn, 2002). And yet a detailed list of journalism codes of conduct is available on the Editors' Forum website at www.sanef.org.za.

This comes as no surprise given the trimming of staff and the gradual erosion of other newsroom resources for more than a decade. Among the suggested remedies for this ethical impoverishment were to teach journalism students more ethics before they enter the newsroom. But it is quite obvious that, as the BBC in the United Kingdom had found out, media ethics and law are best learned 'on the job', combined with a chance to reflect. In many respects learning ethics in the workplace beats doing so in the theoretical environment of an academic lecture hall.

The value of learning theory is not doubted, let us be clear about that. The challenge is to ensure that it can be applied in the workplace. If we use the term ethics to refer to ideas, values and principles, and morality to refer to correct actions and behaviour, then it is morality that is learned in a newsroom. Ethics, at an intellectual level, can certainly be learned from reading. But it is only in practice that ethical principles become entrenched. But ethics can also be under threat from other vested interests which may use the term ethics to organise media coverage which is favourable towards those vested interests. For example, the Media Institute of Southern Africa reported on their website in May 2007 that Zambian provincial minister Joseph Mulyata threatened Sky FM, a commercial radio station in Monze, about 200 kilometres south of the capital Lusaka, with closure for what he termed 'unethical and unprofessional' conduct in reporting on his personal business transactions.

In a South African newsroom, you might expect to find a number of senior reporters who act as mentors [*advisers*] for newcomers to the profession. There would also be a 'code of conduct' – sometimes called a 'code of ethics' – stating what to do and not to do. But where a newsroom has been stripped of its senior

Definitions

Ethics

Morality

staff, there are too few senior reporters to learn from and whatever mentoring might take place will probably amount to rewriting copy – a sub-editing function.

⑤ MINUTE TASK

Which senior journalist would you like as your mentor and why? Explain your reasons in terms of ethical guidance.

We may expect ethical codes of conduct to supply the way forward by assisting reporters not only to perform according to the rules of their profession but also to develop professional character. However, it is useless to have declarations of ideals which are not internalised by the majority of the reporters. They become hollow. Furthermore, the text of a code is open to differences in decoding. It may come to mean very different things to different people and do more harm than good.

Debate over journalism codes usually focus on the precise meaning of words such as 'confidentiality' and 'conflict of interest'. What these words mean in the culture and language of those who use them is seldom taken into account. Also, evidence shows that codes of conduct do not feature boldly in most newsrooms, except when a crisis emerges and attention is drawn to them. To take the brave step of scrapping a code, as American philosopher John Kultgen writes, would work only if its principles and ideals are internalised and "incorporated in the lives of individuals who act on the social scene". (Kultgen, 1988).

⑳ MINUTE TASK

In groups or as a class, debate the topic, "The code of conduct for journalists has no value or place in the 21ˢᵗ century."

We sometimes find a strong emphasis on technical competence in journalism training. But while technique is an important beginning point, journalism is more than technique, just as it is more than general communication. There is no doubt that computer technology has enhanced journalists' capacity to work more speedily and to manage information more efficiently. However, intellectual and critical skills still remain the stock-in-trade of journalistic competence. The real challenge is to develop communicative competence.

Journalism was born in the political struggles of the modern age and leans towards the liberal arts from which it significantly draws its intellectual lifeblood. The collective contribution journalists have made to their profession over the

years was done so with resources derived from their intellectual development in other fields. All this material was committed to the process of moulding the craft as it was learned 'on the job'. All these resources have become part of the tradition of how journalists understand their practice. The late American media scholar James Carey (1935 - 2006) says that journalism naturally belongs with political theory, which nurtures an understanding of democratic life and institutions. But Carey, (Carey, quoted in Adam, 1993) goes much further. Carey, who was professor of international journalism at the USA's Columbia University, also links journalism with literature, which provides a heightened awareness of language and expression and an understanding of narrative form. And Carey also links journalism with philosophy, so it can clarify its own moral foundations; from history, which forms the underlying layer of its consciousness, and from art, which he says enriches a reporter's capacity to combine the visual and verbal world.

What other disciplines do you think a journalist draws on?

Journalism also involves technology, which includes interviewing, researching, writing and getting the copy or photograph into print, the article or blog uploaded on to the internet, the package aired on radio or television. But technology is brought to life in an imagination fuelled by intellectual resources. The law is not enough to maintain a journalistic identity, and codes of conduct are even less effective. The ingredient is conscientiousness, which brings us to matters of ethics and morality.

10 MINUTE TASK

On your own, list the essential requirements you believe a journalist should have. Compare your answers with your partners.

> The differences between ethics and morality are ...

Ethics and morality

To many people criticising the media, the terms ethics, morality and conscience amount to the same thing, and they use them interchangeably. But this is not always helpful when trying to understand behaviour in the workplace.

The term ethics comes from a Greek word which refers to 'custom'. It applies to personal customs or stable ways of behaving. This indicates that the way a person acts gives us insight into the type of person he or she is. The words morals and morality, however, come from Latin. Both the Greek and Latin words refer to those actions that are blameworthy or praiseworthy with regard to their goodness or rightness.

However, we have come to distinguish between them. Ethics refers to the ideas, values and principles of correct behaviour, and morality to refer to the actions themselves as they are lived out in practice. According to former journalist turned academic Stephen Klaidman and philosophy professor Tom Beauchamp the term morality refers to:

> culturally transmitted rules of right and wrong conduct that establish the basic terms of social life. Morality is not merely a matter of what a person subjectively believes. Individuals do not create their morality by making their own rules, and 'a morality' cannot be purely a personal policy or code ... (Klaidman and Beauchamp, 1997).

For German philosopher Jurgen Habermas (1929 -) morality refers to universal standards of justice, whereas ethics refers to standards derived from culturally specific norms or ideals. For a moral norm to be valid, Habermas says, it must satisfy the condition that "all affected can accept the consequences and the side effects its general observance can be anticipated to have for the satisfaction of everyone's interests" (Habermas, 1993:32).

Conscience

There is a close connection between ethics and morality – at least on the surface. But would a person's ethics and morality be consistent [*in harmony with each other*]? Moral psychology allows for the possibility that a person may hold inconsistent beliefs, which is when belief and desire come into conflict. And if our initial distinction between ethics and morality is correct, then these too would come into conflict. This is where conscience enters the picture.

Conscience refers to each individual's moral sense of right and wrong. It is the practical judgement, or power to choose whether an action is good and deserves our consent, or is wrong and should be avoided. Our conscience is a value system that we define and redefine continually – fine-tuning it, as it were. If we ignore our conscience, it bothers us until we come to accept the consequences of our actions as acceptable, and thereafter the conscience no longer bothers us, and has become lax. So conscience is not perfect and is not in any respect a final judge on right and wrong. It is not a feeling, but a matter of right judgement, expressing our ethics and our morality.

Has your conscience ever 'bothered' you? Why? What was your response?

In the history of ethics the conscience has been looked upon in different ways. It has been described variously as:

a reflection of the voice of God;
a human faculty;
the voice of reason;
a special moral sense;

Conscience

intentions /
thoughts

vs

experience /
actions

I know what I'm doing.

I decide how I act.

I'm responsible and accountable for my own actions.

I act of my own free will.

Types of imperatives

Moral

Religious

Social

an innate sense of right and wrong resulting from our unity with the universe; and

an expression of values instilled from the instructions of our parents.

The consciences of different people within a society or from different societies do vary, and in some areas quite significantly. Moral philosophers have applied their minds to the phenomenon, and generally tend towards opposite poles. At one extreme are those who believe that our moral sense is innate [*qualities that a person is born with*]. In their thinking, conscience acts as the originator of moral behaviour. At the other extreme are those who consider conscience as both a rational power of discrimination and as something acquired from the experience of having to make moral judgments. A wide range of compromises lies between these extremes.

Moral fact

Not all instances where a journalist has made a mistake in a report or article automatically imply moral failure. If a journalist has taken all reasonable steps to apply his or her mind to how a story is reported, has checked and double-checked information and consulted with colleagues and yet has committed an error in the report, the matter is not normally a moral failure.

We in fact have moral experiences and feel obliged to act in ways that we think are good, whether they are good or not. This experience is characterised by feelings of praise or blame, stemming from a sense of responsibility for our actions. We are not compelled to act one way or another. It is me who decides how I will act. Nonetheless, morality manifests [*shows*] itself as an order [*moral imperative*] that wants to be obeyed. Our moral appraisal is connected to the intention of the person who performs the act but at the same time we do not judge morality simply by the intention of the person who acts.

How does a journalist behave in a situation in which the personal urge to judge conflicts with the professional need to report on a story? If, for example, you were personally anti-abortion but had to interview a medical team which conducted abortions, how would you respond?

There are other imperatives too, which can get confused with the moral one. For some, there is a religious imperative, which orders us to act in ways that are in tune with our spiritual beliefs. The social imperative orders us to conform to social expectations. The difference is that while the social and religious come from 'without', the moral imperative springs from 'within', or from the demands of our nature to be a good person. The moral imperative carries the sanction [*penalty*] of personal failure in relation to what it means to be a good person. It is linked to what is right and wrong, irrespective of what others consider this to be.

Have you ever felt motivated by one of the above imperatives to do the 'right thing' in the face of opposition?

The moral imperative imposes itself on me: I feel that if I go against it, I will lessen myself as a person. This is why I can follow my conscience rather than obey peer pressure, no matter what others think of me. Thus morality supposes an autonomous [*independent*] being, responsible and free, thinking and acting for myself. Responsibility means I can be called to answer for what I do, that my acts depend on myself as its true origin and source. Morality, then, concerns free persons who are responsible for what they do, who know what they are doing, and who decide to act or not to act.

Definitions

Virtue

Virtue ethics

Virtue ethics

If we are free to choose, the fundamental question is, 'How should I act?' According to the doctrine that value is measured in terms of usefulness [*the utilitarian principle*], we should choose that which achieves the greatest good. Or we may choose that which respects the human dignity of all persons. Moral principles like these discussed above focus primarily on actions.

But ethics consists of more than principles which seem to reduce life to something regulated by rules. A number of ethicists challenge this tendency, saying that it ignores an important principle, more fundamental than rules: virtue. Virtue ethics, according to the New Zealand philosophy professor Rosalind Hursthouse emphasises moral character, in contrast to an approach which emphasises duties or rules or one which emphasises the consequences of actions. (Hursthouse, 1999).

Virtue ethics has its origins in the ancient world of the Mediterranean, hundreds of years before the birth of Christ, particularly in the writings of the ancient Greek writers Plato (around 437 BC – 347 BC) and his prize student Aristotle (around 384 BC – 322 BC). Among the questions philosophers of virtue ethics ask are: What is the good life? What part does virtue play in leading a good life? Are moral reasons independent of individuals' particular concerns? Is morality captured in a set of values, or is the sensitivity of the virtuous person central to ethics?

Virtues are attitudes, dispositions, or character traits – honesty, courage, compassion, generosity, fidelity, integrity, fairness and so on – that enable us to act in ways that develop our human potential. But not all virtues are moral. There are intellectual virtues also.

Can you add other virtues that you think are important in being a good journalist and a good person?

Approaches of Ethics

Virtue ethics

Deontology

Utilitarianism

Teleology

" Virtues are learned and developed. "

Have I/observed/copied/ learned/practised these virtues to be a virtuous/ ethical person?

Personal development is not an isolated endeavour but is achieved within the communities to which the person belongs. A person belonging to a journalistic community, for instance, will develop traits instilled in that community through role models like senior journalists, or the stories told about those best remembered. Moral life, then, is not simply a matter of applying rules to specific situations. It is also a matter of trying to determine the kind of people we should be both in the communities to which we belong and in ourselves as authentic human beings.

Virtue ethics provides a useful way of understanding questions of right and wrong in the practice of journalism, instead of these questions being a matter of external regulation. Put another way, we know from history that journalism, for all its faults, is a practice driven by a fundamental moral impulse to expose wrong-doing and to serve public life.

Journalists' ethical dilemma

For democracy to succeed it is essential that the press and by implication journalists, are both trusted and believed and therefore act in an ethical manner. So what constitutes an ethical manner?

What is legal under law may not be considered ethical from a journalistic point of view. There are many cases where journalists have been jailed for refusing to reveal their sources when the identities of whistle-blowers or sources of information have been demanded by the courts.

The ideals of journalism are sometimes in conflict with the laws of the land and most journalism codes of conduct expressly forbid journalists from revealing their source of information. This has led many governments to turn to the courts of law to force reporters and news organisations to reveal sources and source material. Governments believe that the courts must be able to compel any citizen or organisation to provide evidence, if demanded by the court. However, journalists believe that their promise not to name their sources promises the trust of anonymous sources present and future (and therefore protects them) and in this way allows journalists to keep a country's electorate adequately informed, thereby ensuring the functioning of democracy.

While journalists and governments obviously disagree on this issue, each side can claim to hold the ethical high ground [the belief that you are right] – governments, so that they can justify the current legal status quo; and journalists, so that the public will continue to trust their reporting.

Journalists and their principles are often in conflict with the legal situation. By looking at cases in practise, it can be seen how journalists must proceed to maintain both the confidentiality of their own sources and the trust of the public. It is a never-ending battle. In 2006, the National Director of Public Prosecutions attempted at the last minute to stop the weekly *Mail & Guardian* newspaper, edited by Ferial Haffejee, from publishing a report into its investigations into an organised crime network. The matter was taken to the Johannesburg High Court, which ruled that the public has a right to be informed of matters that affect their lives. Nor is this constant legal battle limited to South Africa. In April 2007 in Lesotho, according to the Media Institute of Southern Africa, Bethuel Thai, the editor in chief of *The Public Eye*, was summoned by the Criminal Investigation Department of the Lesotho Mounted Police. The police demanded that the news-paper become a state witness in a case in which opposition party leader Anthony Manyeli is charged with criminal defamation in the magistrate's court. The editor refused. In May 2007, the Associated Newspapers of Zimbabwe, publishers of the banned *Daily News* and *Daily News on Sunday*, lost a Harare court effort to be licensed, thus effectively stopping them from exposing anything.

Forcing reporters to reveal their sources of information is a global phenom-enon. In the United Kingdom, for example, the main judicial tool used to compel journalists to disclose their source is section 10 of the Contempt of Court Act of 1981. According to the book McNae's Essential Law for Journalists, the Act actually gives limited protection to journalists but requires disclosure under three exemptions. The Act states: "No court may require a person to disclose, nor is any person guilty of contempt of court for refusing to disclose, the source of information contained in a publication for which he is responsible, unless it is established to the satisfaction of the court that disclosure is necessary in the interests of justice or national security, or for the prevention of disorder or crime." (Welsh et al, 2005:302).

The courts therefore can demand disclosure while providing no protection to the source if it is considered in the interests of national security, justice, or to prevent crime. If a journalist fails to comply, he or she may be fined or imprisoned. However, since the European Convention on Human Rights was signed in Italy in 1950 by the European Union state members, this convention has given journalists working in the United Kingdom limited protection. Article 10 of the Convention provides the right to freedom of expression, subject to certain restrictions that are "in accordance with law" and "necessary in a democratic society". This right includes the freedom to hold opinions, and to receive and impart information and ideas.

Article 10 of the European Convention which gives the right to freedom of expression has been interpreted in the European Court of Human Rights as giving journalists the privilege to refuse to disclose confidential sources due to the role of an independent press as a government watchdog. A government must there-fore give reasons why it is necessary to limit a journalist's freedom of expression. And government can only limit freedom of expression in proportion to the need to serve the public interest. According to author Jeffrey Nestler, author of *The*

Underprivileged Profession: The Case for Supreme Court Recognition of the Journalist's Privilege, European conventions and courts have been more generous to journalists than Britain's Contempt of Court Act. Court Act (2005:228).

It is not just the compulsion to name sources that British journalists, and many journalists around the world, have to worry about. The United Kingdom's Police and Criminal Evidence Act of 1984 can be used to force journalists to hand over any materials that they hold. A judge has to believe that the public interest is being served by making such an order and override special regard given to journalistic material, note Tom Welsh, Walter Greenwood and David Banks in *McNae's Essential Law for Journalists*. But, they warn, as with the Contempt of Court Act, judges generally side with the police against journalists. (2005:306-7).

In the United States, in contrast, the freedom of the press is protected by the First Amendment to the Constitution, adopted along with the Bill of Rights in 1791 to limit the power of the federal government. The first amendment guarantees press freedom.

The text of the first amendment to the American constitution limits elected politicians from both the Senate and the House of Representatives, otherwise known as the Congress, the legislature of the United States' federal government: "Congress shall make no law respecting an establishment of religion, or prohibiting the free exercise thereof; or abridging the freedom of speech, or of the press; or the right of the people peaceably to assemble, and to petition the Government for a redress of grievances."

The limitations of the American press to refuse to answer subpoenas (court orders) are governed by a 1972 ruling known as *Branzburg versus Hayes*, a landmark United States Supreme Court decision which very nearly went the other way (the case was decided on a vote of 5 to 4). This case, the only time the American Supreme Court has considered the use of reportorial privilege, involved three reporters, all of whom had refused to testify before grand juries (a special type of jury used in the USA to determine if there is enough evidence for a trial, which normally proceeds in secrecy). Paul Branzburg of *The Louisville Courier-Journal* newspaper, in the course of his reporting duties, had witnessed people manufacturing and using the illegal drug hashish. The others were Earl Caldwell, a reporter for *The New York Times* newspaper, and Paul Pappas, a Massachusetts television reporter, who had both conducted extensive interviews with the leaders of The Black Panthers, a militant African American organisation founded to promote civil rights and self-defense which began in the late 1960s.

The court ruled that journalists have no right to refuse to provide testimony when subpoenaed by a grand jury. Only two exceptions to a subpoena were allowed, when enquiries were not in good faith and when enquiries were specifically designed to disrupt a reporter's relationship with a source.

The protection afforded American journalists by the First Amendment is similarly muddled over the issue of newsroom searches. The USA's Supreme Court ruled in 1978 that news organisations had no right to prevent police from raiding newsrooms to seize materials - only for legislators in Congress in the national capital of Washington to pass a law two years later prohibiting newsroom searches unless journalists were suspected of committing a crime. (Jost, ?:306).

In the United Kingdom, according to the publication *Journalism Studies*, the National Union of Journalists' code of conduct states that "A journalist shall protect confidential sources of information." (Harcup, 2002:114). This is reinforced, according to the British Journalism Review, by the UK's Press Complaints Commission's code that states "journalists have a moral obligation to protect confidential sources of information." (Coulter, 2005:67).

This of course does not always happen. The longstanding violent troubles between Catholic and Protestant militias over who controls Northern Ireland, which is based on the same island as the independent country of Ireland but falls under the UK government, have provided numerous instances when journalists have refused to expose their sources. However, this approach was contradicted by Northern Ireland journalist Nick Martin-Clark, who vowed to a pro-British-rule Protestant loyalist terrorist already in jail that he would not reveal what was about to be told. The man being interviewed, Clifford McKeown, revealed that he had murdered a Catholic taxi driver. The journalist, Martin-Clark, voluntarily went to court as a prosecution witness to ensure that McKeown was jailed. (Martin-Clark, 2003:39). Martin-Clark was subsequently expelled from the National Union of Journalists and had to enter a witness protection programme after receiving death threats but continues to work as a freelance journalist specialising in Northern Ireland.

It could be argued that in such circumstances journalists face a dilemma between short term pragmatism [*practicality*] in securing a conviction and longer term benefits which may be secured by protecting sources. From a utilitarian stance it is a choice of what will bring about the greatest good for the greatest number of people. The National Union of Journalists in Britain believes that over time journalism will do greater good by not revealing a source's identity than anything achieved by a one-off disclosure to obtain a prosecution. However in the modern climate of terrorism, where the greater good may exist may well depend on what side of the argument you find yourself.

A reporter who betrays a promise given to a source is seen as untrustworthy and therefore their future reporting will not be accepted. It would also stop other sources coming forward who might be able to expose illegal acts. Failure to protect a source might ruin the profession as a whole. Journalists are convinced that the use of confidential sources is the only way that serious wrongdoing can be exposed to the public.

On the other hand, a case was brought by Belgian brewer Interbrew to try to force several British newspapers to disclose the source who had supplied them with forged documents detailing a proposed takeover bid. The source intended to cash in when the newspapers published the information and the financial markets responded accordingly. A court order was obtained when the newspapers refused to disclose the source despite the fact that they knew they were protecting a criminal, a case where even lawyer-client confidentiality could be broken. (Preston, 2005:49).

What do journalist unions in your country or region have as a code of conduct? Has action been taken against members who have contravened the code?

If journalists consider that they are going to be pressured into revealing their source or sources, they can protect themselves legally by preparing for what might occur. John Coulter says "the simple rule is, if you can't keep your word, don't do the story." (Coulter, 2005:67)." But if you may succumb to legal pressure to reveal a source, it is perfectly legal in the UK (not everywhere in the world) to prevent the seizure of documents by destroying them before they are requested by a court. An alternative is to allow the journalists' union to move the documents or photographs out of the country to somewhere beyond the courts' jurisdiction. Similarly, it is prudent [*wise*] to be discreet when communicating with a source in case phone or email records are seized.

In South Africa, the right to privacy is enshrined in the Bill of Rights. But section 32 of the Constitution enshrines the rights of all people in South Africa to access any information held by the state or any information held by another person that is required for the exercise or protection of any rights. Journalists can expect continued legal challenges. In 2007, the Parliamentary Portfolio Committee on Home Affairs heard public representations from several media organisations on the Film and Publications Amendment Bill. Officially, the legislation is meant to curb the easy availability of pornography, especially child pornography. In practice, according to the Freedom of Expression Institute, the new amendment would remove the media's long-standing exemption from the Act. As a result, media would be subjected to pre-publication censorship by the Film and Publications Board, in violation of their editorial freedom.

What has happened since then in the legal battle for freedom of expression and protection of sources?

Introducing Journalism and Media Studies

(20) MINUTE TASK

Find recent examples of pressure being brought on local journalists to reveal their sources or their documentation. What was the response of the journalists, and those who objected to the stories, and what was the response of their employers?

Suggested Reading

Adam, Stuart (1993). *Notes towards a definition of journalism: Understanding an old craft as an art form.* St Petersburg: The Poynter Institute for Media Studies.

De Beer, A.S. and Steyn, E. (2002). South African National Editors' Forum (SANEF) 2002 South African national journalism skills audit: An introduction and the SANEF report regarding the media industry. *Ecquid Novi* 23(1): pp 11-86

Grossberg, Lawrence, Wartella, Ellen. & Whitney, D. Charles (1998). *Media Making: Mass Media in a Popular Culture.* Thousand Oaks: Sage.

Gurevitch, Michael, and Blumler, Jay. (1990). Political Communication Systems and Democratic Values. In Judith Lichtenberg, (ed) *Democracy and the Mass Media.* New York: Cambridge University Press.

Habermas, J. (1993). *Justification and Application: Remarks on Discourse Ethics.* Cambridge, MA: MIT Press.

Hackett, Robert, and Zhao, Yuezhi. (1998). *Sustaining Democracy? Journalism and the Politics of Objectivity.* Toronto: Garamond Press.

Hursthouse, Rosalind (1999). *On Virtue Ethics.* Oxford: Oxford University Press

Keeble, Richard (1994). *The Newspapers Handbook.* London: Routledge.

Kieran, Matthew (1997). Objectivity, Impartiality and Good Journalism. In Matthew Kieran (ed). *Media Ethics.* London: Routledge.

Klaidman, et al (1987). *The Virtuous Journalist,* pp 14-15

Klaidman, Stephen. Beauchamp, Tom. (1987). *The Virtuous Journalist.* New York: Oxford University Press, Ibid, pp 4-5

Kultgen, John (1988). *Ethics and Professionalism: Parentalism in the Caring Life.* University of Pennsylvania Press, pp 220.

Lambeth, Edmund (1992). *Committed Journalism: An Ethic for the Profession.* Bloomington: Indiana University Press.

Schudson, Michael. (2001). *The objectivity norm in American journalism.* Journalism 2(2).

Singer, Jane. (2003). Who are these guys? The online challenge to the notion of journalistic professionalism? *Journalism 4(2).*

Windschuttle, Keith. (1997). *The poverty of media theory.* Equid Novi 18(1).

Zelizer, Barbie (1997). *Journalists as interpretive Communities.* In Dan Berkowitz (ed.), *Social Meanings of News.* Thousand Oaks: Sage.

3 Media literacy

Outcomes

At the end of this chapter you will be able to:
- Explain the basic communication process.
- Define media literacy.
- List the aspects involved in being media literate.

Do you think you are media literate?

Do you think you are media literate? Do you read newspapers and magazines, watch television news, listen to radio current affairs programmes, follow events on the internet? A media literate person would be able to answer the following questions after reading a media text – and reading, in this context, is something you can do whether it is an article, an image, a sound or a programme which you are reading. You can read an article, an image or a programme, for example. So, after reading a media text, can you state:

Who is communicating, and why?
What type of media text is it?
How do we know what it means?
Who receives it?
What sense do we make of it?
How does the media text present its subject matter?

There are many different definitions of media literacy. Here are a few:

The ability to choose and to understand the media we consume.

The ability to question, to evaluate and to respond thoughtfully to the media we consume.

Can you add another definition of media literacy?

The ability of a citizen to access, analyse and produce information for specific outcomes.

American academic Art Silverblatt, says critical thinking enables audiences to develop independent judgement about media content. (Silverblatt, 2001:2). We simply cannot accept at face value everything we read, view or hear. Our interaction with the media must be active. We have to engage with the content critically, otherwise the outcome could be disastrous. Media literacy should promote the critical thinking skills to enable us to make informed decisions in response to the information we receive through the media. Maintaining a critical distance from the content received through the media helps us make informed and independent choices. Silverblatt says media literacy goes further, including:

Understanding the process of mass communication.

An awareness of the impact of the media on the individual and society.

Developing strategies with which to analyse and discuss media messages.

List other important elements you think should be considered.

Awareness of media content as a 'text' that provides insight into our contemporary culture and ourselves. An understanding of culture can give us perspectives and insight into media messages.

Cultivating enjoyment and understanding of media. (Silverblatt, 2001:4).

Media literacy should not detract from your appreciation of programmes and should not be merely critical. Critical interpretation should enhance your enjoyment of media at its best: insightful articles, good reporting, great theatre. In the case of media communicators: the ability to produce effective, responsible and well researched media messages. To be a good journalist or media practitioner you must demonstrate an understanding of the mass communication process as well as a mastery of production techniques and strategies. But to truly improve the media industry, media communicators must also appreciate the challenges and responsibilities needed to produce thoughtful programmes, reports and articles that serve the public interest best.

Are you influenced by the media?

Survey on influence of the media

Question	Strongly Agree
1. Does the media influence society?	80%
2. Does the media influence you personally?	12%

Source: Silverblatt, 2001

⑤ MINUTE TASK

In pairs, what can you deduce from the above survey? Why do you think people won't admit to being influenced by the media?

Fill in your favourite:

TV soapie

TV programme

Radio Station

Radio DJ

Radio / TV advert

Comic/cartoon strip

Art Silverblatt, a professor of communications and journalism at Webster University in the USA, refers to the survey attitudes revealed above as elitism [*exclusiveness, superiority, snobbery*]. He says that the results of the above survey are both intriguing and disturbing. Why? Because the participants had no problem with seeing the media's influence on others while denying its influence on themselves. A follow-up survey found that education was not a significant factor "in this wide disparity between perceptions of effects of the media on others and on themselves." People, no matter what their level of education, were able to recognise the impact of the media on others while denying its impact on their own lives. You may know a number of highly intelligent and educated people who watch the television soap operas each night but would never admit to that in public – another example of the same trend. One possible reason why the educated deny the influence of the media on their lives is embarrassment. But they - and we - are as susceptible to the influence of the media message as the general public. Therefore an important step in becoming media literate is to agree that the daily messages that you receive through the media can and do affect your attitudes, values and behaviour.

Audience behaviour

Another aspect that needs to be taken into account is patterns of audience behaviour. During the communication process, audience members are selective in what part of the message they store and assimilate [*incorporate*] into meaning. Audiences may also be involved in other activities at the same time, such as eating dinner and watching television, or driving a car and listening to the radio. Because their primary attention is focused elsewhere they may be susceptible to other messages that can affect their understanding of the message and thus affect their attitudes and behaviour. How often have you heard people protest: "But I thought he or she said/meant/implied..."? As a result you may be receiving an altogether different message from what the message communicator originally intended. In other words the message sent is not the message received.

Examine what you do while watching television news. Does this affect what you remember and your understanding of the message?

Another issue we have to take into account is audience expectations. We are not always inspired or in the mood to analyse media content. Yet the only way to 'discover media messages is to look for media messages' as Art Silverblatt points out. (Silverblatt, 2001).

Audiences on the whole tend to believe media messages simply based on the fact that 'if it is in the news it must be true'. You only have to consider the number of people who are fooled by bogus [*false*] messages that are put out each April 1, otherwise known as April Fool's Day, in many parts of the world. Newspaper readers, radio listeners and television viewers believe the message and do not analyse it for credibility simply because they believe the media.

Can you think of an example from the internet where people surfing the world wide web have done so without analysing it for credibility?

Government messages are treated much the same, that 'they must be true because the government says so'. Often what appears on screen, although appearing real, is constructed and staged by the media. It only represents a version of reality. Indeed, the very presence of the media can affect the event it is intended to capture. Also the clever use of camera angles and selective editing of the event can portray a very different picture.

(10) MINUTE TASK

In pairs:
- list three examples of government messages via the media that have misled the public and suggest why the public were so easily misled.
- Give a recent example of when you critically challenged the news.

Signs and symbols

Media literacy, apart from often requiring a certain level of education, also requires an understanding of the signs and symbols used in the media. The level of language used in a message can also affect the way audiences receive the message. The message may be latent [*hidden, indirect*] and consequently escape our immediate attention. Latent or hidden messages may be used to reinforce a more direct message.

Emotive appeal

Communicators influence the attitudes and behaviour of audiences by appealing to their emotions. Even if you do not understand the language, view a news clip of German chancellor Adolf Hitler (1889 – 1945) raging to the German people during the late 1930s and early 1940s, in preparation for launching World War Two. The old newsreel will give you an idea how appealing to the emotions of a nation can win widespread support even though the message had dire and abhorrent consequences. Visual (seeing) and aural (hearing) media (photography, film, television and radio) are particularly well suited to emotional appeals, as Art Silverblatt points out. (Silverblatt, 2001). The clever use of colour, light and movement, camera angles and size can be used to evoke emotional responses that can convey meaning. Or block meaning.

Can you think of a current political leader who utilises the emotional appeal of television to influence the behaviour of citizens?

Representation

Media content nearly always reflects the values and ideology [*framework of ideas and beliefs*] of the communicator. The production techniques chosen are often selected to bring those views, biased or otherwise, across to the audience. Some messages appear so repetitively that they begin to form new meanings, independent of any individual article, production or programme. Examples of this may be in the messages we are bombarded with regarding gender roles, race, definitions of success and cultural stereotypes [*labels*]. In hip-hop music videos, how are women portrayed, for example?

Communication process

If you want to become media literate, it is important that you understand the communication process. Communication is a dynamic process, demanding your total attention and focus. When somebody speaks to you, you become engaged in what is known as the communication process, a rapid set of actions that involves the following:

    Receiving the message.

    Decoding the message by selecting the relevant information.

    Forming an appropriate response.

    Responding to the message.

After you have responded in a face-to-face conversation, or in an email or Skype or telephone interview, the roles are often reversed and you go from being the audience to becoming the communicator. What does this entail? The basic communication model consists of the following elements:

The communicator: the person who delivers the message.

The message: the information being communicated.

The channel: the medium through which the message is being conveyed – the media, voice, facial expression, theatrical performance, radio interview, photograph.

The audience: the person or group of people who receive the message.

The list is endless but the media serves as a channel to communicate information to large groups of people (the audience) who are separated by time and/or distance from the communicator.

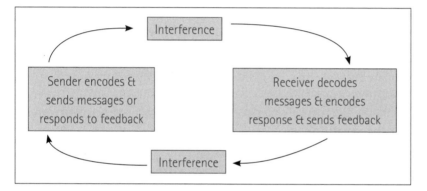

Figure 3.1 - Communication process and model

There are three different types of communication:

Intrapersonal, which takes place within us.

Interpersonal, which is face to face communication with another person or persons.

Mass communication, which are messages communicated through a mass medium like the media.

To communication effectively there must be mutual trust and respect between communicator and audience. Can you think of many examples of this in normal life? The communicator and audience must formulate rules of communication that govern their conduct and both parties must agree to abide by those rules. For example, participants in a discussion agree to maintain a comfortable distance from each other and not invade each other's body space. This may be different depending on one's culture and other circumstances.

In pairs, dramatise how you would greet:

▶ Someone from your own culture.

▶ Someone from a different culture

▶ Someone much older than you.

▶ A good friend.

For people to trust the media there must be an implicit contract between both parties that governs their behaviour. During the second Iraq war (March 2003 and ongoing at the date of publication) public opinion about this war in the Middle East changed substantially in many countries due to the images that were shown in the daily television news. Some people lost faith in the independence and reliability of reporters when the public was constantly fed information about the capture of a town only to find that the incident had not occurred. Because some media were considered less biased, some people decided to switch allegiance to satellite television stations actually based in the Middle East. Others demonised such television channels, including the English-language 24-hour-a-day Al Jazeera television network, for reporting on 'the enemy' and not simply repeating American and British military claims. A diversity of media provides options when a contract between audience and communicator is breached. Nonetheless, the reporting of unreliable information leads to an eroding of the trust between the communicator (the media) and their audience (the general public).

For good communication to take place and to avoid misunderstanding, the message sent must be the same message that is received. In order for this to occur two elements are critical to the communication process: feedback and interference.

Feedback

Feedback provides the audience the opportunity to respond to the communicator. Listeners may ask questions directly or comment by text message or email in order to better understand what the communicator is trying to say. Feedback is also important to the communicator because the communicator then knows if the message sent is the actual message received. In some cases, with eye contact, all the feedback required is a nod of the head. In print media, sometimes the feedback can be the reduction or increase in sales or a shift in sales as a desired audience moves elsewhere. A drop in ratings is sometimes the feedback for electronic broadcasting, and in both cases, as figures are publicly available, the advertisers soon notice. Results may be due to a lack of trust in the message or the communicator, so it is vital for the media to maintain trust with its audience. Always remember, a press that is not trusted is a press that is not listened to, watched or read.

Interference

Interference refers to multiple factors that obstruct the communication process and can occur at all points during the process. Anger and frustration are often the cause of communication interference, whether on the part of the communicator or the audience.

Some examples of communicator interference are:

When communicators obstruct the messages by not expressing themselves properly. Expressing yourself clearly is an essential skill for a media worker like a journalist.

Using words or expressions that the audience does not understand. This is particularly pertinent during intercultural and multilingual communication.

When the communicator has not thought through carefully what he or she wants to say and might ramble on.

When the facial expressions of the communicator do not seem to match his or her verbal message. Think of those people you know who tell jokes or tease people with a deadpan (hard-to-read) expression on their face.

Some examples of channel interference are:

When a piece in a text has not been edited properly and vital information has either been misused or left out.

When there is distortion at a vital moment in the radio broadcast or somebody in a cinema coughs or talks during an important piece of dialogue.

Some examples of audience interference are:

When you have totally misunderstood an advert.

When the audience impedes the communication process. Often an audience's choice of what to read or hear is based on their own personal values and interests. People often seek those views that concur with their own and avoid communications that offer a different perspective.

When content is distorted by bias, prejudice, and preconceptions.

It may be that audience interference will increase, as new technologies get in the way. How will people try to pay attention to communication while simultaneously juggling iPods, Walkmans, cellphones, Blackberries and pagers? Audiences also have a tendency to be selective in what they choose to remember and tend to tune out of a discussion in which they have a low level of interest or in topics they know nothing about. Consider how often you do that during lectures and lessons? Some people who do this regularly are accused of having a low attention span but it is a legitimate interference factor - one that your lecturers and teachers have to fight against all the time.

Finally, audiences often filter message through their egos in that they only concentrate on parts of a discussion that pertain to them, ignoring the rest of the communication. Often the audience is not paying attention when the other party is talking because they are busy formulating answers and replies or impatiently awaiting their turn to talk. How often does that happen to you during a class debate?

⑮ MINUTE TASK

You may wish to pause at this point to consider a few examples of communication interference. What have you done as an audience to eliminate that interference? Remember, good communication is a two way street. In groups, explore the following:

▶ An example of miscommunication due to cultural misunderstanding.
▶ An advert you did not understand.
▶ An example where your interpretation of an event or person(s) has been distorted by your prejudice.
▶ Words or meanings in this chapter that you did not understand.

My favourite TV personality is?

Because

Mass Communication

What we have discussed so far pertains to all forms of communication but there are some significant differences between interpersonal and mass communication.

Canadian researcher Marshall McLuhan (1911 – 1980), also known as the patron saint of *Wired* magazine, famously said, "The medium is the message." He was suggesting that the media have changed the traditional face-to-face communication model as shown in the figure below. The channels of mass communication have now assumed a primary role in determining content, choice of communicator, and the audience. An example of this is that many news readers and talk show hosts are chosen on the basis of their looks, acting abilities and voices rather than their journalistic ability. Can you think of any examples?

"The characteristics of the medium also affect the message," notes Art Silverblatt, a professor of communications and media studies in the USA. "In order to take advantage of the visual capabilities of the medium, television news often emphasises events rather than issues. News programming is also influenced by the entertainment sensibility of television". (Silverblatt, 2001). Stories are often selected because they are dramatic, sensational, have an identifiable cast of characters and have a clear narrative structure with a beginning, middle and end.

My favourite print journalist is?

Because

Communication Model		
Interpersonal Communication Model	Mass Communication Model	American Mass Communication Model
Communicator	Channel	Channel
*	*	*
Message	Communicator	Audience
*	*	*
Channel	Message	Communicator
*	*	*
Audience	Audience	Message

Source: Silverblatt, Art. (2001). *Media Literacy.* London: Praeger.

4 Media ideology

Outcomes

At the end of this chapter you will be able to:

- Define ideology.
- Identify powerful groups in society.
- Explain the links between power and ideology.
- Explain four different approaches to ideology.
- List ways in which propaganda and censorship are used to shape public opinion.

Why should we care about ideology?

Media provides an articulate and coherent way to define and interpret the world around us. Television, film, radio, the internet and newspapers provide us with examples of appropriate behaviour and attitudes. But who decides what is considered appropriate? The issue of representation - the way certain types of people, events, and places are depicted - is a fundamental or basic part of ideology's power. Media texts provide us with models for current attitudes, behaviours and appropriate roles in society. The problem we have to consider then is how do the media represent appropriate roles of men and women, parents, children, leaders and workers, and so on? How does the media define success?

① MINUTE TASK

In pairs, list four or more people or groups in your community who have power and suggest why they have this power.

Definitions

Ideology

The concept of ideology is key to the study of media. It is essential that when we talk of ideology we are careful to define what we mean by the term. The term ideology refers to:

Sets of ideas which usually give a partial and selective account of the social world.

The relationship of these ideas or values to the ways in which power is distributed socially.

The way that such values and ideas are normally explained as 'common sense', 'natural', and 'obvious' rather than socially constructed.

USA researchers David Croteau and William Hoynes, describe ideology as "a system of meaning that helps explain the world and that makes value judgements about that world". (Croteau and Hoynes, 2003:160).

Can you add to these definitions of ideology?

Ideology is closely related to concepts such as world view, belief systems and values. Ideology therefore is not simply about politics but takes into account how we define our world. When we examine ideology, the key is the relationship between the words and images in a media text and the ways of thinking about the social and cultural issues involved.

British academic Jonathan Bignell says "Ideologies are always shared by members of a group or groups in society, and one group's ideology will often conflict with another's." (Bignell, 2002:24). But, as Bignell notes, the situation is subject to alteration: "The dominant ideology in society is subject to change, as the economic and political balance of power changes." (Bignell, 2002:25). Ideology then is always changing and always dependent on history. What was self-evident and common sense in one decade or century might not necessarily be acceptable later. In the nineteenth century it was believed that men were superior to women, which was why women were not allowed to vote in much of the world. In South Africa, most adults only received the right to vote in 1994. Neither view would be acceptable today. And commonly held views of today – your own strongly-held views - may well be discredited in the future.

(15) MINUTE TASK

In groups, consider three beliefs or values that have changed over the last 20 years. What can you deduce from this?

"Politicians have long perceived mass media, both news and entertainment, as sites for the dissemination [*distribution*] of ideology," note American scholars David Croteau and William Hoynes. "That is one reason why the media is so frequently the subject of political debate. Indeed, prominent politicians routinely identify mass media as facilitator [*someone who assists*], and sometimes a source of social problems." (Croteau and Hoynes, 2003).

Politicians from all persuasions regularly attack the mass media – radio, television, movies, music and the internet – for being ideological. They criticise the selling of certain messages and world views that do not coincide with their own ideology. Because the views expressed in the mass media are often well received by the public, it is logical to assume that large numbers of the public agree with the ideology expressed, even if they do not use the term. There has been a long debate between those who argue that the media promotes the world view of the powerful – the dominant ideology – and those who argue that mass media includes more contradictory messages. The latter group argues that mass media expresses and supports the dominant ideology but also, more importantly, challenges those views.

Ideology and media texts

It can be argued that media texts are sites where cultural contests over meaning can be debated, rather than being sites that provide a single expression of an ideology. Media texts are sites where ideological perspectives, representing different interests with unequal power, can engage in debate. Some ideas will have an advantage because they are perceived as being more popular and build on familiar media images. Other ideas will be disadvantaged and less popular. Such ideas may live around the fringes of the debate waiting to be used and popularised at a more opportune moment (maybe never) by politicians, activists and academics. And some ideologies might find more congenial homes in particular media, such as the internet, even though they may be banned by law from use in the media. Neo-Nazis are not allowed by legislation to disseminate their hate speech in Germany, but they find ways to colonise cyberspace.

Some definitions of ideology describe it as 'belief systems' that help justify the actions of those in power by distorting and misrepresenting reality. Most ideological analyses of mass media concentrate on the message content – the stories they tell – rather than on the effects of those stories. In the context of media, the term ideology refers to the underlying message that media texts convey. We will consider a few that have affected media in the last hundred years, and continue to influence behaviour and analysis.

The Marxist approach to media

The German-born philosopher, political economist, and revolutionary, Karl Marx (1818 - 1883) questioned the supposedly natural but deeply unequal order of things in society. He analysed the new profit- and market-dominated system of capitalism and the power of the two classes within it: the rising industrial manufacturers or capitalists and the working class or proletariat.

Definitions

Capitalism

Economic
determinism

He emphasised the importance of class difference, or people's different relationship to the means of production [factories, banks and so on], as key to the kinds of values and political ideas they will have. Do they own the factories, banks, and country estates? Or do they have to earn their living by working for the owners of factories and banks?

Karl Marx was particularly interested in capitalists' relationship to their employees, the working classes whom, he argued, had the power to change history by their united action. He explained how the capitalist class protected and preserved its economic interests, even during years of unrest and revolutions, in the following way:

The dominant or most influential ideas of any society are those who work in the interests of the ruling class to secure its rule or dominance. Those that control the means of production thereby control the producing and circulating of the most important ideas in society. This is the key to why the bodies that make meaning, including the media, represent political issues the way they do. To successfully challenge the ruling class the proletariat needs to develop its own ideas and the means of circulating those ideas. The basic needs of a social order are met by institutions like the media, religious structures and cultural life. The dominant class is thus able to make workers believe that the existing relations of exploitation and opposition are natural, inescapable and inevitable. This power conceals how existing conditions could be changed and conceals the interest it has in preventing such change.

Gramsci's approach to media

Italian revolutionary, politician and Marxist critic Antonio Gramsci (1891 - 1937) formed a key way of thinking about how dominant value systems can change through struggle. Gramsci describes how people are influenced into accepting the dominance of a power elite who impose their will and world view on the rest of the population. Unlike Karl Marx, Gramsci argued that particular social groups in modern democracies continuously struggle for ascendancy, dominance and power, using persuasion (including persuading the media) and consent as well as force (including sometimes forcing the media to comply).

Because this power is never secured once and for all time, it has to be constantly negotiated, which makes the media a key player in this struggle. From our perspective it is important to note that people are not forced, or tricked into a 'false consciousness' [*false sense of reality of the world*]. Rather, citizens have their consent actively fought for, all the time - and nowadays this struggle is often exclusively waged through the media.

Antonio Gramsci argues that the elite are able to rule because we allow them to do so. In this context, notes Phillip Rayner, the ideological role of the media is to persuade the population that it is in their best interest to accept the dominance of this elite. (Rayner, et al, 2001:82). Gramsci noted, however, that power is also wielded at the level of culture or ideology and not just through the use of force. He suggested that when power is wielded at the level of culture, in the realm of everyday life, people will agree to the current social arrangement. Citizens consent to a 'cultural leadership'. Institutions such as schools, universities, religions and the media help the powerful elite exercise this cultural leadership. All these institutions are sites where we produce and reproduce ways of thinking about society. Hegemony is therefore subtle, operating at the level of common sense in the assumptions and decisions we make about everyday life and the things we accept as normal. Gramsci, as quoted by David Croteau and William Hoynes states, "one of the most effective ways of ruling is through the shaping of commonsense assumptions. What we take for granted exists in a realm that is uncontested, where there is neither a need nor room for questioning assumptions." (Croteau and Hoynes, 2003:166).

⑩ MINUTE TASK

In groups discuss how your favourite cultural institution, your religion (or lack of it) and the local media exercise cultural or ideological leadership.

Who has power now?

The processes identified by Antonio Gramsci are not permanent. Gramsci saw hegemony as a daily struggle about our underlying conceptions of the world. It is a dynamic and continuous process, always in the making depending on historical conditions and responses to it. To wield power in this manner requires that the level of 'common sense' in people must be continually reinforced. Otherwise, people's actual experiences will lead them to question the current dominant ideological assumptions. "People are active agents, and modern society is full of contradictions; therefore hegemony can never be complete or final. Some people will not accept the basic hegemonic worldview and some people may resist it," he wrote.

Althusser's approach to media

The Algeria-born French communist and philosopher Louis Althusser (1919 – 1990) developed an idea of human society as a network of interrelated elements and structures of power, often referred to as structuralism. Althusser argued that parts of society's economic superstructure are relatively autonomous, or operate independently of each other. Class rule is sustained by two kinds of organised and related power:

The repressive state apparatus, including the army, police, prisons and law courts, which wins and maintains power by force; and

The ideological state apparatus, including education, the church and other religious bodies, party politics, the family and the media. These maintain power by producing imaginary relations to the real structures of power. It does this by naturalising assumptions [*making matters appear natural and acceptable so that people consent to the existing social order*].

Louis Althusser's approach is rigid. It implies there can be no way out of ideology, as anything which appears as 'common sense' is always to be distrusted. (Of course, this fails to account for his own work, as noted by David Croteau and William Hoynes. They point out that in theory, Louis Althusser must be outside the influence of ideology to write about it at all – perhaps this offers us some hope!) (Croteau and Hoynes, 2003).

Other analysts argue that those who control large portions of the media, such as Australian global media executive Rupert Murdoch or American entrepreneur Bill Gates, founder of the computer company Microsoft, share in the privilege of the dominant class. Therefore they ensure that the social imagery and knowledge which is circulated through the media is broadly in the interests of those at the top of the social pyramid, so as to reproduce the system of class inequalities from which it benefits.

Increasing the concentration of power within a few media conglomerates will inevitably lead to a decline in the range of material available to the public. The voices of those lacking economic power to challenge this concentration of economic power will continue to be silenced.

Foucault's approach to media

Definitions

Discourse

Discourse analysis

French philosopher and social critic Michel Foucault (1926 - 1984) introduced an alternative concept as the term ideology became unfashionable. His focus is on discourse analysis, a form of mass communication analysis which concentrates upon ways in which the media convey information, focusing on the language of presentation. It goes into detail, including linguistic patterns, word and phrase selection, grammatical construction and story coherence. In particular, according to the *Dictionary of Media and Communication Studies*, by James Watson and Anne Hill, Foucault's analysis tries to account for the form in which the mass media present ideology to its readership or audience. (Watson and Hill, nd:92).

Society, according to Michel Foucault, creates institutions with their own practices and discourses. Those working in them soon learn to adopt the practices and style which is considered acceptable, the common language, attitudes and behaviour in that institution. Therefore, you are unlikely to be allowed to join and remain within an institution unless you are able to demonstrate compatibility [*be able to exist, live, or work together without conflict*] with the practices that are already in operation. You can see examples of this in 'old boys' clubs' and networks in society. Conformity, compliance and obedience here is the key. Clearly, as South African-born, Australia-based researcher Eric Louw points out, this limits what one is able to think, say and write and restricts the knowledge and ideas that can appear.

How should I speak and behave in this particular situation?

Michel Foucault shows how this becomes a powerful tool for social control, because certain questions or issues can simply be excluded from participation. This ends debate and obviously people who cannot engage in the debate will not be able to influence any conclusions. As academic and former journalist Eric Louw points out a lack of debate predetermines what conclusions may be reached. (Louw, 2001:29). The 'free enterprise' discourse can, for example, prevent its promoters from admitting or considering the notion that capitalism may disadvantage certain sectors of society. (Louw, 2001:31).

10 MINUTE TASK

In groups, consider a newspaper, radio or TV station you worked for (or your educational institution if you are not yet employed). Did you follow a specific discourse – in terms of language, dress, politics, gender or religion – which helped or hindered your attempts to be employed or educated?

Propaganda and censorship

Governments and the power elite or ruling class use propaganda when they believe they need to control and shape public opinion. They use propaganda in both coercive ways [*using force, or having the power to use force, to make people do things against their will*] as well as ways which are proactive [*taking the initiative by acting rather than reacting to events*]. This can be achieved in a number of ways but the most favoured are:

Censorship [*the suppression of all or part of a publication, play, or film considered offensive or a threat to security*] of sensitive information.

Only giving information (normally selective information) to certain trusted journalists.

Only allowing particular accredited journalists into certain areas such as war zones.

Banning certain material that may show the government in a poor light.

Applying direct pressure on the media not to report certain issues or to report in a selective way.

Trying to get the media to self-censor.

Can you add any other ways in which propaganda is used by those in power to control public opinion?

✓ SELF-STUDY TASK

In the light of the information in this chapter, analyse your local daily newspaper, radio station and television news in terms of ideologies presented. Compare and contrast two newspapers which have different ideologies but cover the same event from different perspectives.

---

5 Media representation

Outcomes

By the end of this chapter you will be able to:

◗ Summarise the basic issues in media representation.

◗ Analyse media for fairness, accuracy and objectivity.

◗ Define media concepts.

◗ Assess articles, news report images and other media texts in terms of form and content, context and message and language.

◗ Understand the concepts of signs, codes, body language, denotation and connotation and stereotypes.

◗ Explain the concept of the signified and the signifier.

◗ Critique media texts.

How the media represents the world

Definitions

Representation

Reality

The media is an important source of information about the world at large and a powerful means of shaping our attitudes and beliefs. Because the media is a principal source of our understanding of the world, it is therefore important that the media's representation of the world is as accurate, fair and as free from bias [*prejudice*] as possible.

There is a great philosophical debate over what constitutes 'reality', so it is important to remember that there is no one-size-fits-all, totally-accepted, global, single reality. For our study, we will assume that there is an external reality, and that a key function of the media is to represent that external reality to us, the audience.

How fair, accurate and objective?

We must always remember that the media offers us a representation of reality, not reality itself. What is represented to us by the media has been reshaped and constructed by the media. We need to ask ourselves the following questions:

Can we trust the representation that is being made to be an accurate interpretation?

To what degree has the context [*background*] determined the nature of the representation?

To what degree has the audience's expectations determined the nature of the representation?

In whose interest is it that the representation is made in this way?

We usually associate the word 'text' with something that is printed or written but in the case of media studies the term refers to any media product such as television programmes, photographs, radio programmes, advertisements, newspaper articles, web pages, media on cellphones and the internet and so on.

15 MINUTE TASK

If you were asked to describe an incident that took place at college today, how would you describe it to:
- A college friend who was not present but knows all concerned?
- A non-college friend?
- Your parents?
- MySpace.com?

How would you represent the above incident to each of the above? Would your representation vary? How? Why? What factors would influence your representation of the events? How would you select, edit and prioritise the information you wish to present?

Image analysis

'Seeing is believing' is a common phrase in the English language: most people rely on their sight so much that they neglect their other senses of hearing, taste, smell and touch. The concept is so powerful that the majority accept it as true. In reality, what we see can often be very misleading.

One of the best examples of the eye providing misleading information to the brain and not always giving the true answer can be illustrated by watching a

televised boxing match. What you will notice if you concentrate on the commentary as well as the action is that in many cases, the commentators seem to commentating on a different fight and giving an inaccurate description of the fight.

Why?

Well, the commentators are normally at ringside and are situated directly below the action. The images that we see on our television sets usually come from a number of cameras situated above the ring, so in effect, we are not seeing the action from the same perspective as the commentators who may have described a punch as having connected, when from our view it clearly did not. This is probably one reason why judges' scorecards in boxing can show such variances: each judge in effect has seen a different fight. So, what our eyes have relayed to our brains is not always an accurate picture of what occurred.

Interpreting the world around us

As we get older, better educated and more experienced, with any luck we start to interpret our world differently than we did as children. This is because we learn to understand what is happening around us. This understanding does not come naturally so the particular society we live in has a profound affect on us. We view the world through that understanding.

When we first start to analyse images it is best to do it as objectively as possible. At the first stage of analysis, denotation, we are merely in the process of identification. For example, if we describe a particular colour as 'red', or a cat as a 'small, four legged, furry, domesticated animal', this is denotation. Theoretically, at the level of analysis, known as denotation, almost everyone will describe an image in exactly the same way. This is not the case, suggesting that even denotation is affected by an individual's understanding of the world.

However, we may later associate 'red', with passion and danger. 'Catty' or 'cattish', in some versions of English, is associated with being spiteful. This is not denotation but connotation. There's more on the topic later in this chapter.

Describe the same scene: three male teenagers wearing hooded jackets and takkies (trainers) walking towards you one evening. We are very likely to interpret the scene using our own life experiences and will read into the various modes of dress, attitudes, race, gender and expressions. Women, often victims of sexual abuse, might read even more into the scene.

What would go through your mind in this situation? How would you react and why? Under the circumstances, what would be an appropriate response if you were a journalist? How would you combat any automatic assumptions [guesses] about the situation?

If we consider the situation further and look at each individual's body language, we find even more coded information which we can interpret. These signs and

Definitions

Interpretation

Denotation

Connotation

symbols are part of what is referred to as non-verbal communication. Try watching a television programme (not the news, which often carries subtitles) with the sound turned off. Or watch a television programme in a language you don't understand. See how much information you can pick up from the visual clues?

Reading images

Every day we are bombarded with different images, whether still or moving, that we have to interpret. Television, film and internet images, graffiti, advertising, warning signs, photographs in books, magazines, newspapers and mobile phones all have to be interpreted (understood) in order for us to make sense of them and to make a value judgement as to the message being conveyed to us, the audience.

When we analyse a photographic image, or any other media, it is important to distinguish between its form and content.

> Form is how the image is created, taking into account the camera position relative to the subject of the image.

> Content is simply what is in the image.

What is in this text/image (content)?

How is it created (form)?

Form

Information regarding how an image was created or cropped (edited) is usually not available, although some file-sharing websites provide highly technical information about the digital camera used. Normally, however, we have to make these assumptions [*guesses*] from the image itself. And some information can be added or subtracted independently of the cameraperson, so a South American photographer can have his or her work cropped and reframed by an editor in London, without his knowledge or permission, and the caption altered. Consider the following:

Framing

The frame defines the position from which the image was created and is the border of the space we are allowed to see. This relationship is important, particularly when making a film. The formal aspects that the frame does not determine are the depth of field (what is in focus) and the quality of the film or digital image.

Dimension and shape

All frames have a shape and are usually only significant if they are unconventional. The standard cinema film dimension called the Academy ratio was standardised in the 1930s when sound transformed the silent movies, and remained until the wide-screen revolution of the 1950s. Although screen and print sizes will vary, the relationship between the image's height and width, called the aspect ratio, will not.

Angle

The camera's angle in relation to the vertical is referred to as the angle of vision. The most common angle is the straight-on position. Low angles are used to indicate positions of power – the audience is required to look up at the subject. High angles are used to portray the subject in a subservient position (audience looks down at the subject). A high or low angle might be the only positions available to the camera – for example, in a war zone, many cameramen crouch or lie flat to take pictures to protect their lives - and therefore should not always be assumed to be portraying power or subservience.

Distance

Distance refers to the distance of the object from the camera. Categories range from the extremely long shot used for landscapes, the medium shot used for one or two people and the extreme close-up of part of a face.

Depth of field

Depth of field refers to the distance between the nearest and furthest points from the camera which are in focus. Deep focus will have the whole scene in focus, whereas a conventional shot will have the subject in focus and the background out of focus. By using special filters, a soft focus effect can be achieved by preventing the appearance of hard edges in the image.

Mobile frames

Mobile frames are used to achieve a moving image. They include the following:

> The pan: the camera moves horizontally, up to 360 degrees, from a static position.

> Tracking or dolly: the camera moves on tracks to give a smooth movement.

> Handheld: gives the frame a shaky look.

> Zoom: technically not a movement, the camera is held still and the focal length is altered during the shot bringing the subject closer, zoom and wide-angle takes the subject further away.

Using cellphone cameras, many of which come equipped to take both still photos and video (moving images), it can be useful to film the same person saying the same thing or doing the same task from different angles and in different styles (zoom versus handheld, for example) to see if the different techniques support or undercut the person's presence. Do certain angles or techniques make the content of the message easier to understand or harder to understand?

(20) MINUTE TASK

In groups, analyse three photographs from your local newspaper or magazine, in terms of the aspects of form above.

Content – mise-en-scène

The French term *mise-en-scène* means 'to put on stage' and is used in film to describe the director's total control of what appears in the frame of the film. It is important to assume that everything in the frame is there for a purpose and has meaning. In other words, everything you see in a television, advertisement or film text is a series of codes waiting to be interpreted.

There are three main components of mise-en-scène analysis:

the subject;

the lighting; and

the setting.

Subject

The subject of an image can be a person, a group or almost anything at all. It may represent reality or be totally abstract. To make sense of the subject of an image we must employ our cultural knowledge and the norms of society prevailing at the time that the image is meant to depict.

The positions in which the subjects are placed in the image is referred to as the composition, or arrangement, of the shot. A convention used by photographers – the 'rule of thirds' – is to place the subject a third of the way in from either end of the frame. This is aesthetically or visually more pleasing than placing the subject in the middle which would divide the image in half.

Lighting

This refers to how an image is illuminated. Lighting can be natural, artificial or a combination of both. Lighting is used in a number of coded ways to arrive at different effects in the image. Shadows are sometimes used to conceal something or someone and are often used in film noir – dark suspenseful, detective thrillers. In most of the images you will study, the lighting will not be natural and will be used to achieve a particular outcome.

Setting

When we discuss setting, it is useful to divide the image into foreground and background. The subject, which is usually the most important element of the shot, is usually in the foreground with the setting as the background.

> ## 15 MINUTE TASK
>
> In your previous groups, analyse the same three photographs used before, from your local newspaper or magazine, in terms of setting, lighting and subject.

Definitions

Code(s)

Context

Contact

Production of meaning

What the codes of meaning (see the description of denotation earlier) actually do mean depends on consensus [*compromise or agreement*]. This is the level of connotation. Codes should not be analysed in isolation because their meaning is usually determined by other factors such as the context and message.

Context, contact and message

The context is the social situation in which the message is embedded. If one of the variable in an image is changed this would affect the message.

> ## 10 MINUTE TASK
>
> Visualise a picture of a cowboy wearing a wristwatch. What would that tell us about the context?

A film in a particular genre [*type*] sets up particular expectations in the audience. In a cowboy (western) film which appears to be placed in the American pioneer era, the appearance of a wristwatch would obviously profoundly change the context. The context in which the image is viewed also sets off different expectations. So does the company in which the image is viewed. Young teenage boys viewing an adult film at home on a Digital Video Disk (DVD) or video may react differently than if they sneaked into a cinema to see the same film. And they would certainly respond differently if their sister, mother or grandmother showed up in the next row! The context, therefore, is external information that influences how a text is read.

The contact is the channel of communication and the manner in which the audience receives the information. The text most often affected by contact is film. Film is best seen in a cinema but is most often watched on television where the quality is poor and there are additional distractions, resulting in the various audiences seeing different products. The sound and visual effects of blockbusters are usually lost or diminished when shown on television or video, and even more so on laptop computers or in cars or buses which can run DVDs. However, video and DVD-using audiences do have the advantage of being able to rewind, review, pause, and stop. This privilege is not enjoyed by the cinemagoer, although television users can now access it as well if they can afford the relevant additional technology. Although many directors feel that it is better to enjoy a text in the medium for which it was intended, others have embraced this diversity and issue special releases meant to be used on DVD, with extra interviews and extended scenes.

Contact has possibly the least influence on the meaning generated by the communication. Information is being sent to the audience. But there is no certainty that the message will be received and read by the audience in the way it was intended. Advertisements are often misread and misunderstood by their audiences especially where an advert made in one cultural or social context is shown in another. Often texts are misunderstood because the audience do not understand the codes employed. For this reason media texts are often reinforced by the use of images and words to anchor [fix] the meaning. In most case images are used to illustrate and reinforce the message. Clearly, in the early silent cinema and when using foreign languages without subtitles, the image must carry all the information about the narrative.

⑤ MINUTE TASK

Consider how the same message, for example a similar item of news via television, radio, internet, newspaper and magazine, is received by audiences.

Canadian media researcher Marshall McLuhan (1911 - 1980), who also coined the phrase 'the global village', said "the medium is the message."

This is an oversimplification of the act of communication but his words do illustrate how the medium can transform the meaning of the message the audience is receiving. Television, for example, relies more on words to deliver its message. This is because visually, it is not as powerful as cinema, although recent technical advancements in home entertainment systems and high-definition television are rapidly changing that. The television message has to be unambiguous [unable

Message

Ambiguous

Image + words = clearer meaning

What are the codes used in this text?

to be misunderstood] and easily understood. Although images play a vital role, words are still important because they present a lesser chance of the possibility of any ambiguity in the message. Radio, on the other hand, has to rely only on sound and words to transmit its message.

What should be remembered is that the message should be unambiguous [*unable to be misunderstood*] and easily understood. Although images play a vital role, words are still important because they present a lesser chance of the possibility of any ambiguity in the message.

⑤ MINUTE TASK

In pairs analyse an advert (TV or radio) that you have difficulty in understanding. Suggest why this is so.

Media text

In order to make meaning of media texts, it helps to comprehend the various codes, rules and conventions by which signs are put together to make meaning.

Language itself is a set of codes with letters making up words, words in a specific order and according to rules forming sentences, with sentences in turn forming paragraphs and so on. So, just as we learn to read and use language in our younger days, so we can learn to 'read' media codes and language. We soon learn that sound and/or images can be joined in a specific sequence to work as codes to give specific meanings.

According to British scholar Jonathan Bignell "there is no perfect analytical method for studying the media because there are so many different ways to approach the task." (Bignell, 2002:3). Two ways to consider the meaning of media texts could be:

A detailed analysis of the text.

Asking individuals how they interact with the specific text.

Think of your favourite adverts on TV, radio and in the press. Consider how the sounds, movement and images have been put together in order to arrive at the advertiser's message. Deconstruct [*analyse*] one of the adverts into its essential codes.

Definitions

Signs

Semiotics

Semiotics

The word semiotics derives from the Greek word for sign and is the study of signs (such as words, pictures and symbols). Semiotics also looks at the role played by signs in the construction and reconstruction of meaning in media texts. Semiotic approaches view language and the structures of language as creating the opportunity of representing the world in a particular way.

Using a semiotic approach, the media, far from distorting the reality or providing a barrier between the audience and some mythical real experience, is seen as a place where particular meanings are formed, playing a part in actually producing and framing or outlining the way in which people begin to understand their social world. According to United Kingdom researchers Lisa Blackman and Valerie Walkerdine, the media is part of a wider apparatus. It reproduces and produces, through the particular organisation of signs embodied within the media text, wider cultural values and beliefs. (Blackman and Walkerdine, 2001:20).

Semiotics can be a challenge when you are exposed to the concept for the first time. But Jonathan Bignell, currently based at the University of Reading in England, argues that an advantage of the semiotic approach is that it is applicable to a much wider field of "meaning-making which includes, for instance, fashion, theatre, dance, literature and even architecture." (Bignell, 2002:1).

Can you think of ways in which semiotics might influence journalism?

Signs

Language is the most fundamental and all-encompassing medium for human communication. Semiotics takes the view that language works as the basis for all communication and all other sign systems. We use language to explain the relationship between things and the reality around us. For example, we use the word 'children' to describe and identify a group of very young people as distinct from adults who in turn share common features. In different parts of the world the word child may have a slightly different meaning depending on legal, social, religious and cultural status etc. However, what makes the sign 'child' meaningful to us is the distinction between 'child' and 'adult', according to the normal conventions of our culture.

⑤ MINUTE TASK

On your own, define and write down the following terms:
A child is a ...
An adult is a ...

Compare your answer with your partner's answer.

Language is a sign system which shapes our reality and acts as a channel to pass on meaning. "All our thought and experience, our very sense of our own identity, depends on the systems of signs already existing," writes Jonathan Bignell. "It is language which enables us to refer uniquely to ourselves by giving us the sign 'I'." (Bignell, 2002:7).

Different types of signs

Symbolic signs represent an object or a concept solely by the agreement of the people who use them. Phillip Rayner, writes that there are no obvious connections between the symbolic sign and the object it represents. (Rayner, et al, 2001:33).

car

CAR

For example, there is no obvious connection between the 'car' and a mode of transport. It only works as a sign because we understand the rules of the English language that when the letters are put in a certain order they signify a certain mode of transport. In another language, the letters CAR, in capitals, might mean something totally different, such as Central African Republic, a country in Africa, or nothing at all.

You will appreciate "that at this point the sign says nothing about any real car out there in reality," as Jonathan Bignell, from the Centre for Television Drama Studies at the UK's University of Reading, points out. "The sign is made up of entities, signified and signifier, which are joined together in the minds of the language users. The sign cat does not refer to any particular cat, but to a mental concept." (Bignell, 2007:62).

⑤ MINUTE TASK

On your own, write down three examples of symbols and their meaning. Explain their meaning to your partner.

Arbitrary signs are arrived at by agreement among their users. "These types of signs do not have any direct or intrinsic connection with what is being signified" says Phillip Rayner "This means that arbitrary signs can have several meanings that are contested [*argued about*], or about which people do not agree." (Rayner, 2001:33).

⑤ MINUTE TASK

Give three examples of arbitrary symbols and explain their meaning to the person next to you.

Iconic signs bear resemblance to that which they represent; they look like it or sound like it and can be images or graphics. Photographs can also be considered *iconic* because they have physical similarities to the objects they represent or signify. We have many iconic symbols in everyday life. For example, wherever we go in the world, we will usually be able to find the men's and women's toilets by the iconic signs on the doors.

⑤ MINUTE TASK

On your own, write down three examples of iconic symbols and their meanings. Explain their meaning to your partner. Discuss your partner's examples as well.

Indexical signs are those signs that have a direct connection with what is being signified. Road signs are good examples of universal indexical signs. So are many of the symbols (emoticons) used with SMS text on cellphones.

⑤ MINUTE TASK

Write down three examples of indexical symbols – perhaps from your route to campus today, or from your cellphone. Explain their meaning to your partner. Consider your partner's examples. Are they indexical symbols or another type of symbol?

Definitions

Anchorage

Polysemic

Preferred meaning

What is important is that we accept that media texts are usually complex messages made up of all the different signs we have discussed. The act of watching television makes meaning from a complex set of signs that the audience has become used to reading. Because they understand the meaning of the signs and how they work, the audience is able to interpret the media text.

Iconic signs, for example, are important because they appear so natural and closely related to what they represent. It is therefore easy to forget that what we are observing is a sign and confuse the sign with reality itself. This is also important for the way in which we read the representation of reality in the media. Media texts can have several possible meanings depending on the way in which the signs are read and the background knowledge and experience of the reader. The signs are open to many interpretations (polysemic). Sometimes, however, a particular or preferred meaning is indicated by the way in which the text has been produced and presented to the reader. Many adverts are ambiguous until we notice a particular sign, usually the advertiser's name, which anchors the meaning, giving it one preferred interpretation. Anchorage is the fixing or limiting of a particular set of meanings to an image. One of the most common forms of anchorage is the caption underneath a photograph.

Signified and signifier

Definitions

Signifier

Signified

Signs are dynamic and work as part of a structure that is in place at a given point in time. For example, denim clothes used to be work-clothes since their use became widespread in the America gold rush around 1850. Denims – once only worn by sailors in the port of Genoa in Italy - became clothing signs in a code for manual labour. Then, in the 1950s in the USA, jeans became a sign whose meaning was 'youthfulness'. Now it is a sign meaning 'casual'. The dynamic coded meaning of jeans depends much more on their relationship with, and difference from, other coded signs in the clothing system today.

There are two components to every sign:

Signifier

The signifier is the vehicle that expresses the sign, like a pattern of sound which make up a word, the marks on a paper which we read as a word or words or the shapes and colours which make up a photograph used to depict a particular image. The signifier is the vehicle which immediately calls up the signified or concept in your mind.

Thought/mental concept of car/signified.

Signified

The second part of the sign is called the signified. It is the concept that the signifier calls forth when we perceive it. When you perceive the word 'car' written on this page, you perceive a group of marks, the c, a, and r which are the signifier.

Colour/shape/ words e.g. c-a-r/ experience/signifier.

The sign is an inseparable unity of the signifier with the signified, since we never have one without the other.

"The division of a sign into a signified and a signifier made it possible to describe how language divides up the world of thought, creating the concepts which shape our actual experience," says Jonathan Bignell. "The signifieds or concepts in our minds are shaped by the signifiers that our language provides for us to think and talk with." (Bignell, 2002:13). If it shapes language, semiotics certainly will shape journalism as well.

Codes

Signs often work through a series of codes that are usually socially constructed or created by a particular society and therefore agreed upon by society as a whole," notes Phillip Rayner (Rayner et al, 2001:63). In media texts there are many different codes at work and some of the most obvious and common are: dress codes, colour codes and non-verbal codes. They depend on culture and context which are open to change.

Definitions

Code(s)

Dress codes relate to what we wear in a specific context. For example, we normally associate people wearing bathing costumes with the beach or the swimming pool. What is appropriate to wear in one situation is not in another. On some occasions dress rules are deliberately broken.

---

(10) MINUTE TASK

In groups, suggest what is appropriate to wear at the following functions: job interview, cinema and wedding.

Colour codes also vary from culture to culture. The colour black is associated with death and mourning in the Western world and in parts of Africa and South America that have been heavily influenced by Christianity. But in some parts of

Asia the colour white is worn at funerals and cremations instead. Consider the different meanings the colour red has for different cultures: in some it is the sign for danger or sex; in some cultures it is used for a bride.

10 MINUTE TASK

In pairs, consider the different meanings of different colours in your respective cultures.

Non-verbal codes are what are normally referred to as body language and gesture. These also vary from culture to culture. Let's consider how personal space varies from culture to culture. In some cultures men, when greeting each other, will stand arm's length apart and shake hands. In others they may embrace or even kiss each other two or three times. However, in these same cultures, a man might greet a woman with only a slight nod of the head, keeping a fair degree of personal space between the sexes. Any form of intimate contact, like touching or kissing between the sexes, might be considered taboo.

Body Language

Body language or non-verbal communication is an important channel of communication which human beings use mostly unconsciously. Argyle, in Nick Lacey's book, describes eight aspects of non-verbal communication:

Facial expression;
Gaze;
Gesture and other body movements;
Posture;
Body contact;
Spatial behaviour;
Clothes and appearance; and
Non-verbal aspects of speech such as the tone in which it is delivered.
(Lacey, 2000:11).

Each of the above aspects has its own codes. As members of society, we are able to interpret them. Most of these codes are culture specific. Like language, these codes are learned. Just as children we learned to use language, so we learned the non-verbal language associated with our specific culture, and learned it so well that we do not have to think consciously when we use it. We know, for example, that when a person's gaze is too long it becomes a stare and is considered inappropriate. In some cultures it is appropriate to look a person in the eye when addressing them. In other cultures, to look an elder in the eye when addressing them would be the height of bad manners. The clothes we wear, (when and how) and our hair styles all make a statement about who and what we are and where we wish to position ourselves in society.

Like language, non-verbal codes are learned and dynamic, changing as society changes. We spend all our time unconsciously interpreting the information our senses receive from the environment by using the codes we have learned in order to give meaning to our world.

(15) MINUTE TASK

In groups, analyse the way you greet members of the opposite sex (your own age and older) in your culture, using non-verbal communication.

Denotation and connotation

French literary critic, philosopher and semiotician Roland Barthes (1915 – 1980) noted important aspects of the transmission of a message.

Definitions

Denotation

Denotation, according to Barthes, is simply a process of identification. "Denotation is what an image actually shows and is immediately apparent," says Argyle, in Nick Lacey's book. (Lacey, 2000:38). Denotation refers to the facts in the text. "Denotation is what an image actually shows and is immediately apparent, rather than the assumption [best guess] an individual reader may make of it." Denotation can be considered the labelling function of signs to denote a fact. But denotation is still open to confusion and misinterpretation.

Connotation

The second stage, connotation, is the act of adding meaning - information, insight, angle, value and so on - to the same media text. The reader of media texts goes through various stages when deconstructing the meaning of a sign. The reader adds his or her own information and opinions to the text. The reader attempts to translate what the sign is signifying by using his or her cultural background and experience. Connotation is arrived at through the reader's cultural experience.

For example, a photograph of Durban denotes a city. This is the denotation or labelling function. Because Durban is a sub-tropical city with wonderful beaches and sunny weather all year and South Africa's holiday capital, the name Durban no longer denotes simply the name of a city but can be used to connote care-free holidays and happy times. This is the connotation.

In groups, work out the denotative and connotative meanings of the following:

▶ rastafarians

▶ BMW cars

▶ feminists

How would you represent the above example to each of the above? Would your representation vary? How? Why? What factors would influence your representation of the information? How would you select, edit and prioritise the information you wish to present?

Metaphors and metonymy

Media texts often connect one signified idea with another or one signifier with another, in order to endow people and things with mystic meanings," writes James Watson and Anne Hill in the *Dictionary of Media and Communication Studies*. Watson and Hill say there are two ways in which these associations work:

> One is called metaphor, a figure of speech which works by transporting qualities from one to another. For example, the English-language phrase 'The camel is the ship of the desert'. It works by making one signified appear similar to another different signified. (Watson and Hill, nd:191).

> The other is called metonymy and as Jonathan Bignell writes, metonymy works by replacing one signified with another signified. Metonymy is a selection of one available image to represent the whole; "sceptre and crown" represents royalty in the Western world, while "scythe and spade" represents Medieval European peasants. And from that selection flows our interpretation or understanding of the whole. (Bignell, 2002:17).

Thus the selection of a piece of film of rioters in confrontation with the police acts as a 'trigger of meaning' for the way the rioters and the police are defined. For this reason, as James Watson and Anne Hill write "metonyms are powerful conveyors of reality, indeed so powerful that they can come to be accepted as actually being reality, the way things really are." (Watson and Hill, nd:192).

British media researcher Andrew Ruddock observes that "news and drama are united by the fact that they are first and foremost signifying practices that transform everyday experiences into something else ... news production procedures spin reality by systematically excluding certain voices from its accounts."

(Ruddock, 2001:122). An example of this would be a programme that tells of the war in Iraq from the perspective of the ordinary soldier or aid worker or Iraqi family rather than with the voices of Western politicians.

Some criticism of semiotics:

> All signs can have different meanings depending on the reader's interpretation. Because of this, it is difficult to judge which interpretations are valid.

> It is difficult to measure the impact or influence of signs on a reader or audience.

> The denotation stage is artificial; all readers automatically add their own meanings.

Stereotyping

Stereotypes are the media's shorthand method of representing different groups of people. Stereotypes are a necessary mode of processing information because the media need to simplify their texts in order to make it easier to represent various different groups of people to their audiences.

Rather than representing people as individuals, stereotypes provide us with sets of expectations and assumptions that we can access when we encounter groups of people who are different from us and events that we are not familiar with. These groups, often minorities (like gay men and women, recent immigrants or possibly opposition parties or atheists) are made up of people who come from all walks of life. Stereotypes are specifically used to represent them as all having the same attitudes, characteristics and behaviour. Because of this manifestly unfair representation, stereotyping is unfortunately often the result of, or accompanied by, prejudice. Stereotyping therefore, characterises whole groups of people by attributing to them qualities which may be found in one or two individuals. These characteristics are often exaggerated, and entire groups or nationalities are reduced to these specific characteristics.

The use of stereotypes reflects the power relations within a society and tends to subordinate stereotyped groups by opening them up to ridicule, suggesting that they are intellectually challenged or that they are more prone to criminal or other deviant behaviour than the rest of the population.

In groups, consider the following, how are the following groups portrayed in the various media:

▶ Gay men
▶ Nigerians
▶ Drug dealers
▶ Muslims
▶ Lawyers

Stereotyping, although an unfair representation, is a useful media device and a short-cut method used to represent a particular group in the media. It also allows media producers to condense complex information into a character who is easily recognised by the audience and simple to deal with.

The use of stereotypes does support the argument that the media are prejudiced and encourage prejudice in others. The problem with stereotypes is that they become reality to some. Communities can be very sensitive about their media stereotypes. There have been instances of so-called innocent comments being the cause of much controversy and forced media apologies to the outraged victims of stereotyping.

10 MINUTE TASK

In groups, consider the last few films that you have seen and discuss any offensive racial stereotypes portrayed.

An hour or two watching your favourite TV station will reveal that there is a good deal of gender stereotyping. Television characters are stereotyped according to certain formulas, which make the characters easily recognisable to their audience. The main character is usually a white, middle-class, youthful, good-looking male with positive character traits. Women and minorities are often portrayed negatively. For females, as American researcher James Potter writes, there are two primary stereotypes, mother or whore:

> If the woman is single, she is often portrayed as a sex object. There is a strong emphasis on the female body being attractive, desirable, and youthful. If a woman is a mother, she is usually portrayed as wise and nurturing. The profile of women on prime time television has not changed much in 50 years. Older characters, especially males, tend to be cast in comic roles. The elderly are likely to be treated with disrespect and are often shown as stubborn, eccentric and foolish. (Potter, 2001:120).

Other stereotypes you are sure to recognise include:

The strong, self-reliant, police detective who is continually in conflict with his authoritarian boss but always succeeds using his own unorthodox methods.

The nurturing mother who has strange kids and an idiot husband.

The sexy, young, intelligent female lawyer/doctor/nurse/professional who has plenty of girlfriends but struggles to find a suitable male partner.

Stereotyping can marginalise and devalue the worth of whole groups of people in society. If one looks at the way refugees are often portrayed as all living together in crowded, substandard accommodation, it can suggest that this is a matter of choice rather than the harsh economic and social reality that they have been forced to endure.

On the positive side, stereotypes make it easy for viewers to recognise character types easily and thus process stories quickly. However, on the negative side, they are inadequate, biased, resistant to social change and can serve as impediment to rational assessment.

Frequent media messages and themes

It is interesting to examine the messages that we receive from our mass media daily, you will notice certain themes such as:

Material consumption is good and should be strived for.

The world is a dangerous place.

Males are more powerful than females.

Work status is highly valued and professional work more highly considered than manual work.

A high number of programmes depicting strong language, sex and violence.

There are a disproportionate number of law enforcement programmes.

Sex and celebrities are used to sell almost everything.

Can you add to these messages and themes?

---

⑤ MINUTE TASK

In groups, debate and critique for truth and accuracy the above frequent messages and themes.

---

6 Narrative

What is narrative?

Definitions

Narrative

Restrictive

Story

Plot

Narrative or story-telling can be defined as the way in which a story, whether fictional or non-fictional, is told in media texts. From the Latin word which means 'to make known', narrative can be defined as 'to convey information'. However, this definition is far too restrictive [*limited*], considering that arrival and departure boards at airports and railway stations give information. Would we consider the information they give as narrative? No. Narrative is distinguished by the fact that it presents information as a connected, logical sequence of events. So to be a narrative there must be a sequence of at least two events. The 2003 statement 'British football star David Beckham sold to Real Madrid' is not a narrative as it stands but add 'and Manchester United fans are in uproar', then a narrative does exist.

In 2007 Beckham moved to Los Angeles in the USA to join LA Galaxy. How would you construct a narrative for the story now? Can you construct a narrative for a local sports team or athlete?

Although the term narrative is associated with non-fiction texts such as newspaper stories and fiction and media texts (such as films and novels), it is important to note that photographs are also narrative texts. The narrative can be seen as a means whereby media producers shape and control the flow of information to an audience by sequencing information about events into a logical and cohesive structure in time and space.

Story and plot

With narrative, the concept of sequence is crucial. Without development, there is no narrative. To describe development further we need to distinguish between two more concepts – story and plot. Story can be defined as 'the chronological order of all events explicitly [clearly] presented and inferred [implied] by the media text' and plot as 'everything that the text explicitly presents.'

American researchers David Bordwell and Kristin Thompson (1993) quoted in Nick Lacey's book use the following example to show the distinction between story and plot.

Story	a) Crime conceived	Plot	e) Detective investigates
	b) Crime planned		f) Detective reveals a, b, and c.
	c) Crime committed		
	d) Crime discovered		

(Lacey, 2000:17).

If the text is a detective or crime story, it makes no sense for the plot to show the audience the crime being conceived [thought about], planned, and committed because we would then know who did it – which gives this genre its nickname of 'whodunit'. Indeed, the progress of the plot, as the detective or team of detectives investigates and reveals aspects of the investigation, consists of the reconstruction of the crime. Commonly, say Bordwell and Thompson, the crime, in all its details, is revealed at the end by the detective. (Lacey, 2000:17).

Can you think of ways to distinguish between story and plot for other genres – for example, a romance and a history?

The plot is what the reader perceives. The plot is the narrative as read, seen or heard from the first to the last word or image. It is the signifier, that which calls up the concept in your mind. The story, on the other hand, is the narrative in chronological order, the order of events as they follow each other. The story, therefore, is the signified, the concept. As Bordwell and Thompson point out, the story is what the reader conceives or understands. (Lacey, 2000:18).

Narrative construction

Journalists are busy people. Those writing for daily publications or on a daily shift at a broadcaster or internet site may have to write several stories every day. Their work will require them to compile a vast array of detail that must be processed in a short time to meet deadlines. This requires the journalist to decide on what story to tell, how best to communicate that story to the newspaper or broadcaster's audience and then to polish the story via a number of drafts before the finished article is completed. Journalists on radio and television are faced with a similar problem, sometimes with worse deadlines, and although they do not use the written word in quite the same way, they still have to think of an appropriate way in which to tell their story.

Storytelling has always played an important part of our lives. We all love stories. For many of us our earliest recollection of storytelling will be the bedtime stories read to us by older family members or at story time in pre-school. The narrative is important because it acts as an organising function that helps us interpret and make sense of the world. The early fairy stories and fables helped us as children to see the world in equilibrium, the triumph of good over evil and the assurance of a 'happy ever after' ending.

What was your favourite story and how did it end?

"For media producers, narrative is an important tool for organising seemingly random and incoherent events into a coherent and logical form that an audience can assimilate," says Philip Rayner (Rayner, 2001:74).

In a busy newsroom, time is always in short supply. Most journalists, therefore, rely on a number of tried and tested formulas to produce their stories and these will be dealt with in detail later.

The most popular news gathering formula is the 5W's+1H where the journalist answers the following questions: Who? What? Where? Why? When? How? The questions do not necessarily have to be in that order, and the questions are asked on behalf of the audience.

10 MINUTE TASK

In groups, analyse a news report that uses the 5W's+1H technique.

Another popular news writing formula is the inverted pyramid. This formula demands that the journalist answer the 5W's+1H at the start of the story and then adds the descriptive detail, in decreasing levels of importance, in the following paragraphs. The advantage of this form of news reporting is that you get the gist of the story at the beginning and if you do not require any further information you can stop reading. The inverted pyramid is easy to edit because if it is too long it can be cut from the bottom up without losing the essence of the story.

⑩ MINUTE TASK

In groups, analyse a news report that uses the inverted pyramid technique.

The *Wall Street Journal* method draws attention to a person who becomes the focus but not the subject of the story. Other popular reporting methods include beginning the story with a gruesome description, conflict, or unusual quote. Some journalists like to start their stories with an anecdote, a short narrative, used to illustrate a general issue. "Anecdotes are often used in media coverage to heighten the emotional aspect of an issue," say James Watson and Anne Hill (Watson and Hill, nd:8).

⑩ MINUTE TASK

In groups, analyse a news report that uses the *Wall Street Journal* technique.

"Narrative can be used as a potent means of influencing the responses of an audience to a particular event," writes Philip Rayner. "This is often determined by the way in which the information is presented. Certainly when we are being told about a conflict, in a western or gangster movie for example, the narrative often unfolds in such a way to make us 'take sides' in support of one party. The narrative can thus be used to position an audience in such a way as to limit the range of readings available to them from the text." (Rayner et al 2001:45). An example of this is the popular American gangster television series *The Sopranos* where the hero is the mob boss Tony Soprano. Soprano is guilty of murder, extortion and adultery but is portrayed in such a way that the audience identify with him as the 'good guy', deserving of their sympathy.

Can you remember taking the side of the villain in a story? Why?

The simplest narrative

It has been argued that the underlying structure of all narratives is basically the same, the only differences being in the characters, setting and the context.

Franco-Bulgarian theorist and philosopher Tzvetan Todorov (born in 1939) reduced the concept of narrative to a simple recurring formula:

Equilibrium (harmony) → Disequilibrium (disruption) → New Equilibrium (harmony)

This can be explained by the following example: A narrative starts by describing a peaceful community/family (harmony). Enter the villain (disruption) and there is a break down of social order. This is followed by the intervention of some outside agency and the force of evil is overcome. Order (harmony) is restored – leading to a new equilibrium.

Todorov's plot is easily recognisable with the television evening news. The opening sequence is always the familiar (harmony) introduction of the news studio and news reader. Disequilibrium and disruption then follow as we are introduced to the tragic events taking place in the world - reports of wars, famines, crime, political debate, and natural disasters. Finally, at the end we are offered some amusing anecdote to provide us with some relief from the depressing news (disorder) before returning to the familiar (harmony) of the news reader shuffling papers saying goodbye in the closing sequence. The equilibrium of our familiar world is re-established.

(10) MINUTE TASK

In groups, analyse a news report that uses Todorov's technique.

Definitions

Character

Functions

Fairy tale narrative

A Germano-Russian structuralist, Vladimir Propp (1895 – 1970) used fairy stories to establish a number of character types and events associated with them. Propp, whose Russian folklore research was only translated into English in the 1950s, called these events 'functions'. Feature films, television and media rely heavily on his 31 character types.

Propp's 31 characters and functions include the following:

The hero;
The villain;
The donor (who offers gifts and magical properties);
The dispatcher (who sends the hero on a mission);
The helper (who aids the hero); and
The princess (who is the hero's reward);

⑩ MINUTE TASK

In pairs, using the above list, identify some of the characters in any film or TV programme that you have seen in the last year.

You will notice that character has an important role in cause and effect in Vladimir Propp's analysis. Characters act out of motive and when certain characters are introduced we are usually able to work out what their goals are. These motives are likely to be the cause of events that unfold around this character: marry the girl, save the world, win the race, and so on. These motives will drive the character and become the cause of action within the text. This will naturally bring the character into conflict with other characters within the text who may be acting out different motives and intent on achieving different goals. Conflict is central to the functioning of the narrative because it is important in getting the audience to take sides.

⑩ MINUTE TASK

In pairs, identify the conflict in any film or TV programme that you have seen recently. What triggered it?

Roland Barthes

The French academic Roland Barthes (1915 - 1980) whose work is explored elsewhere in this book, argued that narrative works through a series of codes that are used to control the way in which information is given to the audience. Philip Rayner (Rayner et al 2001:56) argues that two of Barthes' codes, enigma and action, are of particular importance to our understanding of how the narrative function works in media texts.

Enigma is a narrative device that teases the audience by presenting a puzzle or riddle to be solved. The obvious example here is the detective story where the audience is invited to solve the puzzle of who committed the crime.

One use of enigma is in the use of programme trailers where the audience is given just enough information about a programme to be shown or broadcast at a later date to tease them into watching the programme or continue listening to the radio. In print journalism the same device is used when constructing headlines and posters. Only enough information is given to tease the audience into reading the article. Wouldn't you want to read the story introduced by the headline "MAN BITES DOG"? Advertisements do the same, trying to convince readers to buy the advertised product.

Definitions

Enigma

Action

" Man Bites Dog! "

In groups, can you identify a film, television programme, music video or advertisement which relies on enigma in its narrative?

Audiences get a lot of pleasure from trying to predict the outcome of a particular narrative. Barthes' work on enigmatic narratives helps explain the popularity of detective and police shows on television where the audience is positioned alongside the detective in solving the mystery or crime.

Barthes' action code is a narrative device whereby a resolution is produced typically through action or violence - often on the part of the hero. The action code is therefore seen as a traditionally male genre, where problems are resolved through action.

5 MINUTE TASK

In groups, can you identify a film or television programme which uses the action codes identified by Roland Barthes?

Mode of address

Definitions

Mode of address

Voice-over

The concept of mode of address refers to the way in which the media text talks or communicates with its audience. It has important implications for the way in which the audience responds to the text.

Voice-overs, where the narrator addresses the audience directly, are a popular means of addressing an audience when there is a need for authority in the tone of delivery. Voice-overs are seen as an excellent method of delivering information that the author does not wish to be challenged. The choice of the voice is very important because it must exude authority and reinforce the message and for this reason the distinctive voice of a well-known actor is normally chosen. Voice-overs are normally used in news, current affairs programmes, and documentaries where the commentary not only develops the narrative but holds it together.

In film, voice-overs are normally used to address and confide in the audience. This makes the audience party to information that may not be common knowledge to the rest of the characters. Voice-overs offer the audience privileged information about what is occurring and we usually accept, without question, the information being communicated by this off-screen voice. But be careful: this narrative device might be used to trick or mislead the audience.

He sounds authoritative but is it true?

Modernism, Postmodernism & Structuralism

Useful terms that crop up often in any discussion on narrative are modernism, postmodernism and structuralism.

Modernism is often seen as a response to the ruptures in society caused by the First World War (1914 - 1918), which broke up four empires and caused the deaths of millions of civilians and more than nine million soldiers. In a conventional narrative, readers and viewers and listeners expect events to follow in a logical fashion towards a resolution but in a modernist novel, "texts draw attention to themselves as texts," say Bordwell and Thompson. In a modernist novel:

> Non-events can also feature.
> There is an ironic distance between the narrator and the characters.
> There is no need for realistic settings.
> The promised resolution (or resolutions) might never occur.

Can you think of a story that could be described as modern? Give reasons for your answer.

Postmodernism is a bit more difficult to explain. Postmodernism can be defined as cultural, social and political attitudes and expressions. It incorporates psycho-analysis, the 'talking cure' based on the theory of how to treat the unconscious mind in order to alter and free conscious behaviour, which was developed by Austrian neurologist and psychiatrist Sigmund Freud (1856 - 1939). Postmodern-ism also includes architecture, abstract art and fiction which incorporates the continuous random flow of thoughts, according to James Watson and Anne Hill. Five features have been identified in post-modernism:

> The distinction between culture and society is erased.
> Style is emphasised at the expense of substance and content.
>
> The distinction between high culture (art) and popular culture is broken down.
>
> There is confusion over space and time.
>
> The decline of absolute ways of describing reality (meta-narratives).
> (Watson and Hill, nd).

Can you think of a story that could be described as postmodern? Give reasons for your answer.

Structuralism argues that identifying underlying structures is all-important in undertaking social analysis. Certain social structures like the family unit may be common to most cultures. Likewise, in terms of linguistics, all languages have a similar underlying grammatical structure (so that we are born with the capacity to learn them).

The above techniques may influence the way a story is told. These techniques also influence how newspaper, television and radio reports are constructed.

7 Genre

The usefulness of genre

Genre – pronounced jhan-re as it comes from the French word for *sort* or *type* – is the classification of media texts into groups with similar characteristics. Genre can be applied to television, radio and print texts as well as film, internet websites and video games. The concept of genre is useful in looking at the way in which media texts are organised, categorised and consumed. Genre analysis normally concentrates on the producers, directors or audiences of the particular media texts, rather than on the users or consumers of the media.

Genre implies that there are story types which are recognised through common elements such as style, narrative and structure, that are repeated to make a particular type of media genre, such as a science fiction movie, or a Bollywood musical romance from India, a Nollywood action film from Nigeria or a Chinese

Definitions

Genre

kung fu action movie. An important element in identifying a genre is the 'look' or iconography of the text which constitutes a pattern of visual imagery which remains common to a genre over a period of time.

Can you identify particular genres in a single edition of a newspaper or a television news broadcast?

British academic Jonathan Bignell, writes, "It is clear that identifying a film's genre relies on identifying particular signs, and their membership of one or more codes. But the analysis of a particular film will involve comparing and contrasting the signification in a film with that of other films and with texts in other media." (Bignell, 2002:199). This is part of intertextuality - the shaping of texts' meanings by other texts. Intertextuality, a term coined by Franco-Bulgarian poststructuralist Julia Kristeva in 1966, will be dealt with later in the chapter.

"The concept of genre reminds us that films are not self-contained but are structures of signs and texts which exist within a broader social context," Bignell notes. (Bignell, 2002:200). Part of the pleasure of seeing a new film is the viewer's ability to recognise and predict meanings appropriately.

Iconography

Iconography – the study of images - has been defined by Philip Rayner "those particular signs that we associate with particular genres, such as physical attributes and dress of the actors, the settings and the 'tools of the trade.'" (Rayner et al 2001:56).

Genre as a critical tool

Media texts have been categorised into different genres for centuries. Some examples include tragedy, comedy, farce and drag (when men wear women's clothing, or the reverse). Other examples include the sonnet (a type of poem) and novels. Traditional African praise poetry in honour of the ancestors would be a genre, for example. Grouping media texts according to type makes it easier to critique them within the context of popular culture and audience appeal.

Can you read something in each of the above categories? Could you identify reasons why each text would fall in a particular category?

But placing a particular media text within a particular genre might mislead and detract from what the text has to offer. Some texts may look similar but are sufficiently different that they should not be grouped together. Sometimes a category becomes too generalised to be helpful. Although the concept of genre can be applied to all media texts, it is usually most helpful when studying film and television and only of limited use when applied to newspapers, magazines, internet and radio.

> ## ⑤ MINUTE TASK
>
> In pairs, pick a genre and then describe the dress and setting of a typical film or book.

Relationship between narrative and genre

Studying different film and television genres will reveal that the narrative is formulated in a different way for each genre. Different narrative devices [*methods*] are used to engage the audience with the text:

The cliff-hanger is designed to create suspense for the audience and ensure they tune in to the next episode of a soap opera or series. It has been used by British writers Charles Dickens (1812 - 1870) and in the modern era, Alexander McCall Smith, who both wrote daily, weekly or monthly newspaper instalments of stories which were later published as novels. Movies designed to have a sequel – such as The Matrix or X-Men – and comic books can also rely heavily on cliff-hangers.

The bomb under the table method was often used by British-born Hollywood director Alfred Hitchcock (1899 - 1980). Here suspense is developed by making the audience aware of information not shared by the characters on screen. For example, a bomb is under the table ready to explode but the on-screen characters are totally unaware of it.

The linear presentation of the narrative means that normally, a narrative will follow the basic chronology of a story. However, if an author wishes to withhold or control the release of information to the audience, a number of methods can be used to realign the story. Former South African president Nelson Mandela's autobiography, *Long Walk to Freedom*, uses a linear format.

One method is the use of **flashbacks** where the narrative allows a character to recall past events to explain current events within the narrative. The Hindu epic poem *The Mahabharata*, originally written in Sanskrit some five or six centuries ago in what is now known as India, is an early example of flashbacks, as the main story is narrated through a framing story set in a later time.

Another method, referred to as **parallel action**, normally used for complex narrative, allows for the juxtaposition [*being placed side by side*] of events taking place simultaneously but in different locations. The *Lord* of *The Rings* trilogy by New Zealand director Peter Jackson, based on the fantasy books by JRR Tolkien, is an example of this.

The anti-narrative occurs when a character who has already died, suddenly and inexplicably reappears and then later disappears again. American director Quentin Tarantino's gangster film *Pulp Fiction* with actors Uma Thurman and John Travolta is an excellent example of this technique.

---

(10) MINUTE TASK

In groups, identify the anti-narrative, the cliff-hanger, flashbacks and parallel action, and 'the bomb under the table' in some of the films or TV programmes that you have seen.

Successful genres are formulas that can be repeated over long periods of time and that the audience can recognise. For example, in detective films, we expect to see all or some of the following:

The maverick [*unconventional person*] hero.
The pompous boss – a stickler for conformity.
Car chases.
Villains.
Violence.
Corrupt police or corrupt politicians.
Beautiful women.

There are also certain performers that we associate with certain genres. In American film history, the late actor John Wayne is associated with Westerns. Actors Robert de Niro and Vinnie Jones immediately suggest gangster movies. Clint Eastwood bridges two genres, the Western (up to 1970) and the detective film (after 1970).

Some genres are so popular that they have reached cult status and have magazines dedicated to them. Television programmes such as the X-Files and Star Trek are but two examples of shows with cult followings.

Can you add other examples of television programmes which have a cult following?

---

(5) MINUTE TASK

In groups, identify standard or formulaic characters in some the of detective or police television programmes that you have watched closely.

Genre and audiences

Audiences prefer certain types of genre because they provide familiar patterns of repetition. The audience knows what to expect. Genre arouses the expectations of the audience and allows them a basis by which they can judge a media text. Audiences become familiar with the codes and conventions of specific genres and it is this familiarity through repetition of the key elements that audiences understand and relate to media texts.

Definitions

Conventions

Docu-soap

Audiences come to expect certain common codes and conventions which save both the audience and the producers from learning and developing new conventions every time they consume or develop a new media text. An excellent example of this is the TV docu-soap, which combine the elements of both documentary and soap opera. Producers of the media text rely on the audiences' understanding and ability to read each specific genre. Docu-soaps such as MTV's reality show *Laguna Beach: The Real Orange County*, which began in 2004 with unscripted situations, real-life locations and no tasks given to the cast (at least, no known ones) are able to satisfy audiences' expectations of both. Often plots are constructed later via editing or voiceovers, with the results resembling soap operas – hence the term docu-soap.

Understanding of a specific genre helps producers market a new media text because audiences understand they are being offered something familiar and are therefore likely to enjoy it. Producers are then able to exploit a winning formula, minimise their risk and hopefully maximise profit.

Although certain genres are very popular with audiences, producers still have to continually find new devices to ensure that audiences do not become bored. In recent years this has lead to the use of technology and in particular computer imaging, which has been used since the 1970s, to achieve renewed interest in familiar texts. Here it is the technology, more than deviation [*change*] from a tried and trusted formula, that maintains the audience's interest. Early examples of computer imaging in the movies include *Westworld* (1973) but more recent examples include two series, the *Pirates of the Caribbean* and *Star Wars*.

Changes in society itself, the way we live and work, have also lead to changes in genres. Producers of media texts have to be careful that their media texts are not marginalised because they have deviated too far from the generic conventions that the audience recognise and accept. For example, although there is *The Gay Detective*, an entire resource book on the sub-genre of detective fiction, many audiences may not be ready for a gay detective who abhors violence, sticks by the rules and sheds a tear when faced with sadness. But genres change: already there has been a gay detective, played by movie star Michael Douglas, on the American television show *Will and Grace* in 2002, and a 2006 film called *Shock to the System*, a gay-themed mystery film. Another stereotype may be even more embedded: when last did you see an African-American actor with a love interest, even a crossover star like Denzel Washington? And how often do black characters get killed off in detective movies?

⑮ MINUTE TASK

In groups, list some of the things that you expect to happen in a romantic comedy, a science fiction and an action film.

Media intertextuality

Audiences enjoy the experience of recognising the reference of one media text in another. This process of referencing is referred to as intertextuality. This is the way in which texts refer to other media texts that producers assume much of the audience will recognise:

Mimicry is a text that is created in one particular medium can be used in some way in another medium. The interdependent relationship between media texts can take a number of different forms and often goes beyond both genre and medium. Music videos and advertising are two genres that use this device a lot to achieve specific effects. Often this borrowing is merely stylistic, to impart a particular effect on the text. For the reader of the text however, the connotative power of the original text is likely to be carried through into the new text. Audiences enjoy this experience of recognising the originality in the way producers play with both genre and style to link their newest product and the original media text.

Pastiche occurs when the elements of one media text are used in a stylistic manner to help in the recognition of another media text. Alexandre Aja's *High Tension* is a 2005 French-language pastiche of '70s American slasher movies, a particularly gruesome type or genre of horror film.

> Is imitation the best form of flattery?

Parody aims at mocking the original text in a critical way. Pastiche is merely imitation. Parody has substance and relies on working through our knowledge of the genre or text being parodied and through recognition of the relationships between the texts. The 2005 film *My Big Fat Independent Movie* is considered a parody of every art-house (or self-consciously artistic) film of the previous decade.

Homage works through a respect for the power and importance of a particular text by imitating it. Film directors are fond of employing this technique where they deliberately create a scene, or even a whole film, in which the intertextual

Introducing Journalism and Media Studies

elements combine to pay respect to an earlier film or media text. Alfred Hitchcock, director of the movie *Psycho* in 1960, was a master of homage.

⑮ MINUTE TASK

In groups, match examples of the above four forms of intertextuality with TV programmes and other media you have seen, not using any of the examples given. Did the 'imitation' work?

Marketing

Intertextuality plays an important role in marketing media texts. A media text is promoted extensively and this advertising is often placed alongside existing products of similar nature and form. This can take the form of film trailers, which are often shown on other media such as television and radio. Other forms of marketing might be in the form of celebrity talk shows, newspaper and magazine advertising and the use of billboards. In all cases, there is an intertextual relationship between one or more texts. Jonathan Bignell writes that "genre allows films to be marketed in ways which inform potential audiences about the pleasures being offered by the film, since posters, advertising etc. contain coded signs which cue [*signal*] genre expectations." (Bignell, 2002:200).

How is a current film being marketed to audiences using knowledge of genres?

Media Reviews

Reviews of media texts appear regularly across all media forms. Film and television shows are reviewed regularly in the printed press. The media have been criticised as being narcissistic (an excessive focus on oneself, derived from an ancient Greek myth about a beautiful youth, Narcissus, who spent all his time gazing at his reflection in a pool) in that they spend a good deal of time positioning themselves at the centre of their own universe.

Definitions
Review
Critique

Do you agree with this criticism?

🎓 SELF-STUDY TASK

Analyse a review by a film critic or literary critic, of a film or book that you are familiar with. Do you agree or disagree with the review? Give your reasons.

8 Media audiences

Outcomes

By the end of this chapter, you will able to:

▎ Summarise the relevant debates on media audiences.

▎ Explain media definitions in relation to audience.

▎ Analyse target audience in relation to market.

▎ Analyse the audience as groups.

▎ List various forms of audience feedback.

▎ Identify the profile of an audience.

▎ Summarise two main audience theories: the passive audience and the active audience.

▎ Examine how the alternative models of the audience sender relationship are implemented in the media.

The media and the public

Definitions

Interpret

Censorship

How do readers, listeners and viewers interact with the media products and media technology at their disposal? Are readers passive [*submissive*] sponges that simply soak up the many messages that they receive from the media? If they were, it would, of course, imply a one way relationship. The media would determine the thoughts and behaviour of listeners, readers and viewers. What this chapter will reveal is that listeners, readers and viewers of media products can actively interpret the messages they have been sent.

For a long time, there has been concern about how negative messages and the 'dumbing down' of media content affects the behaviour of audiences. Even the ancient Greek philosopher and mathematician Plato (428 BC – 348 BC, give or take a year or two) expressed his fears over the effects that storytelling, in its various forms, had on its audience. The following quote from Plato, translated from his longest and greatest dialogue, *The Republic,* must surely be one of the first recorded instances of censorship and audience mind control.

> "Then shall we simply allow our children to listen to any stories that anyone happens to make up, and so to receive into their minds ideas often the very opposite of those we shall think they ought to have when they grow up?"

> "No, certainly not."

> "It seems, then, our first business will be to supervise the makings of fables and legends, rejecting all which are unsatisfactory; and we shall induce nurses and mothers to tell their children only those which we have approved, and to think more of the moulding of their souls."

Audiences for fables and legends have continued ever since Plato's lament 360 years before the birth of Christ. But there is no convenient term to describe people's overall relationship with the media as a whole. Various media are associated with different activities of communicating, viewing, reading, listening, writing and playing. The term 'audience' does not adequately describe all these activities, although media research has traditionally used this term. Until very recently the term audience was heavily focused on radio listenership and television viewership figures. Today, according to British researcher Sonia Livingstone the personal computer, hand-held mobile devices and other media compete with television and radio for our attention, while audiences are becoming more fragmented in response to diversifying content both within and across media. (Livingstone, 2002:8). In a number of important ways we can say audiences are becoming users. According to Professor Livingstone, a professor of social psychology at the London School of Economics, and co-author Leah Lievrouw, audiences are "becoming users because new media and information technologies open up new, more active modes of engagement with media – playing computer games, surfing the web, searching databases, responding to email, visiting a chat room, shopping on-line and so on. Etymologically [*the origin of a word*], the term audience only satisfactorily covers the activities of listening and watching. But the term 'user' better covers this variety of modes of engagement." (Lievrouw and Livingstone, 2002:10). This trend has become even more pronounced since the advent of blogging, networking websites such as MySpace, video-sharing sites such as YouTube, and tagging and bookmarking on sites such as deli.i.cious.

How many of the above activities – playing computer games, surfing the web, searching online databases, responding to emails, shopping online - do you do daily?

Audience / Users

Mass audience

Target audience

It is becoming apparent that the term audience no longer seems adequate and the term user now seems more appropriate - even though user may be considered too narrow because it does not distinguish between the use of media from the use of any other object. So, for continuity, we shall continue with the term audience to describe those who use and interact with the media.

What is a mass audience then? According to James Potter "In order to be a 'mass', an audience needs to fulfil the following four characteristics:

> The audience composition, in general, is not related to each other [heterogeneous].

> The audience members are unknown [*anonymous*].

> There is no interaction between members of the audience – the messages have a direct effect on each person in a direct manner.

> There is no leadership – the audience cannot act with the unity which marks a crowd. (Potter, 2001:245).

In reality, marketers know that there is really no such thing as a mass audience. Consequently, marketers rarely attempt to sell a media product, service or message to everyone. Instead they try to determine how the total population can be divided into meaningful and identifiable segments of people who might need their products. Advertisers specifically target these segments with their message and ignore those segments who don't desire their products, or who need them but cannot afford them.

Until recently, mass media messages do not allow for a one-on-one interaction between audience and sender – you can hardly tell a television comedian to explain his joke or ask the radio news presenter to explain something discussed that you did not understand. Audiences must therefore rely on their own resources to interpret the media message. The advent of interactive television and SMS feedback is likely to alter this dynamic, however.

South African media, like many elsewhere, is predominantly market driven. Therefore, the audience has emerged as the primary consideration in the communication process, a trend that is taking place in many countries where the media is market driven. According to American scholar Art Silverblatt, further changes in the communication model may develop because "in many instances, the audience now determines the choice of the media communicator." (Silverblatt, 2001:90).

In pairs, consider the age of newsreaders and presenters on your favourite TV channel – how many of them are over fifty years of age, female or black? Google them on the internet: how many are trained journalists? Why do you think this is so?

In the American mass communication model, the message is often the last consideration. Media communicators must often pander to [*gratify*] the needs and demands of the audience in order to attain strong ratings, rather than present information for the public good. Often writers are asked to change an aspect of a show simply to appeal to a specific demographic [*population dynamic*]. Many radio stations, television channels, newspapers and magazines now use focus groups to ensure that they meet the demands of their target audience, which is a far cry from the traditional news test of trying to provide what the audience needs to know.

However, the corporate advertiser (the entity that most directly pays for all or most services outside of public entities such as National Public Radio in the USA, the Canadian Broadcasting Corporation, the South African Broadcasting Corporation and DeutscheWelle in Germany) is ultimately sovereign in determining what information and entertainment will be made available and to whom. This is done through both structural practice and direct intervention. This of course goes some way in explaining an observation by American media critic Herb Schiller (1919 - 2000). Schiller, who is credited with documenting key shortcomings in the new information economy years before anyone called it that, said that much of what is made available to audiences through the mass media (and other commercial sources) is "garbage". It is the structural conditions of the marketplace that underlie this situation rather than what people really want to see, read and hear. Rather than a neutral arbiter [*judge*] of supply and demand, the media marketplace, according to this perspective, turns out to be not so neutral after all.

Audiences demand information, entertainment products and services only after they have been exposed to them. Quite clearly, no-one is going to demand to see a film they do not know about and in this instance, supply precedes demand. You would not demand to listen to a Madonna record if you had no idea who Madonna is.

Feedback in mass communication

Without immediate contact with the audience, the media communicator has only one opportunity to convey the message and therefore the message has to be well planned in order to ensure that the message contains no ambiguities or questions

Definitions

Demographic

Focus group

that will be raised by the audience. The media communicator is further hampered by the fact the he or she does not always have the full attention of the audience who, studies have shown, often leave the room or do something else during the communication of the message or even turn off or change channels. Because of this, feedback between audience and media communicator is usually delayed and often leads later to letters, emails or telephone calls to the editor.

One of the major forms of feedback is through the revenue the media channel generates. Revenue [income] is a quantifiable way of measuring mass communication feedback. Newspapers, and television networks and radio stations outside public broadcasting, are often rated by how much revenue they generate.

The internet offers a unique form of almost instant feedback. The internet is a combination of existing media – print, photography, graphics, video and audio - like no other media because interactive communication is non-linear, in opposition to the simple transmission models from media to audience of more traditional media. As a result, individuals are able to control the pace and direction of presentation.

With the internet, information is almost instantaneous and offers a far greater depth of information than other media forms can deliver. However, the use of interactive media has a long way to go because media communicators are still not able to fully harness its potential and many programmes or channels still lean heavily in the direction of text, sound, video or animation instead of combining them effectively in an interactive manner that makes sense to the audience. There is still too much reliance on trying to impress the audience with technical wizardry and this often gets in the way of the communication process. It may be worth pointing out that the internet also lacks the gate-keeping, fact-checking and assessment techniques routinely employed in older media, so some of what appears as fact on the internet is completely invented.

⑤ MINUTE TASK

In pairs, identify three forms of programme feedback for electronic broadcasting.

Audience identification

As discussed earlier, the media communicator has no direct contact with the audience. Because of this, a great amount of time and energy is devoted to audience identification. Media communicators often employ market research specialists to ascertain [find out] for them the exact profile [description] of their audience and what it is that their audience expects from them.

Different sectors of the population have distinct backgrounds, needs and preferences and look for specific indulgences or gratifications in their choice of media. Art Silverblatt says "An audience profile enables the media communicator to develop communication strategies that capitalise on the audiences' interests, concerns, and preoccupations." (Silverblatt, 2001:39). Good media communicators will of course adapt and modify their style of presentation to meet the needs of their audience. For example the advertisers for teenage products must be conversant with the latest teenage trends in music, fashion and slang in order to relate to that specific target market.

In terms of the press, audience identification has gone a long way in determining what news is carried and how that news is presented to reach the intended audience.

One method of identifying the intended audience is to examine the advertising commercials that accompany the media communication. For example, Saturday afternoon sports broadcasts are normally accompanied mainly by motorcar and beer advertising because the majority of the viewers or listeners will be men.

What products are advertised when you watch or listen to your favourite programme? Why do you think that this is so?

Audience breakdown

Media analysts continually give us new ways of attempting to break down and categorise an audience. In many cases their assumptions about audience are mumbo jumbo [*nonsense*], purely aimed at obtaining some commercial advantage. "All media produce content to attract certain types of audience," writes James W. Potter. "Some of those media (newspapers, magazines, radio, and television) rent their audiences out to advertisers who want to get their messages in front of certain types of people. For example, a classical music radio station will play only classical music as well as present interviews and news about specific types of artists in order to attract an upscale, highly educated, older audience. The station then rents this 'audience' out to advertisers such as luxury car dealers, jewellers, and travel agencies." (Potter, 2001:246).

Quite clearly, the identifying of audience or user segments is an important task for media organisations and their advertisers. Over the years this process has become more complex in an effort to generate more precise groupings. Some of the most popular segmentations used are as follows:

Geographics is the oldest form of segmentation and of great importance to newspapers, radio and local TV. Using a geographical base to determine audience preferences works best where the different regions of a country are culturally

Definitions
Geographics
Demographics
Geodemographics
Social Class
Psychographics

diverse, such as Nigeria. It doesn't work as well when a country becomes more geographically homogenised and regions are not so different from one another.

Demographics focuses on the relatively enduring characteristics of each person, such as gender, ethnic background, class, age, income and education. Apart from education and income which can change, particularly in young adulthood, these are fairly stable characteristics and have been quite useful in classifying people into meaningful audience segments. However, the usefulness of some gender demographics as an audience segmentation device has been diminishing with time, as the gender line has blurred.

Geodemographics is a more recent innovation in consumer segmentation. It is a blend of geographic and demographic segmentation. It is based on the premise that we choose to live where other people like us are. Neighbourhoods tend to be homogenous [*consistent*] on important characteristics, and these characteristics change across neighbourhoods.

Social class cannot merely be thought about in terms of household income. Potter says the middle-class is about "holding the belief that it is good to put off immediate pleasure for more important long-term goals." (Potter, 2001:248). Most people at college or university hold middle-class perspectives. Being upper-class does not imply more money but the ability to control more resources (yours and those of others) and wield power.

Psychographics is the 'flavour of the month' [*popular*] amongst market segmentationists. It uses a wide variety of peoples' characteristics to create its segments. "Typically, a psychographic segmentation scheme will use demographics, lifestyle, and product usage variables in segmenting consumers," Potter says. (Potter, 2001:249).

(15) MINUTE TASK

In groups, analyse the demographics of a group of people:
1. watching a particular TV programme at peak time and mid-morning
2. reading a particular newspaper.

Audience theory

Audience research should fulfil a number of criteria, according to Andrew Ruddock:

> Reliability: are the results of the research reliable? Would the same methods applied to the same subjects yield the same results?

Validity: to what degree can we say that what we measure actually represents the concept we wish to discuss?

Generalisability: to what degree can we transpose the observations we have made in a specific research setting to a wider social context? (Ruddock, 2001:18).

The above criteria, although not applicable to all forms of audience research, provide useful ways of thinking about the truth in claims made by various authors and researchers.

The dilemma of what theories we use to try to understand and explain the media is not divorced from who does the theorising. "How we see things in international life that intrigue or depress us depends to a certain extent on our geographical vantage point. No matter how hard we try to compensate for our cultural biases, we can never 'know' the real world in its entirety. We will have biases, priorities, and prejudices that are deeply engrained by our education, national culture, diplomatic history, and the daily headlines – all of which typically express national rather than global perspectives," says Canadian political scientist Kalevi Holsti, who notes that many and varied streams of theoretical activity "deeply reflect the historical experiences of the European states system in the past and the cold war more recently. It would be perfectly legitimate, therefore, for an Indian or African scholar to claim that other historical experiences should help form the basis of theories about contemporary international politics." (Holsti, 1987:viii).

There are other issues to consider as well: "There is also much debate on how much 'activity' or 'passivity' can be ascribed to an audience," argues Dennis Mc-Quail from the University of Amsterdam. "By definition, the audience as a mass is passive because it is incapable of collective action, whereas any true social group has the means and may have the inclination to be active in the sense of choosing a shared goal and participating in its pursuit." (McQuail, 1997:22).

How does the audience interpret media content? In this regard two schools of thought – hegemony, and reception theory - are considered important:

Hegemony

Italian revolutionary Antonio Gramsci, as discussed earlier in this book, stated that a social group or class maintains its power through both domination and consent through 'intellectual and moral leadership'. Social control, in other words, can influence behaviour and choice internally, by moulding personal convictions into a copy of prevailing norms and accepted behaviour. University of Liverpool political theory professor Joseph Femia, in his book on Gramsci, says that "such 'internal control' is based on hegemony, which refers to an order in which a common social-moral language is spoken, in which one concept of reality is dominant, informing with its spirit all modes of thought and behaviour." (Fernia, 1987:24).

Definitions

Hegemony

Passive

Preferred Reading

The media as both a product and a beneficiary of the prevailing system generally reflects the predominant ideology within a culture. The media is also seen as the principal means by which that ideology is introduced and reinforced (and possibly ultimately broken down) within contemporary culture. Jane Ferry, Barbara Finan and Art Silverblatt write that "a central principle of cultural studies is that the world view presented through the media does not merely reflect or reinforce culture but in fact shapes thinking by promoting the dominant ideology of a culture through hegemony; that is, the ability of the dominant classes to exercise social and cultural leadership in order to maintain economic and political control over the subordinate classes." (Ferry and Silverblatt, 1999:4).

According to the hegemonic model, the audience is passive in the communication process. The audience's interpretation of a media text is generally aligned with the values and beliefs of the dominant culture. Rather than imposing their will on the subordinate class by force, the dominant class represent their own interests as being aligned with the welfare of society as a whole. The subordinate class, in adopting this view, willingly consent to the continued superiority of the dominant class. Although a mass media text may be open to several interpretations, the text indicates a 'preferred reading' from the perspective of the media communicator. The audience assumes a passive role.

⑩ MINUTE TASK

In groups, consider a number of media texts, including advertisements and news reports. Discuss what you believe is the 'preferred reading' of the communicator.

Reception Theory

Definitions

Reception theory

Active

In this construct, audience members may arrive at an interpretation entirely different from the preferred reading dictated by the media commentator. For example, women may be more sensitive than men to messages about violence and gender. Art Silverblatt notes that "the audience assumes an active role in interpreting or 'negotiating' the information they receive through mass media." (Silverblatt, 2001:2). Reception theory also deals with personal taste – why certain people derive pleasure from particular media presentations or programmes.

Reception theory suggests the following variables can affect how an individual or an audience interprets media content:

Background: how much does the audience already know about the subject?

Interest level: how interested is the audience in the subject? How attentive is the audience?

Audience attitude: what is the attitude (positive or negative) of the audience towards the subject, prior to the debate/programme?

Concern: what issues are of major concern to the audience? Why?

Audience demographic profile: ethnicity, gender, race, class, nationality, age, education, income and religion.

Psychological profile: self-concept, primary relationships, significant life experiences, ways of relating to others, ways of dealing with emotions, personal aspirations.

Communications environment: audience size? What were the audience doing when they received the information?

Stage of development: Have you ever seen a film for a second or third time and reacted differently from the first time you saw it? Quite clearly the content of the film did not change, so you must have. As you grow older, your life experiences influence your perception of how you view things and will alter how you view media content.

(10) MINUTE TASK

In groups, discuss how critical people are when watching a television news report or reading a newspaper. Explain why / why not.

Probably both the hegemonic model and the reception model offer insights into audience behaviour. Although audiences are encouraged to accept the point of view of the preferred reading, they also negotiate and form their own meaning based on their life experiences. Consider the ways in which audiences comprehend media content:

The shared values, experiences and perspectives of the audiences and how these influence their understanding or interpretation of the media content.

How experiences and perspectives of the individual audience member affect his or her interpretation of the same content.

Audiences are dynamic, never totally passive. Neither are all the members equal. Since some audience members will be more experienced or more active participants than others, their understandings of the media text may differ.

Alternative models

Dennis McQuail identified a number of alternative models of the traditional audience / sender relationship. Some of them are:

Media

Audience

Media←——→Audience

The transmission model: the audience (receiver) is seen primarily as a target for the communicator's message. This could apply to some methods of education and to many forms of advertising. However, feedback is still required via a positive or negative response to the message.

The participant model: communication is defined in terms of sharing of beliefs, increasing the commonality between sender and receiver. In this model the audience are participants.

Media

captures attention of

↓

Audience

The spectator model: the audience are merely spectators. The communicator does not try to transmit information or beliefs but simply tries to capture the audience's attention, regardless of the communication effect. The audience are required for the ratings and the revenue and celebrity status they bring. Celebrity status is often a product of public exposure rather than audience appreciation. Silverblatt notes, "for mass communicators, high ratings (which record attention) offer the least ambiguous and most tradable form of feedback and reward." The audience's attention is temporary and not deeply involved. It implies no 'transfer of meaning', no sharing or deepening of ties between communicator and audience. What counts here is simply the time spent with the medium, even though it might only serve as a time-filling diversion to the audience.

Media

controls

↓ ↑

Audience

The expectancy–value theory: the central idea is that the media offers rewards that are expected (thus predicted) by potential numbers of an audience on the basis of relevant past experience. These rewards or gratifications can be thought of as 'psychological effects' that are valued by the audience. An example of this is 'having a good read'. The feedback is the audience's subsequent choice of reading material.

Media

Rewards

↓

Audience

The simplistic hypodermic needle model: suggests that the media 'injects' ideas into a passive and easily manipulated audience, like giving a patient a drug. In the 1930s there was a school of thought that believed that "the media were a force for pacifying the population"... injecting a 'mass culture' that functioned as a distraction from the mundanity of ordinary daily life. It was further believed that American commercial television and popular cinema 'moulded people into a standardised, passive state of being that allowed them to be easily manipulated'. (McQuail, 1997:22). The main criticism of this theory, according to Philip Rayner et al "it concentrates too much on the text of a programme and does not take into account the audience's interaction with and interpretation of the text's meaning." (Rayner et al, 2001:131).

30 MINUTE TASK

In groups:
1. Discuss how each of the above models are implemented in the media.
2. Analyse the strengths and weaknesses of each model.

Ever-shifting audiences

Today, audiences are much smaller, more numerous, and unlikely to have a fixed and predictable allegiance [*loyalty*] to particular media. Media analysts therefore have a difficult time identifying different audiences. Media providers also battle to retain 'their' specific audiences because patterns of media use are clearly dynamic and a function of ever-changing economies.

How do the media view their audience? A consumer market? Or a commodity to be sold to advertisers with a genuine communicative purpose? What matters, according to Dennis McQuail, "is the composition of the audience, its engagement with the communicators and content, the quality of attention, and response, its loyalty, commitment, and continuity". (McQuail, 1997:22).

It makes less sense these days to talk about a mass audience in the affluent [*wealthy*] Western world, at least not one that is defined by large numbers of people gathered around televisions, watching the same information fed from relatively few providers (although it is true that a number of countries in the developing world still have only one or two television broadcasters and indigenous radio stations with audience numbers in the millions, but satellite and cable television has made inroads here, too.) Consider the following:

> The original time set aside to watch a favourite news programme, preferring instead to tune in and out of various sources. For example, the percentage of people saying their exclusive news source is nightly network or local TV news is dropping in many countries. Those who watch TV news often do so with a remote control in hand.

An audience as a group (or public) must have an independent existence prior to its identification as an audience. In modern society it is very difficult to find examples (except on a small scale) but a good example are publications set up by political or religious organisations as a means of linking with their grass roots membership and creating cohesion and identity within the group.

Probably the best examples of a media audience today would be the listenership of a community radio station or the readers of a community newspaper, where the audience shares a significant social/cultural identifying characteristic – that of shared space and membership of a residential community. Community media contributes significantly to local awareness and sense of belonging. Social and economic forces together reinforce the integrative role of local media.

"However, the group character of local media may, even so, be quite weak since a shared space often conceals a great disparity [*difference*] of other population attributes, depending on the kind of locality. Some local areas are just residential locations without any institutional bonds or common identity, little more than a number of people who share the same shopping facilities but who otherwise live private lives and have a high degree of geographical mobility. It is unlikely that the media on their own can ever be a substitute for an otherwise missing sense of identification. Concentration of ownership and of editorial organisation has often diminished the genuine local character of local media/newspapers." There can hardly be a more diverse population group than that living in London but boroughs such as Camden and Islington go to great lengths to get their residents to feel a sense of community and to feel that they belong. The local community press also goes a long way in trying to reinforce the sense of belonging.

SELF-STUDY TASK

List the community newspapers and radio stations in your community / residential area together with their readership and listenership figures. To what extent are they successful in forging [*building*] a sense of community? Are you part of that community?

However, we should take time to consider the reverse. Consider a country where the population is served by only one newspaper, radio or TV station, probably run and owned by the government. In this extreme example, the audience is everyone and the communication truly mass.

Can you think of a country where the media is government owned and controlled? Do people rely on shortwave radios, satellite transmitters or text messages via cellphone?

9 Ethics and the code of conduct

chapter ◖━━━━━━━━━━━━━━━━━━━━━━━━━

Outcomes

By the end of this chapter, you will able to:

▶ Define and explain ethics in relation to media practice.

▶ Explain the concepts of libel, fairness, fair comment and truth.

▶ Consider the importance of issues of accuracy, objectivity, impartiality, trust and manipulation.

▶ Critically examine the issues surrounding the freedom of the press.

▶ Understand the international code of conduct for journalists and apply the code to your reporting.

Ethics and the international code of conduct

Journalists usually resist when people outside the profession try to guide them about their occupational ethics. In matters of conscience, journalists prefer to be judged by their peers. The ninth principle of the International Federation of Journalists (IFJ) states:

> Journalists worthy of that name shall deem it their duty to observe faithfully the principles stated above. Within the general law of each country the journalist shall recognise in professional matters the jurisdiction of colleagues only, to the exclusion of every kind of interference by governments or others.

The above does not mean that journalists are simply free to do and write what they like. As professionals they must work according to rules about what is news

Definitions

Ethics

and what isn't news, as well as rules about how to write certain kinds of stories, and so on. Journalists are controlled by laws, journalistic traditions, by their employers and by their code of conduct. A journalist must follow the code of conduct or be prepared not to work as a journalist. But all journalists sometimes face situations where they have to make ethical choices. This decision may be a very difficult one.

If we as journalists see ourselves as the public's 'watchdog' to guard against corruption and exploitation, we must make sure that our own morals and values are in order. We have to watch our own behaviour constantly. As one journalist says:

> Journalism being what it is, even the most virtuous journalists operating from what they see as the best of motives, inevitably will produce some morally unsatisfactory results. In either case it is worth understanding what went wrong and how to prevent its recurrence.

We will first consider some aspects of ethics and some problems you could face as a journalist, before looking more closely at codes of conduct.

Libel

Definitions

Libel

Journalists often face the threat of being charged with libel. But what is libel? Libel is usually any written or printed statement, any picture or effigy [*statue*] or figure, not made in the public interest and tending to expose a person to public ridicule and mockery or contempt, injuring his or her reputation.

Many journalists would say that you are not really a journalist if you have not been threatened with legal action for libel. This happens often because it can be hard to judge where a person's right to their reputation is more important than the public's right to know what is happening. A person's reputation is protected by law. A journalist can permanently damage someone's good standing in the community, sometimes without even intending to do so. If this damage is not done in the public interest, it is called defamation and the newspaper can be sued, taken to court and charged. However, the truth cannot libel.

'Cato's Letters' was the name given to a series of political anti-corruption essays appearing in London weekly newspapers in England in the 1720s. Each letter was structured as a letter to the editor and was signed 'Cato', after the Roman statesman noted for his honesty and incorruptibility (although the writers were later revealed to be Thomas Gordon and John Trenchard). In Letter No. 32 - *Reflections upon Libelling*, Cato notes: "A libel is not the less a libel for being true. This may seem a contradiction; but it is neither one in law, or in common sense: There are some truths not fit to be told, where, for example, the discovery of a small fault may do greater mischief, or, where the discovery of a great fault can do no good, there ought to be no discovery at all. And to make faults where there are none is still worse."

Easier if we all saw the same thing

Journalism would be a lot easier (and very boring) if we all reported the same way. As everyone knows, all people are not born alike. Even people who speak the same language do not all understand things the same way. People have different beliefs, cultures, ideas and life experiences and as a result, we simply do not all see the same event in the same manner. Therefore, an act totally acceptable in one circumstance or environment might be totally unacceptable in another.

If you have distrusted the police all your life, it is not easy to understand why someone else does trust them. If you see a police officer doing something, you will interpret their actions differently from someone who has grown up trusting the police. If you do not believe that the law protects you, you will not expect justice from the courts.

Two people seeing the same event will therefore report on it differently. If you compare the reports of different journalists who attended the same press conference you will find that their reports and even their quotes are different. It is important that journalists learn to interpret their code of conduct as their peers would expect them to interpret it, because they must use good judgement in applying it.

Low blow, I saw it.

It was not a low blow, I saw it.

⑩ MINUTE TASK

Think of a situation where you and a friend who was present at the same situation saw things differently. Why do you think the two of you saw it differently?

The role of fairness

Fairness is an essential part of healthy human relationships, because it basically means treating everyone equally and giving everyone an equal chance to be heard and understood. In journalism, the concept fairness means reporting impartially [*not favouring any person or group over others*], as well as reporting completely so that aspects are not left out and striving for balance so that different points of view come through. The code of conduct requires fair reporting.

During the liberation struggle against apartheid in South Africa, the press was continually criticised by both the political left and the political right. Both sides strongly accused the press of unfair reporting during martial law, known as the state of emergency, in the 1980s. Because of the restrictions placed on the press at this time, *The Star*, a daily English-language newspaper in Johannesburg, the country's biggest city, suspended its code of conduct. The code was returned only when the then president, FW de Klerk, leader of the National Party, unbanned all the previously banned political parties, including the African National Congress and the Communist Party in 1990.

Fairness can be interpreted in different ways. Sometimes readers get so little information that they cannot judge whether a story has been reported fairly or not. But this may depend on how much space is available on the page that day, not on anything a journalist has control over. As a result, it may be difficult for the journalist to avoid this situation.

Fair comment

What does the term fair comment mean? Some people - politicians, public officials, entertainers and sports persons - offer their particular talent or service for the approval of the public. Newspapers and other mass media have the right to comment on these people or criticise them. But the comment or criticism must be fair and without malice [*being spiteful*]. Also, the comment should not generally deal with the private lives of the persons concerned. For example, it is fair comment to criticise public officials for their poor performance and point out that they lack ability or specialised knowledge, but it is not fair comment to reveal their sexual preferences. Sometimes a reporter may serve the public best by reporting on a public person's private life. Then this would override the usual rule.

⑤ MINUTE TASK

Can you think of a recent example where a newspaper or internet report made unfair comment? Give a reason for your answer. What would you have done differently?

Striving for truth, accuracy and objectivity

Journalists can talk about reporting the truth. But what is the truth? Philosophers have debated this question for centuries. The early Greeks debated long and hard the issue of how we know reality, and by implication 'the truth'. Steven Knowlton, and Patrick Parsons put it this way:

> Today the term sophistry implies elaborate yet empty argumentation. The original sophists were hired-gun rhetoricians willing to plead, or teach others to plead, any side of an argument. They could do this without ethical qualms because of their belief in the complete inability of humans to really know what constituted truth, or even physical reality. If truth

"Be truthful, accurate & objective!"

cannot be discerned, and may not even exist, they argued, then all points of view became equally valid and the best one can do is simply argue well. (Knowlton and Parsons, 1994:48).

The following extract from *The Moral Compass* should remind journalists of the early origins of the debate over objectivity and the hope that truth does indeed exist:

> Today's journalist may or may not believe in the ability to be truly objective but probably does believe that some objective reality exists. The sophists were not so sure.
>
> The most famous of them, Protagoras, summed it up: "Man," he said, "is the measure of all things." What we take to be real, what we take to be the truth, is simply what we take from a situation, and what we take is heavily influenced, if not wholly determined, by what we bring to it.
>
> Plato however, disagreed with Protagoras – "For Plato, there was a substantive and objective reality..... Truth, however, is not easily obtained, according to Plato. Most people, in fact, avoid it. What people hold to be true represents only the washed-out shadows of the truth. They are poorly thought-out opinions and biases. Knowledge, wisdom and eventually Truth are possible only with considerable effort." (Knowlton and Parsons, 1994:90).

For some people, truth is what they wish to hear and not what they need to hear or should hear. Identifying the truth is a big problem for journalists. James Retson of the *New York Times* is quoted as saying, "You cannot merely report the literal truth. You have to explain it." But to explain the truth you still have to be able to identify it.

Because we have difficulty in identifying the truth, is it possible to be objective? A journalist can deal with this difficulty by interpreting events for the reader and giving as much background information to the news as possible. This doesn't mean that the journalist should mix news and opinion together.

Readers have a right to truthful information and reporting and being trustworthy to the reader is the basis of good journalism. It is therefore our fundamental duty to ensure that the news content is accurate and free from bias, and that all sides have been reported fairly.

Newspaper reports seldom get challenged for not being accurate or truthful but errors do happen when there is pressure on time, as in newspaper publishing. We do our best to avoid them, of course, but somehow the misspelt name or incorrect quote does slip through. Errors of fact and errors of omission [*when things are left out*] must be corrected in good time. Have you ever seen a newspaper apology for an inaccuracy? What have you noticed about the positioning

Definitions

Truth

Reality

Accuracy

Objectivity

" What is the truth? "

of the apology? Corrections should be published, even very prominently when necessary. If a paper or journalist makes too many mistakes they lose the respect and trust of the public. So it is important that you get your stories right the first time.

This is a high standard to aim for and impossible to maintain at all times. A shortage of time and space can limit the journalist's ability to report clearly and fully. There are other constraints too. For example, journalists must ensure that their reports will be understood by the reasonable [*ordinary*] reader, i.e. a reader who does not have specialised knowledge. Thus a journalist may have to cut complex and technical-sounding detail in a report, with the result that the report may lose some fullness and complete accuracy. But at least the journalist must do his/her very best to achieve truth and accuracy.

Reporters must also use quotes from interviews in an ethical way. Only disreputable reporters will deliberately alter or invent quotes to improve the impact of a story. They harm themselves, their readers and their newspaper when they do this. Both they and their newspaper will lose credibility [*respect and trust*] with their readers if they do this.

Sometimes a journalist who is trying to report truthfully and fairly may find that their newspaper does not give them the support they deserve. For example, a former student of mine came to see me one day to express extreme concern. He was covering [*reporting on*] the political violence of 1996 for a newspaper which had strong ties to a particular political party based in KwaZulu-Natal, South Africa.

His problem was as follows: After reading his story his editor insisted that the events that he had described and reported on could not have taken place. The editor then explained exactly what was supposed to have happened, although the only information he had was what this young reporter had given him.

What do you think the young journalist should have done?

The Afrikaners have a wonderful expression: *"Eenoog is koning in die land van die blindes"* (One eye is king in the land of the blind). The 'one-eyed' reporting that this editor was encouraging probably fed the flames of violence that ran through KwaZulu-Natal during the early 90s.

However, this very conscientious young reporter would not write something that he had not checked thoroughly for the facts. He was very concerned that his good name as a fair and accurate journalist was at risk. He has since moved on to another newspaper where he is allowed to do his job properly.

Impartiality: avoiding bias

Impartiality is part of fairness. It means to treat all sides in a dispute [*argument, conflict*] equally. However, it does not mean that the press must be unquestioning, or that journalists and editors cannot offer their opinions on a dispute. The important thing is to have a clear distinction between a news report and an opinion. The writer and the reader must be sure about what is a news report, and what is an opinion. Articles that contain opinion or the writer's personal interpretation should be clearly identified as doing so.

The famous American CBS news anchorman Walter Cronkite had this to say about reporting:

> I made every attempt to keep any hint of prejudice or bias, analysis or commentary, out of news reports.... I believed that the straight presentation of news and a commentary by the same reporter would only confuse the public, although we in the profession know that it is possible for the same person to write a front page, factual unbiased news report and a strong editorial on the same subject.

To be biased means to unfairly prejudice someone or something. For the journalist it means losing accuracy and objectivity in reporting. A story becomes biased when the journalist's or editor's beliefs or values interfere with the reporting and the facts actually get distorted. If you believe that a particular group of people are better than another group, you may favour the one over the other in your writing. For example, sports writers often show a distinct bias towards one team or another: As long as the public rely on the media to play a 'watchdog' role in society, unbiased reporting is essential.

Definitions

Fact

Opinion

News is associated with facts and objectivity.

Editorial / commentary is associated with opinion, interpretation, bias, and prejudice.

" Be factual and impartial! "

5 MINUTE TASK

Do you agree with Walter Cronkite's statement "keep all prejudice and bias out of a news report" or not? Write your response and explain it to a partner.

Public trust

Because the newspaper is one of the most efficient forms of mass communication ever created, millions of people read and trust newspapers. Journalists should guard this public trust in the press carefully. If trust exists, the press can play an important role in society: it can circulate information to enlighten and inform the public. In 1823 Thomas Jefferson the third President of the United States between 1801 and 1809, wrote: *"The press is the best instrument for enlightening the mind of man, and improving him as a rational moral and social being."*

During the liberation struggle in South Africa, the alternative press – among them the *New Nation*, the *Weekly Mail* (later the *Mail and Guardian*) and *Die Vrye Weekblad* - played an important role of keeping the public informed about what was really happening. They paid a heavy price by being constantly harassed by the authorities and in some cases banned.

The press may not always earn approval for playing this role of keeping the public informed,

> The media need not ever be loved or even fully understood to carry out their function in society. But they must be trusted if they are to be credible in their watchdog role over the government, which has the power - with public backing - to restrict press freedom. (Klaidman and Beauchamp, 1987:59).

It is important that the media report fully on what public figures are doing. This helps the public to decide whether they are performing their duties properly or not. However the editor must finally decide what news will be made available to the public. The editor must consider the question: Do people need to know this or, is this information going to benefit our readers? What other questions do you think the editor should ask before deciding what gets published?

The public will trust the press if they feel that the press is working in their best interests as a whole and not in the interests of any particular group. It is a journalist's duty to maintain the public trust at all times.

The press has the powerful ability to affect public opinion and persuade readers. It must not abuse this power. If the press lies to the public, even for a good reason (for example, to catch a criminal), the press betrays a trust and the public will never be sure whether they can trust what they read or not.

Freedom of the press

> Freedom of the press belongs to the people. It must be defended against encroachment or assault from any quarter, public or private. Journalists must be constantly alert to see that the public's business is conducted in public. They must be vigilant against [*watch out for*] all who would exploit the public for selfish purposes.

According to the International Federation of Journalists' code of conduct, journalists have an obligation to defend the freedom of the press at all times. That obligation comes with the job, but it can lead to difficult decisions or painful consequences for the journalist.

Here is an example of such a situation. Some years ago, journalists were asked to leave a mass meeting at the former University of Durban-Westville (now part of the University of KwaZulu-Natal, then a predominantly Indian educational institution) in South Africa. The organisers of the meeting feared more of the negative and distorted publicity that the university had been receiving in the press.

I was one of the journalists at the meeting and I resisted leaving because I believed that the public had a right to know what was happening. Actually, the motion to exclude the press was proposed by a person who usually supported the notion of freedom of the press. He was misguided in his wish to protect the good name of the university. Fortunately, good sense prevailed and I remained to do my job. By excluding journalists, the university would have made the public suspicious and would have further damaged its academic reputation as a free thinking institution. The public had a right to know. Public business must be kept public.

There will always be attacks on press freedom by politicians who accuse journalists of being irresponsible. In 1996, South African president Nelson Mandela accused black journalists of not promoting the transformation of South African society. This was a serious allegation. Mandela met with senior black journalists in Cape Town to discuss the matter. The journalists listened to the president and noted his concerns. But they reminded him that the role of a free press is to inform the public of the true state of affairs so that the public can decide for itself about the performance of government They pointed out that the press has to speak out when the rights and liberties of people are threatened. In other words, don't shoot the messenger. Both parties left the meeting with a better understanding of each other's roles.

⑤ MINUTE TASK

What do you think the role of the press should be in a new democracy?

Influence and manipulation

People often accuse the press of abusing its power by manipulating [*influencing*] public opinion. These accusations often come from government when the press point out defects [*faults, weak parts*] in proposed government policy. It is certainly true that the press has enormous influence and power with the public. And we must indeed ensure that we do not abuse that power.

But what do we mean by manipulation? You manipulate someone when you deliberately influence the choices that they make without actually forcing them to do what you want. You can also manipulate someone by altering the way they see their choices, their idea of what choices they could make. But you do this subtly, in such a way that you don't seem to be persuading them at all.

Manipulation is not always immoral in itself but it can be done for immoral purposes. Therefore it requires explanation and justification. For example, the press itself may use manipulation in trying to influence smokers to give up the habit; but of course it can easily defend this 'good' kind of manipulation.

As you can imagine, manipulation is not used by the press alone. Business people, politicians and others may also wish to influence people's opinions and actions and they constantly try to do this by manipulating the press.

Journalists can influence many kinds of events. A film critic can turn film go-ers against a particular film and therefore influence the box office takings [*the amount of money it makes*] for that film. Sports reporters can lobby [*push*] for the inclusion or exclusion of a certain player from a team. Manipulation may be based on reasons which are not objective. Journalists may also draw people's attention to events that don't need or deserve such attention. So we can influence what happens, in an unjustified or negative way.

In order to maintain public trust, journalists must be wary of manipulating and being manipulated.

The media as leader and change agent in society

The press (print media) as a mass communicator can promote 'nation building' by advocating and promoting good values and by motivating and rewarding people. The press is in a powerful position to foster and promote the good, and expose and condemn evil. "They can promote tolerance, brotherhood and unity, and root out intolerance, divisiveness, enmity and hatred. They can prevent conflicts and violence, and build up peaceful relations, and respect for the rule of law. Media can curb confrontation and help solve problems amicably." (Sawant, 1998:9).

The press can promote discussion and debate to find the appropriate path of economic development consistent with economic, social, and environmental justice to all. It can focus attention on the areas and people which are in need of development and social upliftment. It can debate and propose what is required and ways of implementing necessary change. Corruption, nepotism [*favouritism*], and many other malpractices by those vested with the public power and trust can be legitimately exposed through the columns of the press.

But obviously, to make the right decisions, the free flow of information and ideas is necessary. What is sometimes forgotten is that the freedom of the press is not only an aspect of the individual's right to the freedom of speech and expression, but is essentially, of society's right to be informed. Freedom of the press is exercised for and on behalf of society, for without the reader, the press has no existence. It is therefore the needs and the interests of the reader, which have to be catered to by the press.

The press can also act as a catalyst for change and has the potential to do this and many other things. The press in the west has tried to propagate the idea of development [*upliftment of society*] through democracy. It has dealt with the questions of the disadvantaged members of society and exposed many evils of our system.

The Press in relation to women

It can be argued that the press worldwide has given a lot of attention to the problems of women in disadvantaged communities, the atrocities against women generally and the inequalities they suffer. However, I have a strong suspicion that the extensive coverage of women's interests is due largely to the fact that the subject of women has other attractions. Therefore, the manner in which the women's questions are reported in the press caters to some of the vulgar aspects of the question rather than supporting the freedom, equality and liberation of women as can be seen in the excerpt from the following newspaper article (Special Report – Gender Issues) published in the *Guardian* newspaper in London in 2003.

The Daily Mail is explicitly targeted at women and has a higher proportion of female readers than any other newspaper. So why is *The Daily Mail*'s attitude to women so strange? Esther Addley reports:

A girl's best friend?

What is your "swimsuit age"? Here is a clue. Martine McCutcheon (biological age, 26) has a swimsuit age of 32 because she has "chunky thighs and a lack of visible muscle tone". Philippa Foster (35) "heavy around the thighs" after having a baby is revealed as really being 40 once she dons a swimsuit. Thank the gods, then, for Tracy Shaw (29) who "after defeating anorexia, looks in good shape" – worthy indeed of a 25. The "slim toned" Demi Moore (in her fourties) gets the same score, "whether or not she's had plastic surgery".

How do we know? *The Daily Mail* says so. Last week the newspaper devoted two pages to the issue of "how old stars look on the beach", a collection of paparazzi shots of well-known women in bikinis that was ferocious in its criticism of those who had not expunged every trace of wobble from their bums, tits and thighs by any means necessary.

How does such an article make you feel? Is it a deliciously nasty treat to look through intrusive snatched shots of celebrities on holiday? Or is there something about this kind of article – applauding the body shapes of women who have suffered from eating disorders or had conspicuous cosmetic surgery, while savaging those with residual bulge after having a baby – that seems to be the very definition of body fascism? The Daily Mail is the second-biggest-selling and unquestionably most influential newspaper in the country. And its point is clear: normal women's bodies are not good enough, and will not be tolerated.

"I was absolutely appalled," says one friend about the article, "and yet I looked at every picture", which just about sums up the Daily Mail. The newspaper with proportionally more women readers than any other, is also the paper with the most contradictory – and occasionally apparently hateful - attitude to certain types of women. The paper seems to have a daily article sneering at some woman, usually an ageing one, for looking ghastly, but the Mail and Mail on Sunday, are the only papers to have in Britain to have equal or higher numbers of female readers than men. The paper is never less than committed, and occasionally venomous, in its criticism of working women with families, and yet 1.5m of the daily's six million readers are women who work full or part time. What on earth is going on?

Yet while it [Daily Mail] makes no secret of its socially and politically conservative agenda, its attitude towards women has arguably the most perplexing editorial policy. Are men and women equal, for instance? Well, it depends what you mean. If this is your definition of "feminism" the newspaper unequivocally does not agree that they are. For there are few things the Daily Mail hates more than feminists. In the past year it has run articles blaming "the feminist revolution" for "undermining men".

If such spittle-flecked venom is curious enough, the Mail's attitude to what it terms "career women" is even more perplexing – by turns puzzled, hostile and deeply weird. The newspaper, it seems, just can't quite bring itself to accept that most women nowadays, even if they have children, have to work.

Readers will rarely find this expressed explicitly, though the sense is clear from the stories the newspaper chooses to run and the way they are presented. Why are dubious surveys predicting health risks, loneliness and terminal unhappiness for career women reported so prominently by the Mail, when all other papers tend to ignore them?

To readers who love the paper's mix of popular news, and breezy lifestyle features, and fellow journalists who acknowledge the paper is frequently agenda-setting, this brutal, caveman attitude to women seems, among other things, just plain odd. There is no question that on occasions the Daily Mail is an exceptional product – it is certainly exceptionally successful. Why, then, does it insist on behaving like a boorish, 19th-century husband, demanding food on the table when he gets in from work, and sex with someone who has kept herself nice for him? At times he seems like a bullying abuser, spewing forth a manipulative mix of love and fear.

Or perhaps, it is simply that the paper has identified, and cynically encouraged, the paranoia's of modern women about body image, celebrity and work. And let's not be too sanctimonious; what woman, gathered with her girlfriends and a bottle of wine, has not revelled in giggling bitchiness over another woman's looks? The Mail's cleverest trick is in convincing us that it is not an angry, sexist old man railing over women having let themselves go, but our best girlfriend, who may bitch about other women, but would surely always tell us we still look beautiful? Reader, you must decide which persona best fit.

It seems fair to say that on the subject of women, the press has failed to provide moral and ethical leadership. The press is a mirror of society and in the control of the dominant forces in society, (the rich, the upper and the educated classes) and has often paid insufficient attention to the wishes that intimately affect the disadvantaged classes.

10 MINUTE TASK

In groups discuss how the disadvantaged in society, for example women and the poor, are depicted in your local newspaper from an ethical point of view.

Code of conduct

The code of conduct and principles which follow should cover all the issues we have discussed in this chapter. If you find that one of the principles is worded in a way you find difficult, refer to that part of the chapter which discusses that principle.

International Federation of Journalists (IFJ)
Principles on the Conduct of Journalists

1. Respect for the truth and the right of the public to truth is the first duty of the journalist.
2. In pursuance of this duty, the journalist shall at all times defend the principles of freedom in the honest collection and publication of news, and the right of fair comment and criticism.
3. The journalist shall report only in accordance with facts of which he/she knows the origin. The journalist shall not suppress [*cover up*] essential information or falsify documents.
4. The journalist shall only use fair methods to obtain news, photographs and documents.
5. The journalist shall do the utmost to rectify any published information which is found to be harmfully inaccurate.
6. The journalist shall observe professional secrecy regarding the source of information obtained in confidence.
7. The journalist shall be aware of the danger of discrimination being furthered by the media, and shall do the utmost to avoid facilitating such discrimination based on, among other things, race, sex, sexual orientation, language, religion, political or other opinion, and national or social origins.
8. The journalist shall regard as grave professional offences the following: plagiarism [*copying*], malicious misinterpretation, calumny [*defamation*], slander [*insult, smear*], libel, unfounded accusations; the acceptance of a bribe in any form of consideration of either publication or suppression.
9. Journalists worthy of that name shall deem it their duty to observe faithfully the principles stated above. Within the general law of each country the journalist shall recognise in professional matters the jurisdiction [*authority*] of colleagues only; to the exclusion of every kind of interference by governments or others.

⑤ MINUTE TASK

In your opinion what is the most important and ethical principle that should guide a journalist in all possible situations? Give reasons for your answer.

In the light of what you have learned in this chapter on ethics, analyse a local or national newspaper. You may wish to compare it with another newspaper.

It is important that you debate and commit to memory each of the above principles so that that you can apply them in your profession.

Conclusion

Journalists face ethical and moral decisions daily and it is our duty to know and understand the code of conduct under which we work. We must, at all times, be keenly aware of the interests of society and our readers to ensure that our reporting is ethical. Journalists must refrain from actions that are not morally right. In so doing we maintain and strengthen our readers' trust in the press. Lastly, we must at all times defend the principle of freedom of the press. It is an obligation that comes with the job.

Suggested Reading

Nel, François, (2005). *Writing for the Media in Southern Africa*. 3rd ed. OUP.

10 What is news?

Outcomes

At the end of this chapter, you will able to:

▶ Explain what news is.

▶ Judge the value of news.

▶ Decide whether the information you have is news.

▶ Present news accurately, fairly and objectively.

▶ Reflect on the importance of meeting people's news requirements, especially now that electronic media can deliver the news faster than newspapers can.

Introduction

The very simple question: What is news? is probably the most important and difficult question in journalism. You will find out that there is no one single answer to this question. But it will affect your work as a journalist from day to day.

It is impossible for newspapers to report everything. Therefore we must know how to decide what is news and also what news is relevant to our own readers. We must be aware that what is news today will not be news tomorrow: news is always changing. Also, events are happening all the time but they are not news until someone tells someone else about them. News does not exist in isolation [by itself].

As you read further, the idea of news will get easier to understand. Also, remember that news can change constantly but two important principles of news reporting will never change - the need to report accurately and fairly remains the same.

Before you read this chapter, think of any story that has recently been big news in a newspaper that you read. Then note down your ideas about why this story was news at all. As you read on, compare your ideas with the information in the rest of the chapter.

Defining news

Definitions

News

Defining news is very difficult. There is actually no universal definition of news because news is a relative concept. This means that it is different from newspaper to newspaper, from place to place and from one time to another. You can test this statement by looking at any two local daily newspapers. You can be sure that the news carried on their front pages will not be exactly the same. Clearly, each news editor has a different view on what is the most important news for their readers' needs.

The following versions show how difficult it is to define news:

News is anything published or broadcast.

News is an account of an event or a fact or an opinion that interests people.

News is a presentation of a report on current events in a newspaper or other publication or on radio and television or the internet.

News is anything that is timely that interests a number of readers, and the best news is that which has the greatest interest for the greatest number of people.

News is accurate and timely intelligence of happenings, discoveries, opinions and matters of any sort which affect or interest the readers.

News is everything that happens, the inspiration of happenings and the result of such happenings.

News comprises all current activities of general human interest and the best news is that which interests the most readers.

Thus you can see that it is impossible to reach a satisfactory short description of news. However, there are two aspects of news that I consider especially important. Firstly, news must be new: new to those who hear it, watch it, read it. Secondly, news is any printable story which in the opinion of the editor will interest the readers of his or her paper (or the audience of the broadcast).

Traditional news tests

News requires

1. timeliness
2. proximity/
   relevance
3. impact/
   conse-
   quence
4. prominence
5. novelty/
   curiosity
6. conflict
7. human
   interest
8. sex
9. enjoyment
10. humour

Editors have to sort through many ideas, events and controversies [*arguments going on in society - usually about political or social issues*] every day. They must decide which have real news value. They must also choose those which will actually be reported. Editors throughout the world use similar criteria [*decisive factors*] to guide their decisions.

The basic factors that make news are as follows:

Timeliness: The news in a newspaper must be fresh: today's news is stale tomorrow and nobody wants stale news. Like vegetables, news is a perishable item and goes stale quickly.

These days, television programmes like CNN and Sky News and news websites like www.bbc.co.uk pick up events so quickly that newspapers must continually check the timeliness of their own news. In other words they must print the story of an event as soon after the event as possible.

Proximity/relevance: People like to read or hear news about people and events that are close to them. The closer an issue or an event is to your readers, the greater will be its impact and news value. Thus people are usually most interested in stories from their own neighbourhood, city, province and country – usually in that order. Community newspapers have grown in number although the local news that they contain would not get into the large daily or weekly newspapers. Community media, including community radio stations, include local religious events, local school issues and sports happenings. Readers want news to be relevant and to focus on them and where they live.

Impact/consequence: Any event that can affect a great number of people is obviously newsworthy. Therefore the number of people an event or idea affects, and also how seriously or dramatically it affects them, can tell us how important it is as news. Some events obviously have more consequence for readers than others have. News should be both dramatic and surprising, so that readers say, 'Wow! Have you heard this?'

Consequence is a useful way to measure how newsworthy events such as floods, wars and political campaigns are. But we can't really use consequence to measure the newsworthiness of an event like a football match. Consequence is a good test of news about some kind of conflict, disaster or progress.

Prominence: As we all know, names make news: the bigger the name, the bigger the news. Not all readers are deeply interested in politicians, sports stars, singers and other personalities, but all readers do recognise names. Many readers are interested in what politicians, government officials and business leaders do and say, because it will affect the readers' own lives. Of course, when people are regularly in the news, readers get interested in their behaviour. Although we should respect the privacy of prominent people, they must accept that their prominence makes the public curious about their daily lives.

Prominent people need the press to publicise what they say as much as the press need comments from them to make stories and sell newspapers. Some of these personalities feel that they must be seen with other prominent people. Notice the scramble by film stars, politicians, royalty and other pseudo [*insincere, fake*] personalities to rush to South Africa so that they can meet former president Nelson Mandela and be seen with him, embracing him, if possible. Of course they hope that this will enhance their reputation and political correctness. **Related topics include authority, and what authorities get up to** (especially when it is questioned – for example a high-level traffic official being caught speeding) and **expense** (perhaps involving taxpayers' money).

Novelty/curiosity: People are very interested in the unusual and the bizarre [*odd, extraordinary*]. The first event or last event or a once-in-a-life-time event are news. Once again: If a dog bites a man it is not news because it is a common event. But a man biting a dog is news. Readers love to read about strange animals or striking animal behaviour, such as a dog that escapes from a kennel and walks 200 kilometres to find its owner. People like to read about things that are different, such as a new way to make a living, unusual habits and hobbies, and so on. To have novelty appeal, the reported item must be unusual and provoke people's curiosity. Although most people like to deny it, they are attracted to articles on sex, perversion [*abnormal or unnatural behaviour*], psychic phenomena [things that appear unexplainable by science] and violence. The scholar Jürgen Habermas wrote:

> " Man bites dog "

While most professional journalists today will agree that serious newspapers should avoid sensationalism, such stories do make news. The generally conservative Charles Dana's own creed at the New York Sun was: "I have always felt that whatever the Divine Providence permitted to occur I was not too proud to report." (Habermas, 1993).

Conflict: A quick check through our daily newspapers and television, radio broadcasts and news websites will show you that war, political issues and crime (followed very closely by sport) are the most common news of all. Even when these news items are not directly about war, it is the conflict in them that makes them newsworthy. People love to read about politicians attacking each other in the press; differences of ideology make news. Most conflicts are newsworthy, and physical conflict is especially newsworthy because injury and damage often results. Violence usually makes news because of the emotions it arouses.

War
Politics
Crime
Sport

A fight between two footballers in a match might not get much attention from the editor, but a violent clash between two groups of opposing fans could get front page coverage. Also, conflict naturally leads to tension and suspense which have news value in themselves.

Does the printing of stories depicting [*describing*] violence lead to more acts of violence, or not? Will the perpetrators [*doers*] of violence continue with their activities because they are sure to get publicity this way? I would say no, this argument isn't valid. However, there is much debate about these points and many who feel that we should be very circumspect [*cautious, reserved*] with our reporting of violence. **Corruption, deceit** or **hypocrisy** [*double standards*] are also popular topics.

Human interest: Many stories that appear in our press don't really satisfy any of the above news tests. These stories usually fit into the category of human interest. For example, people love stories about children and animals. Newspapers often use pictures of animals and children to promote various causes. People love to read about people, and today many editors look for a human interest angle in almost all stories. They should have human interest as well as other news value. Although human interest is not strictly a news value measurement, it has important story value. It enriches the news by getting readers to identify with [*feel for*] people they read about. Some stories even get rejected because they have little human interest angle. Sometimes journalists have to look closely at the situation and events in a story before they can decide whether to treat it as a human interest story or as a straight news item.

Sex: As much as some people would like to deny it, sex has great news value. People like to follow the personal lives of the rich and famous. Take for instance the enormous interest that the public show in the divorce proceedings of politicians and celebrities. This interest is continued in the worldwide public interest in members of the British royal family and Hollywood and Bollywood movie actors. Prominence links up with sex as a news value. Sometimes sex links more with novelty, reporting on the unusual sexual practices of a person who is otherwise unknown.

Enjoyment: People sometimes want to sit down and relax with a newspaper. At such times, hard news may depress or stress them; but they will still remain hooked on [*addicted to*] the paper if they simply enjoy reading it. A paper that people buy mainly for the essential information it carries may easily become dull if it does not have enjoyable, easy-to-read articles. These might have human interest or any other news values discussed above. They might also appeal to particular interests such as education, self-help, entertainment, cultural ritual, travel - or just interesting trivia [*small, unimportant items*]. The interest and enjoyment such stories offer is a news value in itself. Let's consider the importance of humour. Cartoons are so popular because people demand a lighter side to the news. People want to laugh. They love trivia and without trivia, newspapers would be very boring. As well as hard news, an important thing that readers want from newspapers is tips and advice on how to improve their lifestyles.

Often, a good news story will incorporate several of these elements. 'Local politician arrested for domestic violence' – if the headline is accurate, the story probably contains proximity, timeliness, authority, violence, sex and possibly, hypocrisy.

Assessing news value

Now that you have looked at some news values, how will you apply this knowledge quickly and efficiently when you are at work?

News must be new.

News must have conversational value. If we don't want to talk about it, it has no news value. The conversational value comes from all the criteria we have been discussing so far.

News must have commercial value. If our readers are not interested in the news that we bring to them they will soon stop buying our newspaper. News, like most things, is a commodity that can be bought and sold. This is very important and we should consider it more closely.

> **Essential news qualities**
> 1. New
> 2. Conversational
> 3. Commercial

Remember that you can decide news value by using a simple, basic measure: what do readers want? This can be different in different times and places and it is risky to ignore what readers want when you are deciding what is news. For example, South Africa launched a Truth and Reconciliation Commission (1995 – 1998) investigating war crimes and abuse during the racist apartheid era. *The Cape Times*, a daily English-language newspaper in the Western Cape, dedicated a number of pages and appointed a number of journalists to cover this important and historic event. The immediate result was a drop in circulation. The general reader of this Cape Town newspaper was not deeply interested in the amount of news about the Truth and Reconciliation Commission and showed his or her frustration by not buying the paper.

5 MINUTE TASK

SABC was doing live radio and television broadcasts of selected Truth and Reconciliation Commission (TRC) hearings at the same time, as well as a weekly television summary of TRC events. In your view, would this have also affected the *Cape Times*' decision? Discuss with a partner.

Another example of this pattern of reader disinterest was the history of the *Rand Daily Mail* (1902 - 1985), a daily English-language newspaper in Johannesburg. The editorial policy showed great dedication to informing the public about the extent of human rights abuse in South Africa, including the use of taxpayer's money to fund disinformation networks; barbaric prison conditions; massacres and the forced removal of long-term black residents from suburbs demarcated for whites. But the newspaper's reading public was not ready to accept this information. Consequently, the newspaper lost advertisers and readership and was forced to close down.

An accurate assessment of our readers' news wants is essential if we wish to remain in business. Many students believe that newspapers should only give readers the facts and what they need to know to make accurate assessments of the situation. While we can admire this attitude, it may not be enough to keep a newspaper in business. A newspaper is a business and needs to sell advertising and copy to survive. As in other businesses, the customer comes first.

How do we decide on the importance of any item of news?

Well, firstly we should measure a news item on how important it is to the readers compared with other news stories which compete for the same space. If it's going to be used, next we should consider how much space it should get. Here we have to be as objective as we can. Finally we should not neglect another important measurement, journalist's intuition [*the power of understanding something quickly, without reasoning it out*].

Here are some ways to measure a story's importance.

> How much disruption was caused to everyday life?
> How many people were affected?
> How close was the event to the readers?
> How long ago did the event take place?
> What was the outcome or result of the event?

Lastly, it is important to bear in mind the mix or variety of our traditional news tests. A car hijacking may not be very big news. However, the first car hijacking which has occurred in a quiet small town is big news for the people in that district. And the hijacking of the car of a prominent person is big news generally. It is even bigger news if it took place outside a police station in full view of high-ranking police officers who took no action because they were off duty.

⑩ MINUTE TASK

In groups look at the front page of any newspaper that is at hand. Reassess the news value of the stories on the page.

Do you agree that all the front page stories have front page news value?

What kinds of news value does each have, in your view?

If you were in charge, would you have put these stories in the same order of importance?

Would you have swapped the lead story for another on that page or even from an inside page? If so, why?

Presenting news objectively, fairly and accurately

So far, we have discussed how the journalist judges what is news and what isn't. But news is not only something 'out there' that the reporter looks for. News is also something that reporters process [*develop, work on*] as they research and write a news story. When readers talk about the news in the newspaper they are talking about the news that the reporter has already discovered, selected and presented as a news story. Important questions arise about this preparation. Whose idea of news are we reading? How accurate is this news? Are we seeing all sides of the picture? Can we trust that it is true? These issues have been raised already in this book. Now you will deepen your understanding of them.

Objectivity and subjectivity

One of the most common accusations that journalists face is the claim that they lack objectivity. But what is it to be objective? It doesn't mean to object! Objective means detached, impersonal, impartial, unbiased and unprejudiced. Subjective, on the other hand, means based on personal bias.

In modern journalism, objectivity is our ideal. But can we achieve true objectivity? The history of the press shows that early newspapers were certainly not objective. They were filled with opinion, with biting sarcasm and with personal bias. It is clear that journalists started to search for objectivity only more recently. However, it is also clear that we don't all see the same event through the same eyes. Thus objectivity in journalism must be difficult or even impossible to achieve.

Does objectivity remain an important goal nonetheless?

Not only do we see events from different angles, we also bring a lifetime of personal experience to every event we witness. No matter how objective we try to be, those life experiences will interfere with our way of seeing things. Subjectivity is sure to enter into our reporting. Why? you may ask. "I reported exactly what I saw happen." In fact that is exactly the problem. Usually the reporter is the observer, interpreter, writer and judge of what information goes into each story. But it is important that we try very hard to be impartial [*fair, unbiased*] when assessing and reporting news. A reporter must consider news value from all angles, and a story must pass through checks and balances before it is printed. All stories must be checked carefully by experienced editors. Your editor will expect you to report without personal bias because he or she knows that is what readers demand.

Is my story objective?

Accuracy and fairness

In seeking news we must look for the truth. *Washington Post* newspaper investigative reporter Bob Woodward helped uncover the Watergate scandal in which the ruling party in America burgled opponents' offices, planted listening devices, and then tried to cover up their dirty tricks campaign. Woodward, whose Watergate stories helped trigger the resignation of American president Richard Nixon in 1974, says we must seek "the best possible version of the truth."

Outside of the letters page and some opinion page articles, newspaper reports very seldom get challenged. But that does not give journalists the right to publish information that is not accurate or truthful. The reporter's idea of news value should never get in the way of the facts. Readers have a right to truthful information and reporting. Good faith with the reader is basic to good journalism. Our first duty is then to ensure that the news content is accurate, free from personal bias, and that all sides have been reported fairly.

Although it is the reporter's job to find and write the facts, the task is not that easy. How does a journalist know when they have achieved the best possible version of the truth? The only answer is that if we are satisfied that our story is accurate and fair, then we have achieved as much as is possible.

Accuracy is the most important aspect of any story. No matter how newsworthy an event is, if you report it inaccurately, your story will not be proper news. Get the facts straight and the rest will usually look after itself. Here are some essential guidelines on accuracy for every reporter:

Is my story fair, accurate and balanced?

1. The spelling of all names must be correct. A misspelt name can and often does lead to embarrassment and possible legal action against the newspaper. You cannot assume you know the correct spelling. And spelling of names should be written down and then checked with the source (not simply checked verbally) because it is easy to misunderstand accents.

2. Every quote must be exactly what was said and how it was said.

3. Numbers must add up. Too many numbers in a sentence or paragraph causes confusion. Be cautious about things like percentages and percentiles.

4. Dates and times must be accurate. Many reporters take down contact numbers of people whom they've already interviewed, so they can double-check information like dates and times back in the newsroom when writing the story – partly to avoid misunderstanding, partly because they can get the latest update.

Even if you have done all this, it is still not good enough. Even if your details are correct, you can still mislead the reader if the details are not placed clearly in context, so that the surrounding events and circumstances are clear. To obtain the best version of the truth, your reporting must be accurate and in context [*background circumstances*]. However, that still does not imply that your story is fair.

What do we mean by being fair? Accuracy and fairness are related but they are not the same. Think of it like this: as reporters we act as the eyes and ears of our readers, with the power to give them information - or to hold it back. How we present a story is how the reader will receive it and react to it. Thus, if we want the public to trust us they must be able to see that we are providing accurate information on all sides or aspects of an issue.

Reporters often have to cover controversial situations in which there are major conflicts of values. There is seldom only one viewpoint in a story and in political stories there will be many viewpoints from opposing sides. For the sake of fairness, everyone involved in the story must get the opportunity to respond. This is especially important for those in the story whose integrity or competence is being questioned.

The more we strive for fairness and objectivity in our stories the more balanced our stories will become. To be balanced, the reporter must let all contrasting points of view be represented. That does not mean that you have to quote every-body, but it means that you must at least acknowledge different points of view. Often that means interviewing people from organisations which disagree with each other. But you can sometimes interview a range of lower-ranking people from within a single institution – a secretary, a cleaner, an artisan - rather than just going to the person at the top of the hierarchy. This often represents a great-er diversity of views. Here are a few rules that you should apply to ensure that your story is fair and balanced:

1. Stick to the facts - never manufacture facts.

2. Do not give your own opinion. If you do, you will be seen as biased.

3. Listen to the advice of your editor - the editor has been there many times before.

4. Go easy with your choice of adjectives - just tell the story.

5. Remember you are an observer and a reporter, not a player in the story.

6. Do not get too close to the story.

7. If someone has something relevant to say, give him or her that space.

8. Remember that your story could ruin a person's good name.

Changing perspectives

One of the modern newspaper's big problems is the fact that other news sources can deliver the news long before newspapers can. Television, radio and the in-ternet can get news to us almost immediately. The Cable News Network, better known as CNN, has been a good example of this since it was founded in the USA in 1980. However, a newspaper is normally up to eight hours behind in its delivery of news. Less than thirty minutes after the horrific 1995 Oklahoma City terrorist bomb blast by right wing Christian Timothy McVeigh , a television station had set up a mobile studio at the scene, where more than 150 people lay dead and dying and close to 800 were injured, and had begun to broadcast. How can newspapers compete with that speed? Obviously, most of their stories will be a rehash of what has been broadcast – although it is also true that many countries in the developing world still lack mobile outside broadcast vans and so newspapers continue to be important.

Because newspapers can never compete with the electronic media for speed of delivery, they must instead try to be more innovative [*inventive, full of new ideas*]. Instead of repeating what has already been broadcast, newspapers must look at the news in more depth seeking a different angle or perspective.

In the case of the Oklahoma City bomb blast, newspapers set up teams of journalists to look for different angles. The first papers tried to link the blast to Muslim extremists. Later papers, looking for their own niche [*angle, approach*], tried to link the blast to local religious extremists. Journalists must try to deliver information that is valuable and difficult for the opposition to copy. Reporters must develop sources rather than theories, and not rely on official press conferences and press releases, which will be available to all.

Newspapers will have to move closer to their readers. They will need to ask very seriously, What do the readers want to read about? What are the hopes and aspirations of the average reader? Newspapers should voice the concerns of their readers and hold politicians and bureaucrats responsible where necessary. Editors and journalists should never forget that their readers are vital to the survival of the newspaper. Newspapers should continually research the wants and interests of their readers.

Unfortunately, hardly any newspapers do true, effective market research. Most newspapers will probably disagree with me when I say that they usually conduct research only to confirm their own existing ideas and not to find out the real situation. For example, a Durban newspaper once used a focus group of four Indian

⑩ MINUTE TASK

Read through any news story in a newspaper that is available. Is the story accurate, fair and as balanced and objective as possible? Explain the reasons for your assessment. Share your notes with your partner/group/class.

Introducing Journalism and Media Studies

families to research their news presentation to an Indian population of almost one million.

If you want to know what people want, ask them! People's interests tend to change, so we must keep re-evaluating our methods of presentation. However, we must be aware that people don't always tell the truth. Most people don't admit to being interested in US singer Britney Spear's underwear but oddly enough, we all seem to know about it. Is it entirely a case of mass media pushing it down our throats, or are we so attuned to celebrity gossip that we cannot filter it out?

Suggested Reading

Brooks, Brian; Kennedy, George; Moen, Daryl and Ranly, Don (1992). The Missouri Group, *News Reporting & Writing*, New York, St Martins Press, 4th edition.

Harriss, Julian; Leiter, Kelly and Johnson, Stanley, (1999). *The Complete Reporter*, New York, MacMillan Publishing, 7th edition.

Teel, Leonard and Taylor, Ron, (1983). *Into the Newsroom - An introduction to journalism*, Prentice-Hall.

Ward, Hiley H, *Professional Newswriting*, (1985). New York, Harcourt Brace Jovanovich, Publishers.

11

chapter

Sources of news

Introduction

People have a deep need for news. They not only need it, they generally demand it. You can see this clearly in people who have been cut off from the outside world for some time. When they return to normal life, they immediately start to catch up on the news in their families, their local communities and the world.

When we meet friends we ask, 'How are you? What have you been doing?' This shows our inborn thirst for news. A reporter responds to this thirst by seeking out the news, evaluating whether it is sound and accurate and bringing it to the readers. Interviewing skills and developing sources are crucial to writing a good news story. Without good sources and good quotes, you cannot write a good article.

The reporter with a nose for news

The ability of the reporter is the most important factor in news-gathering. Old journalists describe this ability as having a nose for news. Not all reporters have this 'nose' to sniff out a story. Those who don't have it must build their skill at news-gathering. They must develop as many contacts as possible who will feed them with information.

Big ears
Good eyes
Good nose
Curiosity
Burning desire
to tell

Stories generally come from outside the newspaper. One study found that approximately 49 out of 50 ideas used in the paper on a particular day came from outside; only one came from the staff. Editors want reporters who go out daily to find new stories and come up with creative ideas. They know that good quality news and creative reporting will put their paper ahead of the others with readers.

⑤ MINUTE TASK

In groups, 'brainstorm' a list of all the things you could do in order to get ideas for stories. Work quickly, don't throw any ideas out and don't try to order your ideas. Now read on and see if your ideas match ours or not.

Find the story

Most story ideas are the result of curiosity, an active imagination and help from fellow journalists. Even the most dedicated and creative journalists run out of ideas now and then. So, we must have a source of ideas that work for any time or place, and especially when the usual well [*storehouse*] of ideas dries up for a while.

There's a story here!

When my students attend their first lecture, I tell them that to be good journalists they will need the following items most of all: big ears to listen, good eyes to observe, a good nose to sniff out a story, curiosity about everything and a burning desire to tell everybody what they have just found out. Obviously, there is more to reporting than these things, but they certainly are a good start.

Here are a few ideas on how to generate ideas for stories:

Read: Read, read, read. The sad truth is that many students do not read - not even for pleasure, even though reading is the lifeblood of all journalists. As a journalist you should read everything that you can put your hands on, including all the opposition newspapers, brochures and magazines. Study the work of the most popular journalists. You can learn from the topics and content they use, as well as the approach to the story and the style. You can try to copy their style of writing,

Definitions

Copyright

Key people

Leads

but not their ideas or exact words; these have copyright. You can take good ideas that you find and adapt them for local conditions and for your own readers.

Listen: This is the most important skill you can develop. Many journalists become boring because they spend too much time talking about their own exploits [*experiences and achievements*] instead of listening and focusing on others. If you listen rather than speak you can learn much. You may well hear something interesting that sparks an idea for a future story. Listening is active, not passive, and it is a skill which can bring you much information.

Circulate: Get around town - go out and meet people. Every month, try to attend an event that you would not normally attend. Meet people out of their work environment when they are relaxed. Listen to their conversations. Find out what interests people, what excites them, what angers them. These people are your readers and there is no better source of ideas than them.

Be friendly: Someone once said, "Be nice to people, not because you might meet them on the way down, but because it is a damn nice way to do business." If you consider yourself better than other people, your arrogance will be your downfall. People are key to your success as a journalist. The best journalists make friends with beggars, street vendors, bartenders, clerks, hotel receptionists, tea makers, police, paramedics and petty criminals. They make friends with almost everybody. In particular, reporters make friends with people who don't look like them, sound like them, and who aren't the same age or sex as them – because they have to be able to see the world through the eyes of many different people.

Identify and meet leaders: Make the effort to identify and get to know key people [*people who have knowledge, responsibility, power*]. Take them to lunch or plan to meet them at social occasions, meetings and clubs. It is easier to interview key people if they know who you are before the interview. You may never need to interview these key people but you should at least establish them as contacts who may introduce you to other key people. The trust of key people is essential. Avoid breaking your word to them, as this will undo all your good work – but be aware that you need to always remain alert against attempts to charm you and feed you propaganda.

Visit your library: Browse through the notice boards at your local library. They will tell you a lot about what is happening in the community. Be alert to local interests.

Read records: Government departments are full of records. Seek out these records and scan them to find out about employment, property sales, financial dealings, new businesses and bankruptcies and indeed all the activities of businesses and individuals that will lead to a good story. Get to know the people who keep and work with the files because they can give you leads to interesting information.

Subscribe: Get on as many mailing lists as you can. The junk in your mail box might be the source of your next story.

Be sceptical: Good reporters are always sceptical. In other words, they suspect that the truth is not quite as it appears. For example, you may hear a story about the charity work of a community leader. But if you speak to the leader's employees, friends and family, you may get a totally different picture. Most people have a dark side to their character and in this kind of story, further investigation may reveal it. Always be aware that the truth may be quite different or even completely opposite to the first picture you get. By checking the facts you may find an alternative story. Even better: you may land an exclusive story.

All is not what it seems to be.

Become an expert: The more you know about a particular subject the better prepared you will be when you want to probe [*investigate*] deeper. You can develop expertise in any subject by reading about experts in that subject or asking them questions. If you can't meet the expert face to face, develop the habit of asking questions as you read. In short, ask as many questions as possible. In this way your knowledge will grow. The more you know about the subject the better you will be able to ask more and more probing questions about that subject.

Check through advertisements: Advertisements, particularly the classifieds, are often a source of interesting stories. You may find someone trying to sell stolen goods or you could find a disgruntled wife selling her adulterous husband's BMW motorcar for R5.

Study community newspapers: Community news can be a rich source of stories. Most of the stories have not caught the attention of the mainstream press but they may be full of possibilities.

Question and consult yourself: Basically, it is you who must be alert to look and listen to what is going on around you. Ask yourself: Why do people behave the way they do? What are they thinking about? What are the fears and anxieties of the people in this situation? Always ask yourself the most important question: why? And then look for the answer. Journalists who attune themselves to people will find a rich source of human interest stories right under their noses.

Developing your own sources

Perhaps you have already noticed that finding ideas will usually connect you with people who provide information in one way or another. As you begin your career as a journalist you will soon start to meet interesting people in various walks of life. As you meet more and more people you should always be alert to find people

Contact

Tipster

Informant

who are influential and knowledgeable about what is going on in their community, organisation or business. Most of the information used in stories comes from a reporter's personal sources - people. Journalists usually divide these personal sources into three groups: contacts, tipsters and informants.

Contact: usually someone whom everyone recognises as the person with information on a specific subject. For example, a company's public relations officer can be considered a contact and may be referred to in a story as a spokesperson.

Tipster: someone who may have information or who may only point to a source of information. A tipster's information is usually unsubstantiated. This means that it is information that is not yet proven or certainly true. Tipsters are usually anonymous [*they don't give their name or they don't want others to know it*]. Their information gives the reporter a start on a story. The reporter is able to question the authorities and seek an explanation for what the tipster hinted at or suggested.

Informants: often referred to as leaks. These will be discussed later.

🔟 MINUTE TASK

In pairs, discuss the following:
- ▶ What kind of people would you look for as sources?
- ▶ How would you know which sources are really useful and which are not?
- ▶ How would you keep your sources going over a long time?

Strategies to develop traditional sources

How can I get their details for my contact book?

Develop your own contact book: As you meet influential and knowledgeable people, write down their names and contact details in a contact book that you can refer to when you need to speak to them. You can use a directory, notebook or file cards for this purpose. It seems mobile phones are being used these days as a contact book but the data needs to be backed up on a computer. And relying on a computer alone is no good, because you need to bring the contact book with you when you leave that particular media house. Your contact book will be your most prized possession as you continue with your career as a journalist. A good contact book takes many years to develop and is something that a journalist never lends out. The contacts that you develop are your eyes and ears and therefore a valuable asset. It may be a good idea to keep a duplicate [*copy*] contact book safely somewhere, in case the original gets lost or stolen. You must be particularly careful with the details of sources who insist on confidentiality (those who refuse to be named or revealed). If you prefer, you could keep their names and addresses in a separate place.

From time to time you should review [*go over*] the names in your contact book to refresh your memory about the people you have met. If you have not spoken to your contacts for some time, it is a good idea to telephone them to keep in touch.

Visit the scene: Always visit the scene of your story. First hand knowledge is basic to good reporting. This means that even when you are not chasing a particular story, you need to be building contacts. Visit all the departments or organisations on your beat [*speciality*] and find a person in each who is willing to talk to the press. Attend as many of the functions, meetings and seminars on your beat as you can. Make a note of those people who seem friendly and positive towards you. Then, when a story comes up you will have a good knowledge of the background context and the contacts you could use.

Remember the 'little' people: Secretaries may not seem to be as important as others but they are excellent sources of information. They have access to the people you wish to contact and usually know what is happening in their organisations. Secretaries can be most helpful in tracking down their bosses or the important information you need just before deadline. Don't forget the 'faceless' people in an organisation - the support staff who are not as visible as the 'professional' staff. Who are they? The tea person, security guards, drivers, clerks and messengers. These people are often very aware of what is going on in an organisation but because they are not seen as powerful, they are ignored. Show them that you consider them significant and you may have a valuable source of information. Your big story may come from them.

Meet influential people: Meet as many of the influential people on your beat as you can. Get to know them and (more important) get them to know you. If you can, take them out to lunch. Or coffee, if your budget is not going to cope with lunch.

Check the telephone directory: The telephone directory is helpful not only for finding people but also for verifying names and addresses. Get to know the layout of the telephone directory and save yourself valuable time. It is a good idea to study your area telephone directory in detail so that you know how the numbers have been classified. For instance, are schools listed together or are they distributed through the directory according to their names? What about government and quasi-government organisations?

Can you add to the above strategies to develop your sources?

You have ten minutes to find the following telephone numbers in your local telephone directory:

▶ two lawyers or attorneys
▶ two schools
▶ the supermarket
▶ the fire station
▶ the hospital or clinic
▶ the member of parliament for your town council
▶ the local police station

Ensure these numbers are accurately recorded in your contact book for later reference.

Good sources make good stories

It is important to remember that strong, authoritative sources make strong, authoritative stories. If you are writing an article about the president's personal expenses, you need to speak to the president, or at least to his or her spokesperson. If you are writing an article about a teacher allegedly sexually harassing learners in his class, you need to speak to the teacher, the principal, the learners (though you may not be able to name them), their parents, other teachers and possibly the head of the state or provincial or even national education department. Securing powerful sources such as presidents and high-ranking officials is by no means easy. You will need to exercise tenacity [*persistence*] to achieve them, but your reward for this will be powerful, balanced, well-read stories.

Seek multiple sources

I must use a variety of sources so that my story is balanced and fair.

You need to develop your journalistic skills in selecting appropriate sources who will lend balance, authority and colour to your articles. While people are the most important sources for journalists, there are many other types of sources, including books, letters, websites, financial reports, old newspaper reports, maps, and so on. It is important to obtain information from a variety of legitimate [*legal*] and authoritative [*respected*] sources and this forms the basis of news-gathering for all types of journalism. If you do not include enough sources in your piece, it will lack credibility [*trustworthiness*] and impact. Never rely too heavily on one source, and never produce a single-sourced story. Obtaining a range of sources will ensure your writing is balanced and fair, as all journalism should be.

You should be looking for sources that are from both genders, different ages and sources that are multi-cultural and multi-racial. Do this so that your story is as reflective of society as possible and so that no reader feels excluded. Obviously, different stories require different sources. If you are writing an article about a group of teenagers who are cycling 1 000 kilometres for charity, your sources would primarily be the teenagers themselves, as well as their friends, families and the beneficiaries of their initiative.

With a good range of carefully selected sources, you will be able to weave a powerful story. Acquiring sources is rarely easy but don't be tempted to fill in any blanks in information with fiction. It should go without saying that you should never, ever, EVER make up a quote or a source. In the media industry, doing so may constitute an offence for which you could lose your job and ruin your career.

You should also not be afraid of asking different people the same question. Let's take an example of a news story: *A local politician has been caught driving under the influence of alcohol.*

To get the full story, you need to ask a variety of people a list of questions. These people may include a police spokesperson, or even better, the officer who caught the politician, any witnesses, perhaps a non-governmental organisation which concentrates on the issue of drunk driving, opposition politicians, and then of course the politician himself. You are obliged, in the interests of making your article objective, balanced and fair, to give him the opportunity to give his side of the story. If he chooses to say 'no comment', you need to include this to prove you gave him that opportunity. In a story such as this, it would be wise to gather as much information about the incident as possible, before approaching the politician. If you are not sure of your information, he might easily dismiss you and then refuse to speak to you later on, when you have found out more. You might also want to visit the scene of the incident to gather details which will bring your story to life. You may gather new information, which will add punch to your piece.

Anonymous sources

Unnamed sources are a no-no unless there is a compelling reason, like someone's life or job would really be in danger if you revealed the source. Any editor worthy of his or her title would question the need for an unnamed source in a story. Of course, there are rare cases when using unnamed sources is necessary.

Perhaps the most famous case of an unnamed source called "Deep Throat" – named partly as a joke around a scandalous porn movie of the time, partly as a tribute to the journalistic concept of deep or intense off-the-record briefings - was the main source in the Watergate political scandal in the United States. Washington Post newspaper reporters Bob Woodward and Carl Bernstein broke the story of the scandal (a complex web of unsavoury events between 1972 and 1974, including spying on the opposition Democratic Party) which led to the resignation of United States President Richard Nixon. For thirty years the identity of 'Deep Throat' remained a secret. In 2005, William Mark Felt, a retired FBI (Federal Bureau of Investigations) agent, voluntarily identified himself as 'Deep Throat' in a magazine article, after which Woodward and Bernstein confirmed his role. They never broke faith with his request for anonymity, for three decades.

Evaluating sources

Definitions

Motives

Leaks

Plants

You may think that it is always the reporter who must find his/her sources of news. The real situation is more complex. American sociologist Herbert Gans said in his book, *Deciding What's News*:

> The relationship between sources and journalists resembles a dance; for sources seek access to journalists and journalists seek access to sources. Although it takes two to tango... more often than not sources do the leading.

Journalists need to have ways of deciding whether sources are reliable and worthwhile or not. This is not easy: the motives of sources are not always clear. Some sources are clearly self-serving. Politicians often fit this type. But the motives of other sources may seem unselfish or they may be self-serving in a rather complex way. Sources can be concerned citizens, dissatisfied employees or people looking for revenge. Their motivation is complex.

Leakers and their motives

There are various types of sources, including those who approach the press themselves.

True leak: happens when a source offers information on a issue or event that the journalist generally was not aware of. The information (and supporting evidence) is often given on condition that the leaker remains anonymous.

The plant: often governments leak information deliberately to the press to find out how the public will respond to a new policy or proposed action. It is a deliberate, authorised leak, known as a plant. A government uses plants to promote its own administration and its interest. Leaks occur most in times of crisis. Although sources have various motives for leaking information they usually have one purpose in common: that is, to serve their own vested interests. Remaining anonymous protects the source because although the journalist gets a story ahead of competitors, the source can deny after publication that he or she gave any information to the journalist.

Why do people leak information to the press? It is important to find out what the source wants. There are widely different motives:

The ego leak - Here the source wishes to satisfy a sense of his or her own importance. This is probably the most common form of leak but the leaks are usually not major ones. Few people do something for nothing. Sources generally supply information with a return in mind. For a charitable source, this return could be something like the benefit of society.

Why is this person giving me this information?

The goodwill leak - Here the source wishes to earn favour with the journalist and probably expects the journalist to return the favour at a later date. Some sources may feel they need the journalist as an ally and may appear to give information freely without selfish motives.

The discrediting or animus leak – derived from the Latin word for ill will or animosity, this type of leak is used mainly by politicians. Its main purpose is to embarrass another person or party.

The policy leak - documents or inside information is used to get attention from the press. In this way public reaction to an impending policy can be gauged [*assessed*]. The issue might not really be worth much attention without the inside information that is leaked.

The trial balloon leak - a controversial policy which is still being considered gets 'leaked' in order to test public opinion before it is officially released. If there is an unfavourable public reaction to the policy it can be modified before it is made official.

The whistle–blower leak - usually happens when a civil servant feels that he or she cannot right a wrong through the usual and 'proper' channels. In this case, the leaker is often willing to state his or her case in public, and be named. Such leakers may risk losing their jobs.

(20) MINUTE TASK

In groups,
- List possible sources of information, including probable leaks, in your community relating to an incident at your municipal office. Why would you identify them as leaks?
- Analyse a current high profile story to decide what type of leak(s) assisted the reporter. Did the reporter acknowledge a leak?

Basic research

I must do some research before this interview.

One of the basic rules of journalism is that the more information you uncover, the sounder your judgement will be and the more accurate your story will be, too. No matter how skilled a writer you are, if you lack information your story will not have a solid foundation. On the other hand, good reporting is frequently backed by good research. Research can equip the journalist not only to report on what is happening but also to give background information and perspective to a story. Ideally, one should research before an interview to prepare the best questions but because of time constraints this may happen after the interview.

Some journalists argue that too much research spoils a good story because it makes you lose focus. Others believe that too much research prevents reporters from meeting their deadlines. There are no easy answers to this. There can be no substitute for good research and journalists have to learn to research economically.

In this section we will look at two resources the modern journalist should use routinely when researching stories; official records and the computer.

Using official records

Interactions between people are recorded in many different ways. We go through life leaving a trail of recorded information that is easily accessible to researchers. Although at first these records may not look very interesting, reporters can use them to obtain fascinating evidence about what people do. Most records are open to public scrutiny [*inspection*]. Anyone may look at them. Here are some public records you may wish to examine.

Police and court records - does the person have a criminal record? How many convictions, on what charges, can lead to an interesting story.

Birth records - if you suspect a person is lying about his/her age and correct name, checking the person's birth certificate can set the record straight. You can also identify who the parents are and the place of birth.

Death records - a death certificate will provide evidence of the time, place and the likely cause of death.

Property register - land ownership is normally registered at the Deeds Office. You should be able to determine the current owner and previous ownership, back to the first owner of the land.

Judgments - these records can help to reveal a person's credit standing.

Other records that you may wish to examine include company records, voter registration or voters' rolls, permits and inspection reports and marriage and divorce records. Not only do these records provide useful information but they also ensure that the information you report is accurate.

You may have to pay a search fee to access records, or you may have to request permission in advance from the relevant authority before examining certain records. Check first with the relevant authority for the correct search protocol [*procedure*]. But never, ever, state the reason why you wish to examine the records, in order to protect your story.

Computer-assisted reporting

Most newspapers today are equipped with computers that are connected to e-mail and the internet. How does this affect journalists researching stories?

The internet has made enormous quantities of information available. It is an advanced tool for learning and research which gives you access to databases worldwide. Wherever you are, you can connect with the best libraries and universities in the world. You can have access to many newspapers in the world (many online), as well as news services such as Reuters and Associated Press. The internet has databases with up-to-date information on almost every subject you can imagine, in many languages. However, there is a strong focus on media from the industrialised economies on the world wide web. You have to hunt a little harder to find media from Africa on the internet, for example.

Secondly, you can share ideas and network with others as you gather information. Internet and e-mail put you immediately and cheaply in contact with people and other journalists around the world. As a local journalist you can become familiar with media issues both here and abroad.

Thirdly, one of the most exciting aspects of this 'power-tool' is that it is so simple to manage for the newspaper or journalist. The reporter doing research can easily access one of the search engines on the internet, such as Google, which is available in several different languages. By entering a key word or phrase, the computer will search all the available data bases quickly and efficiently. The downside is that the information might be out of date, wrong or repetitive.

Finally, journalists who cannot access information by computer may soon become redundant. The internet is obviously challenging traditional means of news gathering and delivery.

The influence and the abilities of the computer will surely continue to alter the practice of journalism. You, as an aspirant journalist, must embrace this technology and grow with it, or you will be left behind.

Whom to interview?

Whom you choose to interview will have a major impact on your finished story. When you are deciding who to interview for an article, try to be creative. There may be others you may not immediately think of who have perspectives that could add colour and depth to your article. If you're writing a piece about an accident at a busy intersection, the first interviews are probably those involved in the accident, the police and any eye-witnesses. But you could gather more information from hospital personnel and residents or shop-owners in the area, who may be able to talk about the frequency of crashes in this spot. Before you know it, you may have another idea: to write a piece on the fears that this intersection is a particularly dangerous one.

Talking to sources

When talking to sources, don't take what people say at face value. Think about the omissions: sometimes what people don't say can be more revealing than what they do say. Be aware and observant. Remember to ask the types of questions that allow you to explore the negatives as well as the positives. Ask open-ended questions that will lead to interesting answers. So if you are interviewing a person who allegedly assaulted someone, you many not want ask them right away "Did you hit the person?" (an answer which could easily be answered "no"). Instead, you might ask, "Please tell me what happened, from your point of view?"

When you're interviewing a source or covering a news event, be observant. Watch sources and situations closely and write down your observations in your notebook. Look at your source's expressions, body language, shoes, cell phone, fingernails, and so on. What do these things tell you about this person? You may not use all the details you collect but it is easy to leave details out of a story if they're unnecessary. But it's impossible to put them in to add colour, if you haven't made the observations in the first place.

Face your partner and study him / her for a minute or so. Then turn your backs on one another for a minute and make a minor physical change to the way you look. Turn back and face one another and see if you can spot the difference. Repeat this three times.

Reflection
- How observant were you?
- How did this exercise make you feel?
- How do you think a source might feel being scrutinised in a similar way?
- How creative were you in changing things about yourself?
- Did you use your initiative in 'borrowing' things from other people?
- How does this relate to news writing?

On and off the record

In dealing with the press, officials often protect themselves by demanding how journalists should describe the way the information came to them. They may say the information is either on the record or off the record.

On the record - means that all statements are directly quotable, by name and title, to the person who is making the statement.

Off the record - information given off the record is for the journalist's knowledge only and is not to be printed or made public in any way. This must be respected. The information also cannot be taken to another source to obtain official confirmation. The source usually provides off-the-record information in order to prevent the journalist speculating incorrectly.

Definitions

On the record

Off the record

Spell names correctly

The first rule of journalism is to ask people how they spell their names. Don't presume it's spelt correctly in a phone book or that a colleague knows how to spell it correctly. Spelling a person's name wrong is a sure way to irritate a source and to make readers doubt your ability as a journalist. If you misspell names, not only will you embarrass your publication, but sources and readers will think that if you can't get a name right, what else have you got wrong?

" So, what's in the name? "
" A lot! "

Obtain first names

While asking sources how to spell their names, ask them for their first names. For many inexperienced journalists, this is a difficult task. You need first names, however, to lend credibility to your story. If you refer to a Captain Naidoo at a police station in Delhi, the identity of the source is immediately questionable, because it could refer to one of many people with the same name. Obtaining a source's full first name (not just initials) makes the person real for the reader, and you should always obtain this information. Be prepared to argue: some people do not like their first names in print.

Ask for background information

While asking for a person's first name, which you may choose to do either at the beginning or end of the interview, you might want to ask for their titles and a short job description of what they do (in a sentence or so), if you think this information might provide useful background for your readers. It is particularly important to obtain ranks and titles of official sources, such as police officers and government officials.

1. Campus official L. Moosa said that the city police were within their rights to tow away the students' cars, as they had been parked illegally.

Without looking at the answer in the text box, can you improve on the lead above, taking into account names and background? Write your answer below.

Introducing sources

In general, introduce sources before quoting them. This ensures that your writing flows better, as your reader doesn't have to absorb and retain all the information quoted before finding out who it comes from. Start a new paragraph whenever you introduce a new source:

2. "I'm outraged! The dean is treating us like dirt," said Thami Shezi, a first-year student.

Without looking at the answer in the text box below, can you improve on the lead above taking into account how to introduce sources? Write your answer below.

Referring to sources again and again

After introducing sources by name and surname, refer to them by surname only on second and subsequent references in news writing. Avoid nicknames or first names (although this is sometimes acceptable for children) as it makes your writing too informal. When you have two sources with the same surname, refer to the source by both first and surname on every reference.

All newspapers have their own style about whether titles are used to refer to people or not, and you need to mirror the style of the publication you are working for. Attributions such as Mr, Miss and Mrs are rather old-fashioned, though some newspapers still apply them.

Never apply academic rules of referencing to journalistic writing. Don't write: "Dumisani Dube said..." and then add (Sunday World, 9 September 2005, page 3). Incorporate your sourcing in a journalistic style, as in "the *Sunday World* newspaper quoted Dumisani Dube in 2005 as saying...".

You can't attribute one quote to more than one person. Specific people say specific things. "I climbed up the beanstalk," said Jack. This sentence is correct. "The giant was huge and hairy," said Jack and his mother. This is incorrect unless they both said it at the same time, which is unlikely.

Referring to age

In terms of age, you should only indicate this if it is relevant to the story in some way. If you are writing about teenagers who drop out of school, and you want to indicate that your source is authoritative because he or she is a teenager, you might want to include the source's age. "Reesha Chiliza, 17, is a high school dropout...". is one example. Don't do this as a matter of course in every news story unless the style guide in your publication requires or encourages it.

Hyphenate ages if they are used adjectivally (before a noun), as in "Charmaine Beukes, a 24-year-old movie producer...". However, if the age is not used adjectivally, don't hyphenate:

"Blessing Gwala has a son who is five years old..." or "Blessing Gwala has a son who is five...".

Don't spell out the age, unless it is between the age of one and nine, as in the previous example or this one: "Nicholas Ndidi, a two-year-old toddler...".

Acknowledging sources

Of course, you always need to acknowledge your sources – that is, to credit them when you have cited information from them. If you don't, you may commit plagiarism, a journalistic sin. Furthermore, your writing may come across as unsourced, subjective and opinionated.

Subjectivity

Avoid being emotive or subjective and always strive for objectivity in your writing. Amateurish news writing is filled with what comes across as opinion. Nearly

Definitions

Plagiarism

Subjective

Opinion

Objective

Facts

everything you say in a news story needs to be attributed to a source, unless it is a well-established fact (such as "People first landed on the moon in 1969."). You do not need to come up with solutions to problems you write about or opinions on issues. In fact, you should not. It is not your job.

"It's times like these that make people want to pack up and run to another country."

1. *If a journalist writes this sentence, rather than quoting someone else saying it, is that acceptable or not? Why? Would it be considered acceptable in another journalistic context – say on the conservative but hugely popular Fox News television channel in the USA, or coming from the host of a local radio station's phone-in talk show?*

"One imperative question still remains unanswered for a mourning mother and sister. Why hasn't justice been served yet?"

2. *If a journalist writes this, is it an example of taking sides and therefore losing objectivity, or is it a fact? How do you distinguish between the two? If the reporter quoted a family friend or a neighbour making precisely the same statement, would that be acceptable?*

Avoid writing "it is believed..." or "it is alleged..." This is a lazy way out. Rather find out the information which confirms or rejects your suspicions, and quote the source directly.

5 MINUTE TASK

In pairs, study the following two quotes. Are they too subjective or appropriate, journalistic writing? Motivate your answer.

1. Alex Shanda, a 23-year-old, was the first involved in an accident on the deadly road. The cause was speeding, but as more deaths occurred on this road the question arose as to what the problem really was.

2. Weeks prior to the incident, Steve Jones had frequently trespassed onto school property and demanded 'tax' in the form of money from several male students. In order to prevent him and his gang of thugs from inflicting grievous bodily harm to them, many of the scared students paid him.

Answer 1

Unacceptable, because it's the writer's opinion.

Answer 2

Acceptable because the journalist is quoting the source directly. Objectivity is maintained.

Don't label people

Be careful not to call people things they might not be. For instance, even if you believe someone has committed a criminal offence, you may not refer to that person as a 'criminal' until they've been convicted in a court. Similarly, you may not call someone a 'murderer' until they've been convicted of murder. So if a body is found in the street, you should refer to the hunt for a person's killer, not their murderer because technically, a person can be killed without being murdered.

Choosing and using quotations

Quotes are the lifeblood of any article. An article with no or too few quotes will be dead and boring to read, and will lack authority.

In general, you need to hone [*sharpen*] your ear as a journalist to listen for quotes that are colourful because they say something in an unusual way, or neatly sum up an opinion or issue. As you hear these words, write down (or record) the exact words the source uses, and reproduce them exactly, without getting a word out of place. Only then are you entitled to use those words within quotes. Reporters who are not 100% sure that they heard the quote precisely can ask for it to be repeated, or can read the information back to the source. This technique is not advisable in more controversial situations in which a source has said something which they will then try to retract or insist was off-the-record.

I'm sure, it's all in my notebook.

Have you written something down accurately? Is that enough reason in itself to include it in a news story? If you don't understand a quote, your readers definitely won't. Here is an example of a poor quote which is difficult to understand, and should not be included in a news story:

> "Some houses have been extended and the value now exceeds R80 000. In this respect they do not qualify for the clearance of rates."

(20) MINUTE TASK

Below is a list of quotes for an article about the martial dance art of Capoeira by a master of the acrobatic technique, Ruben Watkins. In groups, answer the following questions: Which of these are good quotes and which are poor? Which are the top five you'd select if you were writing a short article about the growth of interest in this sport in your area? Justify your answer.

▶ "Capoeira started in the 1500s in Brazil when the Portuguese started taking all the slaves from Africa over to Brazil."

▶ "They split up all the tribes so they couldn't unify, because there were a lot more of them than Portuguese. The slaves started blending all their

> fighting styles together and what happened is Capoeira started forming slowly."
> - "They started using Capoeira to kill their slave masters and unite themselves."
> - "The slave masters made it illegal for the slaves to fight or train so what they did was use music to disguise what they were doing."
> - "The fighting form went underground and was used by street gangs in the favelas (slums) in Rio de Janeiro in the street wars. It got a really bad name."
> - "Capoeira is cool."
> - "Capoeira has been seen as a dirty martial art form in the past, like when it was used in the street wars in Rio."
> - "Capoeira is really catching on here. There are more and more people learning how to do it."

Record quotes accurately and keep your notes

Don't make up quotes or turn your own paraphrasing into quotes! Doing so is unethical. You should never put your own words into the mouths of your sources. If you break this rule, you could be sued. You could certainly be exposed as unprofessional and dishonest. There are many cases in journalism's history where sources have disputed things they've been accused of saying; in cases such as this you need to be able to produce your original notes to prove that's what the source indeed said at the time. You should also keep all your notes together in a notebook, which you should keep forever. You never know when you may want to go back and read your notes for a particular article, or do a follow-up on something you covered, perhaps even years earlier. Many reporters – even print reporters – often tape the interview on their mobile phones or on a minidisk recorder while simultaneously taking notes, in order to have a record which can protect them when unscrupulous people deny being interviewed or deny the quotation.

Avoid repetition

Don't use multiple quotes saying exactly the same thing even if they are from different sources. Your piece will become tedious to read. Similarly, don't paraphrase and then use a quote that says almost the identical thing.

Punctuation of quotations

Different publications have different style rules when it comes to punctuating quotes. It's essential that you understand the style of the publication you are working for, so that your punctuation is correct and your work is professional.

In the United States, punctuation always comes inside the quotation marks, no matter if the sentence quoted is a full one or not. So both of the following examples are accurate, if you are writing for an American publication or one that follows American-style rules:

The prime minister said, "I deeply regret this disaster."
The prime minister said he deeply regretted the "disaster."

But in most European, African and Asian countries, for example, the rules for punctuating quotations in English are more complicated. The general rule for these countries is that if the sentence quoted is a full one, the punctuation mark (such as a full stop or comma) comes inside the quotation marks at the end.

The psychologist said, "This girl is crazy."

If the quote is only part of a sentence, the punctuation mark comes outside the quotation mark.

The psychologist said she thought the girl was "crazy".

You must remember that a quotation, even if it is a full sentence in itself, is still a part of a longer sentence if you are adding "he says" or "she is". So you need to end it with a comma, if you are adding an explanation:

Incorrect: "I am a religious person." says Pete.
Correct: "I am a religious person," says Pete.
Correct: Pete says, "I am a religious person."
Correct: Pete says: "I am a religious person."
Correct: "I am a religious person."

In journalistic writing, always use double quotation marks – " " – when quoting someone. The exception is when using a quote within a quote, when you would use single quotation marks to make the difference clear:

Smanga Zwane, an African traditional healer, explained, "I administer 'im-pepo' [(a herbal concoction)] for sexually transmitted diseases and tuber-culosis."

Respect your sources

You will remember that one of the universal ethical codes for journalists is not to distort what sources say or to use information out of context. Similarly, don't 'manufacture' or sensationalise news by going to sources and inciting them for comment about what you think may be wrong with something. Wait for the angry people to comment and then write the piece.

If you promise to do something for a source, it is vital that you keep that promise. If you say you will not reveal a person's identity, or gather information from someone off the record, you may not go against your word for any reason. In doing so, you would not only betray that person and their trust in you, but you would be harming the professional reputation of journalists in general.

If you promise your source you will send them a copy of the article or borrow a photograph and promise to return it promptly, keep your word. This is common courtesy. Anyway, who knows, you may need to use the same source again in the future. If you promised to read the paragraph or relevant section back to the source prior to publication for fact-checking, do so. Don't promise to let the source know when the story appears in print or airs, which isn't always a promise that can be kept. The longer you spend in the field of journalism, the more you will come to realise how people move up and on in life. A lowly official who tips you off about something in her department may go on to become a high-ranking politician. Show your sources the dignity and respect which you would like to be shown yourself.

> " Keep your promises "

Protect your sources

This is not just good advice. The journalist's code of ethics actually demands it. The International Federation of Journalists says: The journalist shall observe professional secrecy regarding the source of information obtained in confidence. The code of conduct of the South African Union of Journalists, an organisation which sadly is no longer in existence, says: A journalist shall protect confidential sources of information. Journalists have been jailed for not revealing their sources. Most journalists would be reluctant to work with another journalist who did not respect the confidentiality of a source. You must be careful not to write anything that could harm your source, your newspaper or yourself. Many people have lost their jobs because they have spoken to the press.

Suggested Reading

Abel, Elie (1987). *Leaking: Who does it? Who benefits? At what cost?*, New York, Priority Press Publication.

Berry, Thomas Elliot (1976). *Journalism in America*, New York, Hasting House Publishers.

Nel, François, (2005). *Writing for the Media in Southern Africa*. 3rd ed. OUP.

12 Interviewing

<blockquote>chapter ◖────────────────────────────────</blockquote>

<blockquote>
Outcomes

At the end of this chapter, you will able to:
▶ Prepare for an interview.
▶ Plan, conduct and record a successful interview.
</blockquote>

Introduction

Many journalists would argue that you can't separate news-gathering from interviewing. They are quite correct. Interviewing is an important part of news-gathering. We have chosen to deal with interviewing as a separate chapter simply because it is also a specific skill that all reporters need to master.

The importance of interviews

Almost all news stories are the result of personal interviews. Even a reporter who is an eyewitness to an event must talk to other eyewitnesses to clarify facts and to get different viewpoints. The author Brian Brooks says, "Information is the merchandise of a journalist." (Brooks, 1992:99). We collect facts, weave the facts into a story and then tell it to our readers. The quality and richness of the information we sell depends on how we have worked with the people who can release that information to us.

He's trying to charm me. I must be careful.

    As journalists, we must be careful not to be wooed [*charmed, persuaded*] by the people we interview. Most public figures are charming when you get them into the interview situation but that doesn't mean that they will give you the information you need. As François Nel says:

Successful politicians did not get to be successful politicians by being dumb enough to tell reporters the truth, or tell reporters much of anything. (Nel, 1994:72).

Interviews take many different forms. They may be impromptu [*unprepared*] or planned; co-operative or antagonistic [*aggressive, opposed*]; exclusive to one reporter or open to all, as in a press conference. The reporter may need to use different approaches and techniques to suit the different types of interview, the different situations in which they can take place and his or her possible aims for the interview.

Interviewing is a difficult business. You should do all you can to ensure that you control as many aspects of the interview as possible. For example, you should have a goal. What do you want from the interview? Do you want a front-page lead story, a bit of variety to add to an existing news story, a response to a rival publication's article? There is a great scene in the book *Alice in Wonderland* (published in 1865 by a British mathematician, the Reverend Charles Lutwidge Dodgson, better known by his pen name of Lewis Carroll) in which the heroine, young Alice, is lost in a bewildering world and asks a talkative Cheshire cat for directions:

"Would you tell me, please, which way I ought to go from here?" asks Alice.

"That depends a good deal on where you want to go," replies the cat.

"I don't much care where," says Alice.

"Then it doesn't much matter which way you go," is the reply.

"So long as I get somewhere," Alice adds as an explanation.

"Oh you are sure to do that," grins the cat.

You need to have more direction than Alice did! You need to learn much and practise more to become a skilled interviewer.

⑩ MINUTE TASK

In pairs, think about interviewing two different kinds of people: a local politician involved in a controversy [*argument*], and an internationally known musician?

In each case, how would you prepare for the interview? What sort of questions would you ask these different types of interviewee? How would you get the confidence of each of these people?

Preparation, preparation, preparation

The basis of a successful interview is thorough planning before you ask the first question. Research your subject thoroughly. You could easily insult the person by conducting your interview cold [*unprepared*]. However, if you have a thorough knowledge of his or her past and achievements, you will certainly win the interviewee's respect. In addition, you may be able to skip those questions that can be answered by an assistant, book or document. When scheduling the appointment, ask your interviewee to suggest sources of information about the topic you wish to discuss. The interviewee will appreciate your interest and often share valuable sources of information before the interview.

If you can't avoid going in unprepared, admit this openly, and put yourself at the interviewee's mercy. Don't try to bluff your way out, you won't succeed. But don't expect research to solve all your interview problems for you: even when you have planned and researched well, interviews seldom go as they are supposed to, for both sides.

"
Research &
Prepare!
"

Research

What are we trying to do when we research something? Usually we are trying to do one of the following: explain behaviour, predict behaviour or determine the reasons for behaviour. How you actually do your research depends of course on what kind of assignment you have been given.

However, reporters generally use two types of research: asking informal sources, and desk research. It is a good idea to get advice from other journalists who may have done a similar story. These are your informal sources. Then it is time for your desk research.

Before you begin, write down your hypothesis [*your idea of what has taken place*] and what you expect to find out. Your hypothesis is an idea that you have formed by reasoning carefully but you are not totally certain that it is true.

Your ideas will help to focus you in your interview but you should still try to research with an open mind. If you hold your preconceived ideas too rigidly, you may miss something relevant to your story.

When you have developed your hypothesis, you should visit your newspaper's cutting library and then the various data banks and other media available to you. You will certainly need to search the internet.

If you are to do a news story, go first to the cuttings library and review all the cuttings on the subject of the story rather than only those about the personality you must interview. Naturally, if you must do a profile you should concentrate on that personality's interests, friends, career, schooling and so on. Don't be put off if you can't find material on your subject: it means you may be the first! For an investigative story, you will have to concentrate on all aspects. Keep asking the basic question of all journalists: why?

Definitions

Research

Hypothesis

SELF-STUDY TASK

Research a prominent person to interview in order to write a news story, a profile and an investigative report. How different was your preparation for each?

Time management

> "Time is money!"

Arriving late for an interview is a cardinal sin. Time is precious! It is important to plan your time carefully. How much time do you have to do your research and plan your interview, bearing in mind that afterwards you need to do any follow-up research and then write your story or begin the long process of viewing or listening to tapes, logging the shots, writing a script and booking an edit suite? Preparation is no excuse for arriving late. In fact, you can marshal [*put in order*] your thoughts while waiting outside the door, ten minutes before the interview.

Some celebrities or speakers at a conference will allocate you a particular time, say between 11h00 and 11h15. If you arrive ten minutes late, you will have to conduct your interview in the remaining five minutes. Being late for an interview, whatever the reason, is unprofessional and harms your reputation. Your subject probably won't grant you another interview and then you will have an embarrassing time explaining to your editor why there's no interview.

When asking for an interview, it is a good idea to state exactly how much time you require. Do not waste time if you can avoid it. Some television interviews in particular can be very time-consuming because the editing process requires cut-aways – pictures of the subject working, walking or talking – which accompany the reporter's voice. Important people seldom have time to waste. They appreciate those who value time. If the interviewee invites you to stay longer, accept the offer only if there is still important information that you need. Otherwise you can politely decline and leave.

Formulating and phrasing questions

There are two golden rules of interviewing:

> Ask the question!
> Do not ask what you already know, unless it is to check information obtained from elsewhere.

There is nothing more frustrating to an editor than to hear a reporter say: 'I was going to ask that question' or 'I wanted to ask that question.' If you have done your research properly it should have led you to some questions that interest your readers. Asking questions to which you already know the answer – unless you are double-checking information, which is legitimate - is a waste of valuable time. Ask the questions in your head, even if it is the question 'what does that mean?'

It is a good idea to write down at least ten questions in advance of the interview. But interviews seldom follow the question order. Use your list of questions to guide you through the interview and remind you of the important points. Because you have prepared your questions, you will be more relaxed and the conversation can be natural and spontaneous.

Have 10 prepared questions.

The answer to your first question may lead to an interesting new focus, so that the rest of your questions become irrelevant. Therefore it is important to listen actively. Do not be afraid to ask for clarification if you do not understand something. According to François Nel:

> Do not be afraid to let someone know that you are searching blindly. Many interesting details have come from simply asking, is there something else you think may help me?

The way you word your questions is most important. The structure of your questions will often determine whether your interview is a success or not. Badly phrased questions have made reporters lose many good stories. Open-ended questions are less direct and not so threatening for the interviewee.

What is an open-ended question? It is a question that requires more than a direct 'yes' or 'no' answer. For example, if you ask a visiting celebrity, 'Did you enjoy your stay in South Africa?"', then he or she might reply either 'yes' or 'no'. Therefore you have asked a closed question. However if you ask, 'What has impressed you most about South Africa?', you are then inviting the celebrity to answer in a bit more detail. Such an open-ended question is far more flexible. It is a good idea to use open-ended questions, particularly at the beginning of your interview in order to get the interviewee relaxed and talking. Open-ended questions are less threatening and less direct but nevertheless probing.

Of course, there are times when you require a straight 'yes' or 'no' answer. Then a closed question may be more appropriate, although radio and television broadcasters are still warned not to use it because it can be used out of context. However, it is important to know when to ask each type of question. You will learn this from practice and experience.

Vague questions get vague answers. Specific questions are more likely to get explicit [clear] answers. Specific, probing questions also tell the interviewee that you have done your research thoroughly.

Open-ended question

Close-ended question

In pairs, plan and write out 10 questions in relation to the previous self-study task, in which you prepared to interview a prominent person.

In chapter eleven, you looked at the issue of multiple sources, using an incident of drunk driving. Return to that incident, involving a politician, in this case a man. What questions would you ask? These are some of the types of questions you may want to ask:

Who was involved in the accident and why are they newsworthy?

When and where did the incident happen?

How and why did the accident occur? Did he drive dangerously and threaten anyone's safety?

Was the driver considered to be under the influence of alcohol?

If so, when and where was he tested for alcohol? What were the results?

Has he ever been arrested or convicted on similar charges?

What are the consequences of his actions? Has he been arrested? When will he be appearing in court and on what charges?

If he is not being charged, why not?

Who owns the vehicle he was travelling in and what type of vehicle is it? (You may find it was the mayoral limousine, which will add spice to your story!)

What is his response to the incident?

Were there any eyewitnesses to the incident? Do you have their statements? Have you interviewed them? Are they prepared to be quoted?

With all the information that such questions and others will uncover, you can begin to write the story. And it illustrates the importance of making a list of questions – in your head, if it's an emergency, as long as the list exists somewhere.

10 MINUTE TASK

In pairs, each pick three different people to interview about the incident above. Each of you should draw up a list of questions to ask them. How did the questions vary, depending on the person?

Planning and conducting the interview

An important part of good interviewing is the planning you do just before you start the actual interview. Here are some key points on this:

Talk to the correct person: Firstly, ensure that the person you are going to interview is the correct person, someone able and authorised to give you the information you want. You can cause a lot of trouble by approaching the wrong person. You may get a great story from a paramedic who does not fully appreciate the medical problems experienced by a patient. The paramedic is not authorised or qualified to discuss the problem and should have referred you to the doctor concerned. The paramedic gets disciplined for talking out of turn and in the end, no one is satisfied. The problem with interviewing the wrong person is that you usually cause resentment. It is therefore important to go through the right channels to obtain an interview.

Have I ticked off my checklist?

Choose a good time: It is important to time your approach in relation to your deadline. If you phone after 10 am you will usually be well received, but your editor will not be happy if you are writing for an afternoon newspaper with early deadlines. If you phone at 3 am for something that could have waited until later, you will be greeted with anger. Morning radio programme journalists become experts in explaining to sleepy people why it is important that they come on air via the telephone: usually, some story has broken [*just happened*] overnight and if the person comes on air, they have the chance to reach the biggest possible audience. Always try to be courteous and make an appointment whenever possible.

Consider the place: The environment for your interview is important. Most interviews are conducted in the interviewee's office, but if you conduct the interview on neutral ground it could give you an advantage. Or interview the person in a place which brings to life the topic under discussion, so if you are interviewing an education minister, try to do it at a preschool or something similar.

Check your equipment: Before you leave for the interview make sure you have not forgotten your prepared questions, that you are adequately attired [*dressed*] and that you have all the equipment that you will need. What equipment will you need? Spare pens and sharp pencils, notebook, tape recorder or minidisk recorder and spare batteries, a mobile phone which is not going to run out of air time or power, and possibly a digital camera. It is a good idea to make a checklist and tick them off before you go. Make sure that you are on time.

Check your clothes: Remember to dress appropriately. Your source does not have to talk to you. Try to fit in with the environment. If you have to go to a state banquet then it is probably wise to dress formally. If you're going to a construction site, you can't dress as for a party. Many people are offended by excessive displays of skin, gum-chewing, tattoos and facial piercings, which means you have to work even harder at establishing a good relationship with the people you interview. A good idea, if you're not going to a farm, a factory or a game park, is to dress as if you were going for your first job interview.

---

⑤ MINUTE TASK

In pairs, brainstorm and then list the problems you would expect to experience in interviews.

Select two problems which seem more important than the rest and suggest how you might prevent these problems, or how you might deal with them in the interview.

Different approaches to interviews

Arranging an interview is usually easier said than done. Important and powerful people are usually surrounded by protective executive secretaries and public relations people. You will have to get past them. Sometimes you will have to deal with people who are so used to rudeness and abuse that they are always suspicious of anyone asking questions. Let's discuss a number of interview approaches you may need to adopt in these circumstances.

Set the rules of the interview before you begin: be sure your interviewee understands the story you are working on, which media organisation wants it, and that everything they say is 'on the record.' Make sure that your interviewee understands what 'on the record' means. It is preferable to establish these ground rules when making the interview appointment.

Is this on record?

Direct approach: Call the person on the telephone, introduce yourself by first name and surname, and your newspaper or media organisation and tell him/her what you want. Offer your cellphone number and repeat your surname at the end of the conversation, as people often commit to interviews and then when there is a scheduling clash, they can't find the reporter to reschedule the interview.

The assault: This is used on reluctant interviewees. You simply ask your question as quickly and forcibly as possible, "Mr Early, you have been accused of embezzling money from the rugby union. Do you care to comment?"

Begging: Sometimes you simply have to appeal to a person's sense of sympathy. This approach works best when dealing with the survivors of tragedy. "Could you please tell me where I could contact Nithaya Chetty, it's very urgent?"

Being courteous and understanding: when you phone someone who doesn't know you, apologise to whoever answers in case you are interrupting something important. Ask them if they have a moment to answer a few questions. Make sure they know who you are. It is also a great way to go about your business. People who are used to abuse may feel overwhelmed by kindness and will be only too happy to talk to you after hearing, "I know there are at least two sides to a story. I would love to hear yours."

The sit-in: When you get put off by one of Mr Big Cheese's protectors, simply smile and say that you know that he is busy and you will wait until he is free. Take your lunch and a book to show that you are serious. Persistence often works. But don't use this method too much.

Establishing confidence

From the moment you first meet your interviewee it is important to win their confidence, so start by making eye contact, smiling and shaking hands, unless you are in specific cultural situation in which this would cause offence. The interviewee must feel that they can trust you to tell their story fairly, accurately and without bias. Probably the best piece of advice you can get when it comes to dealing with people is: be nice to them. Keep in mind that everyone is different. It is essential to establish a polite rapport [*relationship, understanding*] and a level of comfort for the interviewee. Some interviewees need time to become comfortable talking to journalists. Even though you may only have a short time for an interview, you should not rush your subject. Don't rush your interviewee! If, however, you sense that the interviewee is in a hurry, adjust your timing accordingly. Taking time to get to know your interviewees will prove invaluable in the future, especially when you need to call with follow-up questions or use them as a source for future stories.

   Establishing rapport: A sympathetic, easy exchange between you, the journalist, and your interviewee will make or break the interview. Often the relationship is somewhere between relaxed and strained. This can go beyond one story and affect future stories. One of my students, who was getting her in-service training at a newspaper, did a story on child abuse. The following week she got a telephone call from some parents whose children had been sexually abused. They liked the sensitive way she had handled the story and wanted her to tell the story of their own children's nightmare. The quality of the relationship will decide what type of co-operation you get.

   Listen carefully to your interviewee's response to your questions as this is an important key to how you should continue. But don't be afraid to interrupt when you don't understand! Do not be caught off guard. If you respond too quickly to a question like, "Who told you that?" you could reveal a confidential source without realising what you are doing. If your subject uses scientific jargon or explanations

> "
> Be courteous
> "

> "
> Win confidence & establish rapport
> "

only a few would understand, politely interrupt and ask for further explanation. Never be embarrassed about not knowing something. The point will arrive when you will have to ask the tough and awkward questions that your subject may be reluctant to discuss. When you start asking those intrusive questions, the answers may be too short, unintelligible, too carefully considered, or you may not get an answer at all. When this occurs, maintain eye contact and remain silent. Almost always, the interviewee will begin to feel uncomfortable and begin to explain. If this doesn't work, repeat the question. You may need to ask the interviewee why he or she is unable to answer the question or to supply sources who might be able to answer the question.

Maintain eye contact: Eye contact is important. A reporter bent over taking notes or staring into a notebook can be as disconcerting to an interviewee as a tape recorder or a television camera. While taking notes, try to maintain eye contact as much possible. Learn to take abbreviated notes, looking down only occasionally so you can focus on your interviewee. This will make the interview more like a conversation and enable everyone to be more relaxed.

Before you leave: At the end of the interview ask your interviewee if there is anything that you might have forgotten to ask. You may find the interviewee is eager to share some interesting or important information that you did not ask about or know. Make sure you have a contact number and an e-mail address and arrange good time to call with follow-up questions or to check information when writing. Always ask for other sources. No matter how well the interview went, thank your source for spending time being interviewed.

Controlling the interview

Some interviewees will be friendly towards you, others reluctant or hostile in their response. But nearly all of them, regardless of how they appear on the surface, will also be guarded [*cautious, watchful*]. Often they will ask not to be quoted. Often they will only give the interview off the record. If there is no other choice but an off the record interview (occasionally people will ask for an off the record interview out of ignorance, in which case you can usually negotiate a normal interview) agree to the condition at the beginning of the interview. Then, as the interview progresses and the interviewee relaxes, try to get them to give up their off the record ruling. Point out that the report will be more credible [*believable*] if they go on the record.

Often the interviewee adds this condition at the end of the interview, but it is not retroactive. Nobody can make a normal interview an off the record interview once the interview is done, or well into the interview. It is a good idea to ask during the interview, maybe more than once, something like "I take it that I can use this?" However, if you agree to treat the interviewee's responses as off the record, do not go back on your word.

Often you can get reluctant people to respond if you tell them that you already have some viewpoints from other interviews, and then you mention some of the views expressed, without necessarily identifying the source of those views. You say, "I would also like to hear your thoughts." Quite often the interviewee will respond with, "No, it's not like that at all" and will then tell you their version of events. Others are reluctant due to false modesty and wish to be coaxed into talking.

Most seasoned journalists can recall those first and most difficult interviews when they felt they had been deceived, manipulated or misguided by people they interviewed. In some press cultures, journalists tend to be overly solicitous of [*almost fawning over*] officials and politicians, fearful of the consequences of asking probing questions. Shrewd politicians will take advantage of such situations and ramble, making long-winded, empty statements or giving blunt yes or no responses.

> " Don't be intimidated by politicians and powerful people "

Other tactics journalists should be aware of are:

> When interviewees take an aggressive posture, try to keep calm. Let them vent their hostility and then proceed courteously with the interview. Don't be intimidated by hostile interviewees who go on the offensive by saying things like "That's a stupid question!" Keep calm. Tell them of the sources you checked (if it's safe for the sources) before the question was asked. Explain why the answer to the question is necessary and needs to be answered.

> When an interviewee tries to turn the question around and seeks to interview you, you can reply by replying "I'm sure our readers are much more interested in your opinion on that."

> When an interviewee tries to go off the record, you can explain the need for attribution and urge that the material be placed on the record for the sake of credibility. You can flatly refuse to take the off-the-record response or you can return to the subject later with a rephrased or related question to get the information on the record.

> If the interviewee rambles off the subject, bring them gently back to the question by saying, "That's very interesting, but...".

> If interviewees reply with close-ended "yes" and "no" answers phrase your questions so that they cannot be answered by one word, or ask "Could you elaborate?" or "Why do you say that?".

Finally, you can be provocative without being confrontational. Remember that you're there to collect information, not to fight.

In pairs, role play interview situations. Assign one person the job of acting like a politician who is used to being praised by reporters. Conduct an interview. Switch roles. Discuss with your partner what you have learnt.

> " Do not interrupt too early! "

Usually the best way to start the interview is simply to ask an open-ended question like, "Can you tell me what happened?" Once your interviewee begins to talk, do not interrupt. Let him or her tell the story as far as possible without your help. Only interrupt the interviewee if you need to get the main point of the story clear in your mind. Ask for minor points of clarification only at the end. Don't express your personal reactions much unless the interviewee clearly expects a reaction: if he or she tells an amusing story, it is a good idea to laugh.

Once the interviewee has completed his or her story, begin asking your questions. Start to probe around the main theme of the story, asking questions that will produce an interesting response. Try to get exact answers: "What do you mean by 'fast?'" or "What were the problems you mentioned?" are examples. Ask for explanations if the answers do not make sense to you.

Interviewing is not an exact science. You ask a question but you can never be certain of the response you will receive. The more questions you ask, the more likely you are to hear something interesting, but be careful not to be led astray. Remember the most important answers may come at any time during the interview.

Try to be interested in the answers you get even if they do not appear to be newsworthy. The very excited or self-important interviewee can be a problem when he or she goes off the point or continually repeats information that may not be very useful to you. However, usually he or she only needs to be prodded back to the main theme.

Interview techniques

The first interview technique begins with a sweeping statement (sometimes more than one sweeping statement). The journalist then pins down the generalisations, demanding answers to the what, who, when, why, where and how questions, sometimes known as 'the 5w's and 1h'. This technique appeals to the creative, thoughtful interviewee because it allows for some say in the direction of the interview. The interviewee may go off in a direction that never occurred to the journalist, resulting in a far more productive and interesting interview. The wide-open question not only gives the interviewee room to breathe; it gives the interviewer time to reflect. Another technique starts with hard, fast, specific, close-ended questions, then moves to more general questions.

How do you know which technique to use? Generally, if your interviewee is not comfortable with talking to the press, start with an open, general question. If the interviewee is still ill at ease, make him or her comfortable with a question about something that is easily explained or basic small talk.

Attempts to censor your story

Whatever type of interview you conduct, resist any attempt by the interviewee to censor your copy [*sometimes phrased as 'vetting,' 'checking', 'critting' or 'approving'*]. Occasionally you can make an exception where the story deals with complex technical or scientific subjects, particularly those involving numbers. You might have misunderstood some details. If the interviewee demands to inspect the story in return for giving the interview, say that you will put the request to the editor. Never email or fax the written story to the subjects, who have been known to institute legal action and shut down the printing presses and threaten editors and distributors. Sometimes the problem is not aggressive, it's just that due to ignorance of copyright laws, someone has passed your story on as a press release or sent it to another reporter. If you do need clarification or you want to check some facts, read the relevant sentences out to the interviewee over the telephone. Make it clear, as tactfully as possible, that you want help with the facts only. You are not asking for changes to your style or wording. Make it clear that if a consensus cannot be reached, you retain final control over the article. The interviewee can always write a letter to the editor, request a right to respond on television or radio, or issue a complaint to the relevant ombudsman.

Definitions

Censor

⑩ MINUTE TASK

In pairs, role play a situation where the interviewee is trying to change your story, claiming that it is inaccurate and requires more detail or context. How would you respond? Switch roles.

Recording your interview

Here are a few more tips on managing the recording of your interviews:

Your notepad: The most convenient notepad is a hardback spiral notepad that can be held in one hand. It is easier to hold if you have to stand and take notes. People are also less daunted [*intimidated*] by the sight of a small, unobtrusive notepad. Number, date and keep your old notepads for later reference - you never know when you may have to refer to an old interview.

Taping your interviews: Most reporters tape their interviews, if the interviewee does not mind. The taped interview has a number of advantages:

Total and accurate recall.

You can observe the interviewee's reactions.

The interviewee will be quoted correctly.

"
Review your
notes
immediately
"

A problem with the taped interview is that you can get too much information and it takes time to wade through it all. I personally prefer to use a tape recorder to interview because I feel it leads to accuracy. But I like to take notes as well in order to remember those things that stand out as important.

Review your notes right after the interview: Immediately after the interview has concluded, while the interview is still fresh in your mind, review your notes.

13 News writing

Outcomes

By the end of this chapter, you will able to:

▶ Identify elements of newsworthiness.

▶ Follow basic rules of news writing.

▶ Identify a lead and know what makes a good lead.

▶ Construct a lead.

▶ Identify news angles and select angles for leads.

▶ Identify and write different types of leads.

▶ Provide context to a news story.

▶ Avoid some of the pitfalls of news writing.

▶ Use the checklist grid for self editing.

What makes good news writing?

Introduction

Good journalistic writing is easy to read and understand. But the skills that enable a journalist to convey a message simply are complex and varied. Journalistic writing is different from all other forms of writing that you may use. It is also something that you will hone and perfect your entire journalistic career. One of the joys of journalism is that every story is different, and will challenge you professionally and personally in various ways.

Journalistic writing is concise, succinct writing [*writing which makes points briefly and clearly*]. This style is necessary because editorial space is always limited in newspapers. The space available on any day depends on the amount of advertising space sold. You therefore need to learn how to say as much as possible in as few words as possible, and how to give the most important information at the beginning of each story.

Key terms

Before you learn about news writing and leads, it is important that you understand certain key terms.

Byline: This is the name of the reporter who wrote the story. Usually, this appears at the top of the story, between the headline and the first sentence of the article. Occasionally it is tagged on at the end of the article.

Dateline: This is the place from which the reporter is writing the story. It is usually written in capital letters, and directly precedes the first sentence of the article. Not all newspapers use datelines, and those that do use them only when the reporter is filing the story from out of town. So if the story is for a newspaper circulated primarily in Paris, for example, one would not expect to see a Paris dateline.

Lead: This is the first sentence of a news story.

Basic rules for news writing

The following rules will help you to make decisions about your news writing.

Keep your paragraphs short. Write no more than five typewritten lines per paragraph.

I must remember the basic rules.

Get to the point quickly. You should normally do so in the first two or three sentences, that is, the lead.

Use the active voice rather than the passive. The active voice adds energy and excitement to a story. Active is when the subject is doing the action, as in: "The man hit the dog." Passive is when the action is being done to the subject, as in: "The dog was hit by the man."

Select only the most significant and relevant details.

Write in the present continuous and ordinary past tense, to maintain a sense of immediacy, for example: "A suspected serial rapist has been (present continuous tense) arrested, a police spokesperson confirmed (past tense) this morning."

Introducing Journalism and Media Studies

The news story

A news story, as opposed to a feature article, is usually (but not always) a relatively short piece of about 300 words covering either a particular event or happening, or, more occasionally, a trend. The main point about it is that it tells the reader something new.

Think about how you would tell a friend about an accident you saw. You would get straight to the point and say something like this:

> "I saw this terrible accident on the way to work this morning - between a truck and a car on the highway. Both the drivers were injured and they were being attended to by paramedics. It seems the truck driver had been drinking - he lost control and drove into the back of the car."

Use the same direct approach when you write a lead to a story.

Some articles you write will be follow-ups of earlier events. In this case you must always begin your story with a brief explanation of the previous event. But do not kill your report by reciting all the previous history. Avoid beginning any story with a negative or with expressions that require words like no, not, or unlikely. If there is no news, why should the reader read on?

Usually, the front page of a newspaper is covered in news stories, which editors assign a hierarchical order of importance. The top news story – considered the most interesting, important news for readers – will be positioned at the top of the page, under the largest headline.

News stories also cover the first few pages inside the newspaper. You'll often find a similar layout at the back of the paper, with the strongest sports news stories on the back page, and less important ones inside the first few back pages. Towards the middle of the paper, the content usually changes, to provide more in-depth features and opinion articles. Formulas for the most prominent news stories also exist in television and radio programmes, with the most important news story first in a radio news bulletin and a light story near the end, often followed by a recap [repetition] of the the main story. Listen to the evening news and work out the formula. Likewise the morning current affairs programmes on radio have a formula outside of the news bulletin itself, and the formula usually runs in half-hour chunks. Can you identify it?

The journalist needs to interview a variety of sources, and to juxtapose [put next to one another] different viewpoints and perspectives in the story. A good news story lets the sources do the talking through colourful, relevant quotations – it is essential for the journalist to show, rather than tell. A good news story is 'tight' [uses as few words as possible to say as much as possible]. The information is divulged in a descending order of importance.

Newsworthiness

Is this story newsworthy?

Before you start writing, or even researching your story, you need to be sure it is newsworthy. To recap, or repeat, a good news story will need to have at least one or more of the elements of newsworthiness listed in the margin. Often, a good news story will incorporate several of the elements.

- timeliness (just happened)
- proximity (close by)
- violence
- prominence of people (celebrities or business leaders)
- impact or consequences on wider society
- human interest
- corruption, deceit or hypocrisy
- sex
- novelty or curiosity
- conflict
- authority (especially when it is questioned)
- expense (perhaps involve taxpayer's money)

🔟 MINUTE TASK

In pairs, discuss what elements of newsworthiness the following scenarios have for news stories:

1. A poverty-stricken handicapped woman with no legs has started a vegetable farming business in a poor, rural area and has attracted a major client in the big city.
2. A policeman shoots his wife in a nearby town, then turns the gun on himself.
3. A local principal is fired by the school board after parents complain about rumours that she is having an affair with her male secretary.

How to begin your lead - the first paragraph

How full of facts can we pack the first paragraph? There is much debate about this, and you will have to consider several aspects:

As a writer you must be clear about what is really important and what is interesting but not so important.

The reader should see what you are writing about immediately; there must be no confusion.

All the basic facts should be at the beginning of the story. Some writers try to achieve this in the first paragraph. Others use the first four or five paragraphs.

You will be able to write with better style if you do not have to pack all the most important facts into the first paragraph. We will discuss this more fully later.

Here's an example of a good lead, based on the ideas about multiple sources in chapter eleven:

A politician was caught driving under the influence of alcohol on Thursday night, a city police spokesperson said yesterday.

Better lead:

Deputy mayor Steve Jones was stopped for drunken driving on Thursday night, police have confirmed, not far from a bar where he had been attending a raucous bachelor party.

The second lead is better because it provides more, colourful detail, which brings the story to life. We may wish to name the people involved in the story. Sometimes, if characters are prominent enough, we can use a name and title: "former education minister Kadar Asmal" or if it's for an international publication or on the internet "former South African education minister Kadar Asmal".

🔟 MINUTE TASK

In pairs, list of all the relevant people you could interview in the above news story, and draw up a list of questions to ask them.

Lead sentence styles

The *inverted pyramid* has long been the most common structure for a news story, and this is for good reason. Although its detractors may criticise it as formulaic and predictable, the inverted pyramid provides a structure for journalists which is easy to follow yet flexible.

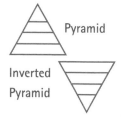

Inverted means upside down. So think of a pyramid with its wide base in the air and its narrow tip on the ground. When using the inverted pyramid style, the journalist places the most important information at the top of the article, and then incorporates information into the article in descending importance. So the least important information will be at the bottom of the piece. This benefits the reader, who may want to read the newspaper very fast, and only skim [*read or scan quickly*] the most important information in it. If this information is at the top of the article it is easily accessible. It also helps the sub-editor, who may have to edit the story because of limited space or last-minute alterations in layout. If the least important information is at the bottom, the sub can simply cut from the bottom up; it is much more time-consuming to sift through a story and decide what is most important to retain and what can be cut.

The *summary lead* is the most crucial aspect of any article written in the inverted pyramid style. It forms the basis of the article, and will determine whether the reader reads on or not. It needs to be powerful without being sensationalist, and informative without being lengthy. A summary lead is usually only one sentence long. It summarises the most important elements for the article. The summary lead should not exceed 35 words, and should form a paragraph on its own. The sentence should contain the "5W's and 1H". The 5W's are Who? What? Why? Where? When? And the 1H is How?

Who? Who is the action about?
What? What happened? What is the story actually about?
Where? Where did it happen?
Why? Why did it happen?
When? When did it happen?
How? How did it happen?

If this is not practical, the summary lead should contain as many of these as possible.

It is rare that a lead will have a perfect set of 5W's and an H, although this is always something to aim for. And sometimes, there could be more than one of any of the 5W's and 1H. Here are some examples of summary leads:

> A gang of youths accused of terrorising a small town with a string of burglaries yesterday allegedly strangled an elderly woman, who caught them breaking into a church.

Who? A gang of youths, an elderly woman
What? Murder allegedly committed as robbery taking place
How? By strangulation
When? Yesterday
Why? It is hinted that she was trying to stop them from robbing a church, or had at least witnessed what they were trying to do; the second why is they were robbing a church, to take something they wanted that didn't belong to them.
Where? A small town

> The city council came under fire this week for stopping all free tea and coffee for municipal workers, though councillors enjoy sumptuous meals after meetings.

Who? The city council
What? Are being criticised for hypocrisy
Why? Because they're stopping tea for the workers, while eating lavishly at tax-payers' expense themselves.
Where? It is implicit that this is the local council because it isn't stated otherwise.
When? This week
How? Not specified how the council "came under fire".

The hardest part of writing a story is writing the lead. You should therefore make sure that you do not forget to answer the 5W's and 1H when you are actually at the scene of your story. Remember these questions when you take notes about what happened and interview bystanders or people who are involved. And take their contact numbers in case you need to ask an extra W or H.

Have I asked the 5W's and 1H?

Working in pairs or on your own, take any daily newspaper and look at the first two or three pages. Identify some examples of summary leads, and write down each of the 5W's and 1H or at least those which are introduced in the lead. Can you find a 'perfect' example of a summary lead - one that has all 5Ws and 1H? Discuss this again after you have read this chapter.

Elements that make a good lead

So, what makes a good lead? According to academic François Nel in his book *Writing for the Media*, the elements that make a good lead are:

A good lead needs a newsworthy action or result.

A good lead appeals to a wide readership.

A good lead gives readers some human interest.

A good lead gives the reader the most important facts.

Let's look closer at these aspects. A good lead needs a news-worthy action or result. News must be new. It must also be informative, educative and sometimes entertaining. You want people to talk about what they have read, "Wow, Martha, have you heard this?" In other words: will people be interested in what happened? Will it affect people's lives? You don't want readers to say, "So what? Who cares?" when they read your lead.

The lead must appeal to a wide readership, from the professor of nuclear physics to the lady who cleans his laboratory.

There must be some human interest. A story which deals with strong human emotions and experiences - (fear, unexpected good fortune, pain, love and romance, anger, reconciliation, death) will appeal to readers.

The lead should contain all the important facts. Although, as we have already pointed out, journalists are always limited by their own picture of the world, every journalist should present the available facts as fully as he/she can.

Guidelines for writing good leads

There are a few guidelines you can generally apply when you write a lead. The following fit in with the basic rules for news writing:

Make your lead less than 35 words if possible. It can be a bit longer if you need more than one sentence.

Make sure you answer the 'who, what, where, when, why and how' questions, but ensure that the answers are relevant to the story.

Get all information that is basic to the story.

Always check names, places, dates and times.

Don't try to cramp too many words and facts into one sentence.

Attribute opinion.

What do we mean by attribute [*credit to*] opinion? First, we should decide what is fact and what is opinion. Let's examine the opening sentence of our example lead:

"A 25-year-old KwaZulu-Natal truck driver, Mr Joe Mkhize, was involved in a collision with a car on the south-bound highway opposite the old power station while under the influence of alcohol...."

Definitions

Fact

Opinion

How do we know that Joe was under the influence of alcohol? Where did we get this information from? Was this just the opinion of the policeman you interviewed, or was Mr Mkhize tested for alcohol? If there is strong evidence that Mr Mkhize was drunk but there is no proof, you must attribute this opinion: that is, you must say whose opinion it was. Here is our lead, rewritten so that the opinion about Mr Mkhize is clearly attributed to the police.

CAPE TOWN: A 25-year-old KwaZulu-Natal truck driver, Mr Joe Mkhize, was involved in a collision with a car on the south-bound highway opposite the old power station while allegedly under the influence of liquor. According to police sources at the scene of the accident, Mr Mkhize smelled heavily of liquor and was incoherent.

This can only be done if the reporter directly interviews the police; if a police press release makes the claim or another eye-witness makes the claim, the reporter needs to make the source of the information as clear as possible.

You should organise your information into two lead sentences when necessary. However, because lead sentences do include a lot of information, you may also need to use some conjunctions or linking expressions to help you link up your story smoothly and logically. In journalistic writing it is customary to start sentences with conjunctions such as 'and' and 'but'. Writing purists [*those who prefer to keep fixed rules about correct style*] may object to you doing so.

(15) MINUTE TASK

Select an important incident that has just occurred in your town or your campus. It should be something you know quite a lot about. How do you think this incident should be covered in your chosen publication? Write the lead paragraph for the story. Do you feel you have met the requirements for good lead-writing? Discuss this again after you have finished this chapter.

Writing a summary lead with an angle

When you actually sit down to write your own summary lead for a news story, you'll no doubt find it difficult. This is the way it should be; your lead should take as long to write as the rest of your article. What you decide to include in your lead sets the focus for your story. Ask yourself what your story is really about. What is the most interesting, important information that you have? Try writing out the 5W's and 1H before writing your lead, to help you focus. Tell someone in one sentence what your story is about. That is what you should include in your lead.

Think about your 'angle'. The news angle is the 'hook' that will catch readers; it's the perspective [*viewpoint*] on the story that you choose to give your readers that you believe to be the most gripping, while not being sensational or dishonest. For example, if you're writing about a robbery, you may decide to focus your lead and story on the suspects, the victims, the police, or anyone else involved in the story. Usually, it's a good idea to have people in your angle and lead, because people naturally like to read about other people.

Here are some possible angles on a robbery:

Suspect angle: Two suspects who allegedly robbed a local supermarket this week have been arrested and will be appearing in court on Monday, police spokesperson Captain Margaret Watson said this morning.

Victim angle: A woman was stabbed to death in a supermarket robbery in downtown Washington this morning.

Police angle: An off-duty police officer apprehended two suspects as they fled the scene of a supermarket robbery in downtown Washington this morning.

Always try to project forward so that your piece is as current as possible. For example, if you are writing about a crime, find out if any suspects have been arrested, and if so, whether they have been charged (and what with). Next, find out if they have already appeared in court on the charges, if they have been released, and if so, on what amount of bail? Have they been asked to plead yet and if so, what is their plea? (You should be able to find out most of this information from the relevant police spokesperson, or from the court).

Try to bring a current element to your lead when your story is a little 'old'. For example, if you write a story about a man who was attacked a week ago, lead with something like: "A 31-year-old man who was beaten and shot by three men who stole his wallet is recovering in hospital."

Once you have decided on your angle and drafted your lead, go back and check it again. Is there a good reason for every single word in the lead to be there? Try cutting out every word to ascertain this. If the lead reads fine without a word, you don't need it. In lead writing, less is more. Make sure that your lead doesn't exceed

35 words. Always ask yourself: "Have I chosen the most gripping angle?" Never 'bury' or hide what should be your lead down at the bottom of your story.

(10) MINUTE TASK

In pairs, read the following leads, identify the angle, and ask yourself if it is a good, gripping one or not. What other angles on the same story could the writer have chosen to follow?

Example 1:
A man was shot twice in the face on a New York City subway platform, the fifth shooting on the city's transit system in just over a month.

Example 2:
A court in northern France has convicted 10 members of a paedophile ring after a trial that gripped France.

Different types of summary lead

In this chapter, you have learnt that summary lead is usually the best to use for a news story. Now we will look at three specific types of summary lead:

Definitions

Summary lead

Immediate identification lead

Delayed identification lead

Multiple elements lead

the immediate identification lead;
the delayed identification lead; and
the multiple elements lead.

The summary lead

Where all aspects of the event are important then it is a good idea to use a summary lead like the following:

AN ALARMING situation is developing at provincial schools, with the chairmen of the governing bodies considering handing back power to the government claiming they would not be competent without money to run schools. (*The Daily News*, South Africa, 4 September 1997, p3)

The immediate identification lead

The main purpose of the immediate identification lead is to name the people involved in the story. Why? Usually because the names are more important than the action or event in that particular story. Take for example the following lead:

London: Princess Diana and her boyfriend Dodi Al Fayed were killed in a car crash inside a Paris tunnel this morning.

The most significant aspect of the lead is the personalities involved.

The delayed identification lead

> Ten people were killed in a car crash inside a Paris tunnel this morning.

Here the action is more important than the identity of the people involved, because none of them were prominent. More information, including perhaps their names if their families have already been informed of their deaths, would be included in the first few paragraphs following the lead.

The multiple elements lead

The multiple elements lead is the most difficult and is used when one theme for a lead would be too restrictive. The combined elements of the lead and story make it more powerful.

> Police have launched an official inquiry into why the number of accidents in downtown Paris has increased dramatically this year, following a crash in which 10 people were killed in a highway tunnel over the weekend.

⑩ MINUTE TASK

In groups, identify examples of the different types of lead in your local newspaper.

SELF-STUDY TASK

Write an example of each of the above types of leads and assess it using the check list grid for self-editing at the end of the chapter.

From the lead to the last word

Writing in the inverted or upside-down pyramid style, your first few paragraphs after the lead will support it with facts and quotes from authoritative sources. Use your most powerful sources, quotes and information first.

The nut graph is usually a summary paragraph, situated high up in the story, perhaps directly after the lead. The nut graph answers the question, "Why does this story matter and what is its significance?" It supports the lead with context and background information and forms a transition between it and the rest of the article. Not all news stories need nut graphs but many do, especially those that are complex. This story comes from a British daily newspaper:

Summary lead

> Thousands of middle-aged professionals who experimented with drugs during their student days will be warned in a major government health campaign this autumn that they may be infected with hepatitis C. (Revill, 2004).

Nut graphs - (incorporating the explanation why this story is important for readers)

> It is thought that up to 400,000 British people may be carrying the potentially fatal virus without knowing it, because there is such a long delay between infection and symptoms appearing.

> Ministers have decided to go ahead with a national public awareness campaign in September, warning that anyone who has ever injected drugs, particularly sharing a needle, used straws to sniff cocaine or had a blood transfusion before 1991, is at risk and should consider having a blood test. However, they are worried about causing mass panic and want to adopt a 'softly-softly' approach by focusing on the treatment available for the disease, rather than its potential consequences. (Revill, 2004).

But don't let your story dribble out when you have no more information – save a good quote for last and always try to end strongly. That said, don't introduce something new at the end. Keep your writing tight and back up everything you say with quotes and facts.

Helping you write your news story

Keep your language objective

Never use "I" or "me" or inject yourself into a news story. There is no place for the first person in hard news.

Details, details

It's usually a good idea to note revealing details. It's also possible to put too many details into a story. Irrelevant facts can become tedious. You will learn to find a happy medium between too many details and too few as you gain experience.

Keep paragraphs and sentences short

Avoid long paragraphs and complex sentences. The longer the sentence, the more difficult it is for readers to read and retain and the greater chance you have of making a grammatical error. Long paragraphs look grey and uninteresting to the reader's eye when laid out on a newspaper page.

Tighter writing

Read through your work and edit out extraneous words to make your writing 'tighter'. "It was already getting quite dark as it was early evening" is repetitive. "It was early evening" conveys the same message in four words rather than 11.

5 MINUTE TASK

In pairs, read over the first two paragraphs of any news article in a newspaper. Which words, if any, could have been edited out, without any of the meaning being lost?

Numbers and dates

For numbers, spell out one to nine. Use numbers for 10 to 999. Use words again for thousands – "five thousand people marched in a protest against soaring child abuse figures today" is the general newspaper style rule. The exception is when it's a specific number: "Police announced 3065 arrests in yesterday's national swoop on outstanding traffic fines." Use 'hundreds' when the word comes up casually: "There were hundreds of guests at the party, according to our society editor,". If you start a sentence with a number, spell the number out: "Twenty people have been hospitalised after an outbreak of gastroenteritis at the arts festival in Grahamstown." Remember, though, that if the number is large and spelling it out would make your sentence unwieldy, rather rephrase your sentence. "At least 278 people have died in an outbreak of Ebola fever in Angola, according to doctors with the World Health Organisation." Avoid using more than one set of numbers in the sentence, if at all possible, or find a useful point of comparison, like this: "Every year we throw away enough waste to fill a row of trucks for 1,400 kilometres, the distance from Cape Town to Gauteng." For dates, the usual style is to use March 5, not the fifth or 5th of March. Time should be written as 2:25 a.m., or 3:75 p.m. yesterday. Sums of money should be written as R72 and not R 72.00 or 72 rands.

Avoid clichés and idioms

You should avoid resorting to clichés, [*over-used expressions*]. Clichés, though instantly recognisable, detract from the power and freshness of your writing. Common clichés: frightened to death, lost track of time, needless to say, couldn't keep my eyes open.

Avoid idioms which not all readers may understand and which are nearly always clichés in themselves. Idioms are common cultural expressions whose meanings cannot be extrapolated [*inferred, deduced*] from the words themselves. In other

Definitions

Cliché

Idiom

words, if the reader doesn't already know the idiom, he or she will not be able to deduce its meaning. Idioms are cultural expressions. English idioms include the phrases such as: raining cats and dogs; take it with a grain of salt; born with a silver spoon in one's mouth.

If you must use an idiom, make sure that you understand it, or your ignorance will impact negatively on your language. You can't 'step up' to the gauntlet, for example, you can only 'take up' the gauntlet. The gauntlet was a glove that was thrown down by knights who were prepared to accept challenges (for things like jousting) in medieval Europe. Knights who wanted to take up the challenge took up the gauntlet. You can 'step up to the plate' in baseball. But it's not recommended in cricket.

---

⑤ MINUTE TASK

Working in groups, write down as many clichés as you can in five minutes. The group with the longest list is the winner! Remember to avoid all of these in your news writing.

Avoid colloquial language

Definitions

Colloquial language

Tautology

Qualifier

While your language should be simple and direct, avoid colloquial language and slang. Don't use 'guys' instead of men, or observe that something is 'cool'. News writing tends to be formal. Some publications don't even like their reporters using contractions, such as don't, can't and couldn't. And never use SMS or mobile phone text style language in an article.

Avoid tautology

Tautology is the unnecessary repetition of an idea. Tautology makes your work onerous [*tedious, heavy*], so cut it out

An official judge – the word "official" isn't needed.
Reverse a car back – the word "back" isn't needed.
The sky went dark as the sun set – "the sun set" would be sufficient. The rest is self-evident.

Of course, sometimes you will use repetition for effect. You will have to discern [*work out*] whether any repetition in your writing is tautological, or is there for effect.

In pairs, study the examples below. What is tautological and what is repetition for effect?

1. The article was printed in the newspaper yesterday, in black and white for all to see.
2. The round circle of the sun shone brightly in the sky.
3. File the document away so you can refer back to it in the coming future.

Keep tenses consistent

Don't chop and change tenses. Choose one and stick to it. When you are writing a news story, it is usually best to refer to sources in the ordinary past tense:

> "The criminals escaped (*past tense*) sometime last night," said chief warder Eugene Harris.

However, sometimes, the present tense is used to refer to sources and quotes. This is used especially in feature writing, to convey the impression of immediacy. In news writing, this impression is not necessary because the news is by definition immediate

> "The problem of prisoner escapes (present tense) is a growing (present tense) one," says chief warder Eugene Harris.

Avoid qualifiers

Qualifiers are words that 'qualify' [*describe*] and can limit the extent of other words: 'quite', 'rather', 'very', 'extremely', 'totally', 'absolutely', 'a little'. If you write, 'The man loved his dog very deeply', the word 'very' contributes little to the sentence. The sentence is just as powerful without the word: 'The man loved his dog deeply'. Qualifiers rarely add much to your writing. Do away with them to make your writing leaner and more powerful.

Keep pronouns consistent

Correct:
One cannot run from one's problems.
They cannot run from their problems.
Incorrect:
One cannot run from their problems.
They cannot run from one's problems.

Use commas appropriately

Beginner writers, often, use, commas, inappropriately. Look at that sentence. Did it need any commas? Use commas only when a pause is necessary (not when you want to emphasise a word or take a breath yourself) or when they separate a phrase or clause from the rest of the sentence.

> The judge, who contestants said was not qualified

Remember, you must either use two commas or none at all when doing this. The judge, who, contestants said, was not qualified.

> Correct:
> Former Iraqi dictator. Saddam Hussein, was executed last week.
> Correct:
> Former Iraqi dictator Saddam Hussein was executed last week.
> Incorrect:
> Former Iraqi dictator, Saddam Hussein was executed last week
> Incorrect:
> Former Iraqi dictator Saddam Hussein, was executed last week.

Suggested Reading

Brooks, Brian S, et al, (1992). *The Missouri Group, News Reporting & Writing*, New York, St Martins Press, 4th edition.

Harris, Geoffrey, (1993). *Journalism Media Manual - Practical Newspaper Reporting*, 2nd ed, Focal Press.

Checklist for self-editing

When you're finished, read over your work carefully two or three times, and critically assess it according to this checklist/grid. It is a useful tool that you can use to assess every article that you write.

	✓	✓	✓
	Yes	Maybe	No
1. Intro/Lead			
1.1 Does it grab your attention?			
1.2 If it's a news story, is it a good summary intro (does it include all or most of the 5 W's and the H?)			
1.3 What is the angle of the piece and is this clearly and concisely communicated in the intro?			
1.4 Is the angle fresh and appropriate?			

		✓	✓	✓
		Yes	Maybe	No
1.5	Have you "buried the lead"? (in other words, left your most powerful info for later in the piece?)			
1.6	If it's a news story and you have opted not to use a summary intro, have you got an excellent motivation for this?			
2. Balance				
2.1	Analyse the sources used in the piece.			
2.2	Are they appropriate?			
2.3	Are any glaringly missing?			
2.4	Are there enough sources to make the piece well-rounded?			
2.5	Who else could you have interviewed to lend your piece more balance, depth and credibility?			
3. Sentence Length & Structure				
3.1	Go through the article sentence by sentence.			
3.2	Sentences should generally be short and to the point. Are any much too long? If so, break them down into shorter sentences.			
3.3	Are all the sentences grammatically correct?			
4. Paragraph Length				
4.1	Paragraphs should be kept short, so readers can easily digest them. Are any paragraphs too long?			
4.2	When a new source is quoted, you should usually begin a new paragraph. Has this been done?			
5. Over-Writing				
5.1	Read through the article and cut out any words that aren't necessary, or find ways of writing more succinctly.			
6. Quotations				

	✓	✓	✓
	Yes	Maybe	No
6.1 Scrutinise the quotes in the story. Have the quotation marks been used correctly at the beginning and end of the quote?			
6.2 Have sources been introduced before they are quoted? (As a rule, they should be.)			
6.3 For every quote you use, you need to have evidence of originally recording it in your reporter's notebook.			
7. Attribution			
7.1 Sources of information must be attributed repeatedly. All statements should be attributed to some source, or the writing will come across as your opinion. Are they?			
7.2 Every person quoted should have a name and a surname spelt correctly.			
8. Poor Expression			
8.1 Is there anywhere in the piece where you have not been clear? Clarify ambiguities.			
9. Numbers & Dates			
9.1 Check you've cited them journalistically.			
10. Use of Tenses			
10.1 Have tenses been used consistently?			
10.2 Have you used the present tense as much as possible (while keeping your writing grammatically correct), to make your story immediate.			
11. Active vs Passive Voice			
11.1 As far as possible, news stories should be written in the active voice. Can you find any instances of the passive voice in the article?			
11.2 Can you find ways to make it active?			
12. Do subject and verb agree (Concord)?			

	✓	✓	✓
	Yes	Maybe	No
12.1 Do your subject and verb agree? e.g. The boy's bag was stolen (singular). The boys' bags were stolen (plural). e.g. She is sick (singular). They are sick (plural)			
13. Do Nouns & Pronouns Agree?/Use of Pronouns			
13.1 Have you chosen the correct pronoun?			
13.2 Check pronouns agree with what they are referring to e.g. you cannot refer to a singular person or thing as 'they'. Do they agree?			
13.3 News-writing should not include the words 'you' or 'I', unless they are in a quotation. Have you avoided this?			
14. Use of Commas			
14.1 Are all the commas in the story used correctly?			
14.2 Are there too many commas?			
14.3 Have you set off all phrases with commas at the beginning and end of the phrase?			
14.4 Are names separated by commas – ie. University of Milan fashion design student, Norah Giovanni, revealed some of the latest trends.			
15. Spelling			
15.1 Can you spot any misspelled words?			
15.2 Are all names and places spelt properly?			
16. Finishing Touches			
16.1 Have you inserted your by-line at the top?			
16.2 Have you written good captions for your pictures?			
Go back and read your lead one more time...			

Source: Greer G, Turkington T, Vahed H.

14 Newspaper language

Outcomes

At the end of this chapter, you will able to:

▶ Use clear and concise English.

▶ Avoid writing long sentences.

▶ Follow the basic grammar, punctuation and style rules that newspaper language uses.

Introduction

The school system seems to produce many common language errors. You may find that you need to work at producing clear, grammatical newspaper language. This chapter cannot handle this subject fully but it will give you a clear understanding of what newspaper language is and what you should know in order to construct a well written article.

5 MINUTE TASK

Discuss with a fellow student or colleague:
What kind of language should be used in newspapers and why?

Why clear language is important

For the journalist, clear and concise English is important because accurate communication is important. In other words, the message we want to send to our readers must be the message they receive. Our writing should be incisive [*sharp and clear*] so that there is no doubt about what we are trying to say. People from many different educational and cultural backgrounds read newspapers. The content must therefore be easy to understand for everybody.

Hartley, in Lucas Oosthuizen's book *Introduction to Communication*, describes the importance of language in our lives:

> ... through language we learn how we should act; within the framework that it establishes we find, explore and understand our own individuality, and through it we gain access to social relationships. (Oosthuizen, 1996:178).

Hartley also points out the ways in which language can play a part in structuring and controlling our world:

> ... language is also a form of social control because people generally voluntarily submit to its rules and conventions. It is also through language that we learn to accept the social forces and institutions around us as natural. (Oosthuizen, 1996:178).

Does my audience understand this?

In short, we live through language. Language and the way it is used is therefore enormously important to those people who read or write newspapers. Because English is the language of choice for mass communication in many parts of the world, it is essential that journalists learn to communicate effectively in English. English is a dynamic, changing, growing language, a language that is constantly being used for hundreds of different purposes by millions of people. Different people are adapting English in different ways as they use it daily. So how do we find an English that is acceptable to different readers?

One answer is that we should accept and even celebrate the changes that happen to English as people use it. However, what is English to some people may be unacceptable to (or not even understood by) others. We therefore need to use an English that as many people as possible will understand and accept.

Some reporters use the following test: ask yourself whether anyone would speak the way you have written. If the answer is No, delete the passage and start again. As Geoffrey Harris says:

> Ordinary speech is a good guide for the correctness of newspaper English though obviously you can rarely tell a newspaper story exactly as you would tell it to a friend: you have to manage with fewer words. (Harris, 1993:77).

And, of course, you need to cut out any forms of English that are understood by you and your friend but not by many other people.

You could also use the English of radio and television news bulletins as a guide. Newspapers need a text that is similar to the broadcast news reader's text - short sentences that read easily and are quickly understood.

Ambiguity

In journalism, above all news, the greatest virtue is clarity. A journalist should never be ambiguous [*confusing, double meaning*] when making a point. What exactly does the following sentence mean? Does 'since' mean 'because' or 'after'?

Ambiguous:

Figures released by the Universities Council for the Education of Teachers show that the failure rate at one institution soared from 3 per cent to around 23 per cent since trainees this year have had to take a test on a computer rather than with a pen and paper.

Unambiguous (correct):

Figures released by the Universities Council for the Education of Teachers show that the failure rate at one institution soared from 3 per cent to 23 per cent **after** trainees this year had to take a test on a computer rather than with a pen and paper.

Sentence length

Is this sentence longer than 24 words?

Some people have the mistaken idea that the longer a sentence is, the better the writing must be. The long sentence is usually difficult to follow, unlikely to flow smoothly and very likely to bore the reader to sleep. So, what can we do? The first golden rule is: Look very suspiciously at every sentence longer than 24 words and double check any sentence longer than 32 words. Try not to write sentences longer than 24 words unless absolutely necessary. Your sentences must be simple, clear and short.

Journalists normally have to write under pressure and although it is possible to write clear long sentences, it is not easy to write clear long sentences in a hurry. It is usually possible to break a long rambling sentence into two short, easier-to-read sentences. But try not to make your sentences so short that they sound like a machine gun.

Try to be democratic with your thoughts and sentences. One thought, one sentence. Write in a direct manner. It is better to say as 'he scored' than 'when scoring'.

Using the right words

Every journalism student should have a good dictionary, a thesaurus and a dictionary of synonyms and antonyms. These three books should be the most used books they own. No journalist should write without these three books at hand, and they should be referred to constantly. Sometimes the change in meaning between two words with similar meanings is slight but important and we can embarrass ourselves if we don't use the right word at the right time.

You have received some information and you are not certain how to describe it. The first word you think of is report - you have received a report. A report implies some ground for belief unless specifically qualified as being false or untrue. No, you feel that the information you received is not so certain. What about rumour? Rumour suggests a report that flies about and gathers detail as it spreads but has no clear source and no clear-cut evidence that it is true. Again, you decide that this does not fit your information. Gossip, perhaps? That sounds better. Gossip applies to idle, often personal chatter that is the chief source of information and also means a propagation of rumours or reports. No, that's not it, it wasn't just idle, personal chatter. What about hearsay? Hearsay stresses the source of a rumour or report, as something heard rather than something seen or known directly. When the word 'hearsay' is used to describe evidence, it suggests that there is only indirect and imperfect knowledge of the facts. You decide this word fits - what you received was not a report, rumour or gossip, but hearsay.

Fewer and less are often confused. 'Fewer trees/less wood' is the basic distinction between number and volume. But there are traps. Some things that sound like numbers - because they are in the plural - don't take 'fewer'. Time, age and measurements of distance take 'less': 'It was less than five miles away.' Sometimes neither 'fewer' nor 'less' will do.

Incorrect: "Teachers get longer holidays and work fewer hours than any other profession."

Correct: "Teachers get longer holidays and work shorter hours than any other profession."

Journalists owe it to their readers to choose their words with care and caution. It is simply not acceptable to choose a word we think is 'close enough'. We must rather select the word that conveys the meaning exactly.

We often look for words to spice up our writing, to make it more varied and interesting to read. One word that we like to change is the word 'said'. Don't be too afraid of using said quite a lot, as the words we use in its place are often much less suitable. Be careful of using the following words: stated, declared, claimed, uttered, or continued. Either might change the meaning and tone of your sentence.

Words like phenomenon, element, effective, virtual, facilitate, utilise and liquidate are used to dress up simple statements and to make biased judgements sound impartial, well-informed and reasonable. For example, a current favourite in the media is 'radical elements'. Avoid words like these.

Words and idioms

Words are the main tools of the journalist. You should use slang only when quoting someone else's words. Dress words in inverted commas - 'goof' - only if you need to emphasise that this is the actual word somebody used. Avoid exaggeration. Use words to fit the circumstances you are writing about.

Ask yourself whether the words you have used really do capture the spirit and style of the event that you are describing. Use words with taste and tact, even when they are the right ones. Remember to use idioms with special care. Some idioms are familiar even to readers whose mother-tongue is not English. However, many idioms may make text hard to understand for some readers.

Getting the tone right

An important aspect of style is tone. Tone shows how the writer sees his or her relationship with the reader. You can offend a person if the tone of your writing does not accurately reflect your relationship with that person. Look at the difference between:

> Answer immediately.
> Could I ask you for an answer?
> I would be grateful if you would answer as soon as possible.

It's not just **what** you say, but **how** you say it!

The first two examples would be used only if you were superior in status to the reader.

Each newspaper has its own tone. Some newspapers use an informal tone and take many opportunities to address the reader directly: "We're asking you, the reader, to tell us what you think about...". Others maintain a fairly formal tone, more distanced from the reader. You will need to understand and conform to the tone of your newspaper. Some journalists may be responsible for a section or column, such as the entertainment pages, which deliberately strike a different tone from the more serious main news and feature pages. It might be worth organising some photocopied articles which block the identity of the newspaper. See if the students can identify the source or at least the type of newspaper.

Slang, jargon and foreign words

Slang, like jargon and technical language, is a special or private language of a particular group. Jargon [*terminology*] is used mainly to impress others. Slang is used mainly to mark a group and its members as special or exclusive. Students use slang to exclude parents, lecturers and other non-students from their communication. Because slang causes strong emotional reactions, it can bring members of the group closer together. It evokes [*raises, calls up*] feelings of warmth and loyalty to the group from members. But it evokes hostile feelings from non-members. You should therefore avoid using slang when your readers do not share the group membership.

Jargon is the use of pretentious [*show-off*] words usually linked with a particular occupation or status. Surfers use jargon to describe surfing conditions and manoeuvres that non-surfers can't understand. Students may do the same in their spoken language. Jargon can annoy or puzzle readers in a way similar to the way slang alienates them. However, do not confuse jargon with technical language. Technical language can be legitimate and necessary for expressing specific meanings of concepts in computer technology, law and medicine. But the use of technical language is only appropriate when writing for specialist readers. Specialised technical terms are inappropriate for a lay audience [*non-specialist readers*]. You should try to find terms that readers will understand better. Remember, our function as journalists is to communicate to people of varying educational levels, including primary or elementary school level English.

Foreign words bring the same difficulties as technical words do. Although the use of foreign words impresses some audiences, there is no place for them in an English newspaper. Words such as compère and entrée are now part of English. But many people who do not speak mother-tongue English will not understand such words and will not understand your news article.

It is best to use ordinary, common speech. Therefore, do not be afraid to use contractions [*shortened forms*] such as didn't, haven't, can't and so on. These are all commonplace in normal speech.

Correct word order

The correct word order in a sentence is the basis of English grammar. It is important to keep together words that belong together. Some languages have relatively free word order but this is generally not so with English. Look:

> The boy loves the girl.
> The girl loves the boy.

Changing the word order changes the meaning of the sentence entirely.

Students frequently have difficulty with the placing of the following adverbs: also, even, just, merely, only, simply. Ambiguity [*two or more possible meanings*] can result if these words are not placed near the word they modify:

> I only lent him my notes.

It is not clear whether the notes were lent to one person only or whether the notes were the only thing that was lent. The following versions are unambiguous and therefore better.

> I lent only him my notes.
> I lent him only my notes.

Commas are useful and show which words should be read together. However, a sentence with too many commas is difficult to read, particularly in newspapers with narrow columns. The best way to deal with a sentence that needs too many commas is to break the one long sentence into two or more sentences.

Variety and readability

Especially if your article is quite long, it needs to be readable - that is, good to read. Variety is what makes English good to read so you should avoid using the same words or using a similar sound continuously. Try to inject rhythm into your sentences. Reading the story out loud to yourself or to others often helps you develop an interesting rhythm or beat. Your final sentence must reach a climax. It should not trail away into nothing

Basic style rules

Definitions

Stylebook

Most media organisations, including radio and television broadcasters, have a set of instructions for writing. As a new journalist at the newspaper or magazine, you will have to learn this stylebook off-by-heart. Indeed, if you want a job at a particular media organisation, you should find a copy of the stylebook and learn to write in that manner.

Every journalist on the paper knows and follows the same rules. This includes everything from preparing copy through to writing style, grammar and also lay-out and design. Conformity [*everyone following the same rules*] is important. Conformity makes it easier for editors and sub-editors to edit your work. The readers know what to expect when they open their newspapers, switch on the television or tune the frequency on the radio dial.

5 MINUTE TASK

Select the same photos and write captions in different styles – for example, for a weekly gossip and celebrity magazine, for a serious weekly newspaper, for a wire service which is sending out material across the globe.

Avoiding common style problems

Prepare your copy: The stylebook will give general instructions on how to prepare and store copy (articles) and how you should transfer this copy between yourself and the news editor and sub-editor. The stylebook will also give specific instructions on how you should type the article and what font and size of font you should use. It is not easy to keep in line with the stylebook but it is essential. The newspaper must conform to a style acceptable to its readers, who are unforgiving about grammar, punctuation and spelling errors. The stylebook tells you what to do.

All writing must conform to the in-house or corporate journalistic style. Very few newspapers today use hard copy (paper versions of articles) so you will do all changes and editing on a computer screen. As you prepare your copy, you should aim to give your news editor and sub-editor as little work to do as possible (and if possible, no work at all) in editing your copy. Make sure that you have checked all the relevant details with sources, by phone if necessary, and have the correct spelling of all names.

Punctuation: The stylebook will also lay down specific instructions for punctuation.

The period (full-stop) must be used at the end of every sentence. It is often used with abbreviations (commonly shortened words, such as Rev. for Reverend, or P. Smith for Peter Smith, Col. Ngubane for Colonel Ngubane, Ford Motor Co. for Ford Motor Company. The period or full-stop should be omitted after headlines, captions, figures and the letters standing for well-known agencies, especially those pronounced by their individual letters, such as NASA, NATO and the UN.

The comma is used in a series: "He selected sweets, fruit juice and biscuits." It is used to separate unrelated adjectives: "It was a long, hard match." The comma is used to set off an introductory element such as the word however: "Therefore, the desperately-poor grandmother went home without her pension this month." It is used to indicate the start of a direct quotation: "He said, 'I am going home to pack my bags for the Olympics.'"

A common error is to use the comma to join grammatically independent sentences: "These days international rugby is not sport, it is war." Wrong! This can be corrected in a number of ways:

Substituting the comma with a full-stop: "These days international rugby is not sport. It is war."

Substituting the comma with a semi-colon: "These days international rugby is not sport; it is war."

Linking the two sections differently: "These days international rugby is a war rather than a sport."

The apostrophe or quote mark (') is often used to show the possession of an item: "Siswe's book is missing" shows how the apostrophe is placed before the letter s, whenever there is a single person or item doing the possessing. "The boys' bags were searched for drugs at the school entrance" shows how possession of something by more than one person in this sentence is clearly signalled by the apostrophe coming after the letter s. An apostrophe is also used to show that some letters have been dropped from a word or phrase, so "Do not do that!" can turn into "Don't do that."

Read the daily newspaper for a week and list examples of misuse of commas and apostrophes.

Suggested Reading

Berry, Thomas Elliot, (1976). *Journalism in America*, New York, Hasting House Publishers.

15 Feature writing

Outcomes

By the end of this chapter, you will able to:

▶ Explain what a feature article is.

▶ Explain what constitutes good feature writing.

▶ Generate ideas for features.

▶ Research features effectively.

▶ Structure a feature effectively.

▶ Write a query letter and sell a feature.

▶ Write professional, innovative feature leads.

▶ Package and submit a feature professionally.

▶ Identify and use figures of speech in feature writing.

What's a feature?

Definitions

Feature

A feature is an in-depth article that may appear in a newspaper, magazine or website. A feature does not depend as heavily on timeliness as a news story, although it might still be about something that happened recently. Some features, however, are timeless. The feature allows the writer to write more creatively and to use more descriptive language than the news story does. The feature also allows the writer to do more research and to fit more information into an article than a news story permits. Features allow a wider and deeper coverage of their subjects than do news stories. They are usually longer than news stories. Generally speaking, features are less formulaic than news stories. A feature's structure is determined by several different factors, including the style of the publication for which the article is written; the readership which the publication enjoys; the type of information which the writer is able to collect from different sources, including people, websites, books, other newspapers and magazines and government reports. Features are usually illustrated with photographs and sometimes with other graphic elements such as maps, cartoons, artwork and graphs.

Types of features

There are many different types of features. Any feature, however, can comprise a mixture of types. These styles should not be seen as a separate and isolated entities but rather as guidelines for potential feature writers.

The news feature

A news feature is based on something that is currently in the news. It is an article which goes 'behind the news' in that it doesn't simply report the facts of an event but tries to provide depth and different angles. You could write a news feature, perhaps after a bad train accident, in which you track down and interview families of the victims or victims themselves, about themselves and their feelings about the accident. Perhaps you attend the funerals of the victims, which can sometimes take place weeks later because bodies are kept for forensic evidence and coroner's reports. After the eruption of a volcano, you could write a news feature on how volcanoes and that one in particular are formed and why they erupt. You could interview geologists, seismologists who monitor volcanos and people who live in the area affected by the volcano's behaviour.

In 2004, American telecommunications businessman Nicholas Berg was the first foreign hostage to be beheaded by militants, after the US-led invasion of Iraq began a year earlier. Shortly after a graphic video showing his beheading was released on the internet, the Washington Post newspaper ran a news feature about what Berg had been like as a person, using information gathered from friends and others who knew him in his home town. Here are the opening paragraphs from the story by Michael Powell and Michelle Garcia:

> The kid known as Berg shows up, in their memory's eye, with his impish smile and his tuft of dirty blond hair atop an otherwise shaved scalp and that brilliant mind, which bounced about like a pinball. Even now his friends smile.
>
> "I remember this freshman comes walking out to the first band practice with his sousaphone and all of his philosophies and funny voices and right there, you knew he was something else," says Luke Lorenz, who was

Definitions

News feature

How-to feature

a high school junior at the time. "We went away for two weeks of practice and that first night Berg takes some scrap of aluminum foil and a Walkman and constructs an alarm system for our cabin."

"If you triggered it, a taped voice started yelling: GET OUT OF HERE! GET OUT OF HERE!"

This was Bergology, aka the Science of Berg. Now Nick Berg is dead and all that's gone forever. (Powell and Garcia, 2004).

Could you select a similar hard news story about a disaster or tragedy and work out how to create a news feature out of it?

The how-to feature

Definitions

The trend feature

The profile feature

The obituary feature

This is a style of feature which teaches readers to do something, usually by laying out a step-by-step process. 'How-Tos' are very practical in nature, such as 'How to Choose Colours that Suit You' for a women's magazine, or 'How to Protect Your PC from Viruses' for a computer magazine. 'How-Tos' might not always incorporate the actual words 'how to' in the headline, but the words will usually appear somewhere in the story.

⑩ MINUTE TASK

In pairs, page through any magazine and find a 'how-to' article. Does your 'how-to' provide readers with a step-by-step approach to doing something? If so, how many steps are explained? Does it include any quotes from sources, such as experts, or is the article written entirely from the writer's point of view? If so, is this satisfactory for the reader or not? Why? Identify some other sources that the writer of the how-to article perhaps could have interviewed.

The trend feature

This is a feature focusing on a particular trend, or something that has developed over time, as opposed to a single event. You could compile an environmental trend story on how global warming is affecting your town or country, a fashion trend feature for a teen magazine on what the 'hottest' things to wear next summer will be, a news feature in which you investigate a trend over the past 10 years in which the world's richest people have grown richer while its poorest have grown poorer, or a human interest trend feature in which you focus on the growing trend of international students travelling to study at your university.

The profile

This is a feature that usually focuses on a single person, or small group of people (such as a band of musicians, or a team of scientists) but it is also possible to profile a place, such as a rural village. Profiles are usually written about people who have accomplished something special, or who readers will find particularly interesting to read about. Good profiles adopt a 'warts and all' approach, providing an all-round picture of a person's character.

Of course, this makes researching and writing a profile a particular challenge. You ideally need the co-operation of the person you're profiling, as well as others who know them well, such as family members, colleagues, friends and even enemies. When writing a profile, try to interview not only a range of sources but a range of types of sources who may know different sides to your subjects – so perhaps the person's husband and children (close family members), colleagues (peers), secretary (employee), boss (employer), childhood friends and so on. The more appropriate sources you interview, the better a picture of the person you will provide.

Often, people are not prepared to say negative things for publication on the record about people they know, so it's the profiler's task to tease out the good, the bad and the ugly about a person, while preferably maintaining co-operation with sources. To do this effectively, think carefully about the questions you ask. So instead of asking an employee, "What's she like as a boss?" (after all, most people will probably say something vaguely complimentary), ask the employee to relate the funniest thing that's ever happened in the office, or to recount an instance in which their employer was under considerable stress.

Definitions

The interview feature

The composite interview feature

The pro & con feature

The seasonal feature

The obituary

An obituary is a profile of someone who has recently died. A good obituary will include an overview of a person's greatest achievements in their lives and provide insight into what the person was like. As with a profile, sources will include people who were close to the person and knew them or worked with them. The element of timeliness is important in any obituary, since its publication is tied to the news event of the person's death. Often, newspapers prepare obituaries of old or sickly famous people, so they can update and publish them quickly when the person passes on. Many newspapers are open to the idea of running a retrospective obituary a month or a year after someone influential has died, showing the gap in the community and paying tribute to his or her work.

The interview

There are different ways of writing up an interview, including the straight question and answer format, and a looser style in which you integrate your discussion with the person into a more conventional feature, comprising a lead, transition sentences and ending. Like the profile, this style works best to feature someone who is in the public eye for some reason, or who has done something noteworthy. It's a popular style for interviewing movie stars.

The composite interview

The composite interview is a feature made up of a series of responses, usually to the same question, from a variety of people. It could take the form of 'vox pops' (from the Latin for 'the voice of the people') where you take a photograph of each interviewee and juxtapose each person's response with their photograph. This might work for a feature on what local people think about a crime wave hitting their area, or about a controversial new road, which might benefit isolated rural residents but runs through a protected wilderness area. Another type of composite interview would be if you tracked down an old school photograph of your country's new president or your town's new mayor, and then tracked down his or her old classmates to find out what they're doing now and to recall what the president was like as a child. You could publish the photograph, ringing the faces of the president and those you've been able to interview.

The pro & con feature

Pro | Con

This type of feature works well when there are clearly two sides to a topic, with different people taking these sides. This works well with controversial topics. For instance, you could do a pro and con (the words come from the Latin for 'for' [pro] and 'against' or 'anti' [con], but you could also think about it as the 'advantages and disadvantages' feature) feature on whether abortion should be legalised or criminalised, depending on the context in your country, or the country you wish to investigate. Or you could select a debate on whether the death penalty ought to be abolished or instated, again depending on the context, or whether priests should be allowed to be openly homosexual or not. You could publish the two sides to the topic side by side, with a source or sources to back up each argument.

The seasonal feature

A large percentage of feature articles are based on seasonal events, such as Mother's Day, Valentine's Day, World Aids Day, International Women's Day, as well as the anniversaries of important dates in history. Feature writers often find themselves in the strange position of having to compile seasonal features long before the actual event itself. There are a lot of seasonal events, though many may not come to mind quickly (did you know there was a World Kissing Day, for example?) Many smaller newspapers welcome freelance seasonal features which you can work on in advance while doing other stories or assignments, such as the anniversaries of the newest and oldest schools, hospitals and churches or mosques in the district.

The human interest feature

This embraces the stories of ordinary people, who have perhaps achieved something unusual or novel. Perhaps it's a feature about an especially inspirational school principal and how she's helped failing students to pass, or the story of a man who dedicates most of his spare time to helping stray cats. Often, human interest features include a 'triumph over tragedy' or 'rags to riches' element: the tale of a factory worker who wins the lottery or the new sports star who came from a home so poor he didn't have a new pair of shoes until he was 10.

The investigative feature

This is an in-depth article on a topical social issue or an in-depth news story, running perhaps to several thousand words. An investigative feature might focus on the declining standards of education, or on how a factory is polluting the air so badly the health of residents is declining. It may incorporate an element of timeliness, such as investigating racism in an area where an upcoming global conference on the issue is to be held. Or it could deal with problems unrelated to a specific news event, such as domestic violence or sexism in the workplace. This is not usually a good place for a writer to start his or her journalistic career because of its complexity.

Definitions

The investigative feature

The quiz feature

The quiz

The quiz is a popular feature in men's and women's magazines in particular, but is a format that could be adapted for almost any publication which publishes features (online quizzes on websites can be fun because they can be more interactive). When compiling a quiz, you need to ensure that the format is clear and easy to follow for the reader and that you compile the answers at the same time as the questions. Provide a range of difficulty in the questions – make some easy, some medium, and some hard. Depending on your topic, seek some expert advice on whether your quiz is sound or not. For example, if you're compiling a quiz entitled "How compatible are you and your partner?" ask a psychologist with experience in dealing with relationships to look over the quiz and advise you.

(10) MINUTE TASK

In pairs, decide on a topic for a quiz, the type of publication it could be published in and the first three questions and answers.

The humour column

Definitions

The humour feature

The travel feature

Humour columns are sometimes found on the inside back pages of monthly magazines and are often based on the writer's personal experience (or an exaggerated version of it). Humour writing is an especially difficult form of feature writing, relying largely on the writer's skill in gross exaggeration (hyperbole), twists in meaning (irony), satire (making fun of something) and others (see the 'writer's toolbox' section).

Gather ideas from humour columns in magazines and newspapers and reflect on personal experiences that have been amusing in some way. Once you've written a humour column, it's useful to get someone whose opinion you value to read through it and tell you honestly and in detail where it's funny and where it could use some editing.

Finish your humorous feature well before deadline, and read it over a few days later – and then again, a few days later. You'll find that some things are not as funny as you thought they were when you wrote them. Rewrite these bits or edit them out. Keep the bits that still make you smile.

The travel feature

So, where is my next holiday going to be?

Only your imagination limits the scope for travel articles. These may range in style from 'how-to' to personal essays, or even profiles of places. Travel writing is in some respects a form where feature and review writing converge. Almost always, your opinion as someone who has personally experienced something you are writing about — whether it's a foreign country or the local aquarium — will be an integral part of your article. That said, the best travel writing, like any good feature writing, is multi-sourced and is packed with information and facts. Good travel writing usually requires good pictures and is informal in tone. It takes the reader (who may be just an 'armchair traveller') somewhere else, through visual writing and attention to detail, and is packed with information and facts. Although it is colourful and descriptive, it doesn't lapse into 'purple prose' (overwritten, non-specific description dripping with too many adjectives). Because it usually depends on the writer's opinions, experiences and recommendations, it is one of the few types of journalism often written in the first person.

> **🔟 MINUTE TASK**
>
> In pairs, devise an idea for a travel feature, based on the place you are living at the moment.

The review

A review is a personal reaction to a play, book, film, website, concert, restaurant, CD, event, experience or artifact. The trick in reviewing is to provide a well-informed and balanced, yet entertaining opinion for the reader. To do this, the review writer often needs to have background knowledge in whatever he or she is reviewing. If you're going to review a play, for instance, read up about the playwright and ask the director and perhaps a lead actor for interviews beforehand.

Once you've written your review, you may want to evaluate it for yourself against the following list of questions:

Have you 'shown rather than told', by packing your reviews with details, including personal observations and 'facts' or background information? Have you attributed your information clearly and in appropriate journalistic style?

Have you achieved an effective balance between your opinion of the piece you are reviewing and background research and reporting?

Is your review fresh and tightly written? (Have you avoided being repetitive or long-winded? Is your use of language original and free of clichés?)

Is your work free of errors of punctuation, spelling and grammar?

Have you discussed the themes of the piece appropriately, without giving away too much of the plot?

Is the length and structure of your review appropriate?

If you've reviewed a film, have you discussed the acting, direction and technical aspects appropriately, showing insight and observation? If it's a book review, have you discussed the style, tone and skill of the writer? If it's about a musical piece, have you discussed the arrangement, performance, lyrics and themes?

Does your review provoke thought about the piece and the issues it raises? Does it allow readers to make up their own minds about the piece, or is your review overly judgmental or smotheringly congratulatory?

What should my readers know about this film/play/book/cd?

> 🔖 **SELF-STUDY TASK**
>
> Write a review of a film or play currently on circuit or on DVD. (You do have to see the film or play first.)

In groups, read through a magazine and try to identify the 15 types of features listed above. Can you find examples where two or more types of feature are merged together? Can you find any examples of features that don't fall into any of the types listed above at all?

The feature writing process

I often say to my students that the term 'feature writing' ought to be replaced with 'feature packaging'. The feature writing process, from the inception of an idea to the delivery and eventual publication of an article, has many aspects to it, not all of which involve writing.

The feature writing process involves coming up with an idea, selling the idea to an editor, researching the feature (including identifying appropriate sources and interviewing people), structuring the feature, packaging it with pictures and perhaps other types of illustrations and finally, delivering it professionally. First, a feature writer has to come up with an idea. There are many ways to come up with an idea including reading regularly (especially news and feature articles in a variety of magazines and newspapers); brainstorming; keeping an ideas book in which you write down ideas as they come to you and maintaining a clippings file of topics which interest you and which you might like to cover in the future.

Do you agree with Walter Cronkite's statement "keep all prejudice and bias out of a news report" or not? Write your response and explain it to a partner.

At almost the same moment you come up with your idea for a feature, you need to start identifying one or more potential target publications in which your article could appear and of selling your idea to an editor. To do this, you need to know the publication you are aiming to publish in very well. You need to know the type of content it publishes, including who its readers are, its personality and the type of content it runs. You need to read back copies of the magazine to ensure it hasn't already published a similar article.

Most print publications today have websites, which can be helpful aids for feature writers to gain insight. Many publications also have a set of writer's guidelines, which may inform potential writers about style, length, submission format, ethics, payment and so on. Look carefully at these guidelines on the website, but if you can't find any, drop the publication a polite e-mail asking if they have any. Reading the writer's guidelines is important, and will stop you making unnecessary mistakes in attempting to sell and publish your article.

Feature writers usually sell their articles by way of a query letter, which is a letter in which they propose their idea to an editor. Some publications, however, prefer to see a completed manuscript before they are prepared to accept an article. While students might write a piece and then think about where it could be published, usually the process works better the other way around: match your idea and the publication before you start writing. This will give your piece focus.

Here are some tips for writing a query letter. A query letter should:

Be addressed to the right person. You need to find out who deals with feature queries, as this differs from publication to publication. It could, for example, be the editor, deputy editor, features editor or content editor. If you're querying a magazine, the contents page may tell you who to direct queries to, or look for information on the publication's website, if it has one. If all else fails, telephone the publication and ask the receptionist the name, position and e-mail address of the person you should query. Query letters not addressed to the right person will not lead to successful publication.

Be fairly formal and polite (though not stiff). If you have not written for the publication before, address the editor using Ms or Mr.

Be concise and to the point. Query letters usually need only be a few paragraphs.

Convey the idea clearly and powerfully to the editor. You may choose to include the lead of your feature in your query.

Be clear and well-expressed.

Propose how long the feature will be, in keeping with the length of articles commonly run in the publication. Don't attempt to sell the publication a 6000-word piece if the longest article it ever runs is 500 words.

Summarise how you will conduct your research (perhaps suggest sources).

Contain your contact details and some information about yourself, including any writing credits you may already have.

Be free of grammar, punctuation and spelling errors. Edit your query letter meticulously. No editor will trust someone who makes elementary writing mistakes.

Definitions

Query letter

On spec

On commission

Kill fee

A brief

Propose ideas for illustration. If you can take your own photographs, explain this and inform the editor you will be able to provide them in his or her preferred format (the writer's guidelines may tell you what this is).

Deliver in the format of the publication's choice, which may be expressed in the writer's guidelines. While most editors today accept e-mailed queries, some prefer hard-copy queries.

Clearly state if the article has been published before and if so, where and when.

Specify when you could deliver the proposed article.

Once you have sent off your query, give the editor a week or so, and if you haven't heard, follow it up with another email, restating your query. If you still don't hear anything, it may be worth giving the editor a call.

Editors may agree to accept a query in various ways. They may agree to take it 'on spec' (speculation) which means that they are interested in your idea and are encouraging you to write the article, but are reserving their rights to purchase your piece until they see the finished product. An editor may also commission you, which means they are agreeing to purchase your article. If an article is not commissioned, the publication may pay you a 'kill fee' (a percentage of what they would have paid you), or the full amount.

Remember when querying that your article must usually be written long before it is actually published. Most monthly magazines have a deadline for writers at least two months before the article comes out (though newspaper and website deadlines are shorter). Also, monthly magazines come out about two to three weeks before the month stated on the cover. So an article entitled "How to Make Your Own Christmas Decorations" would need to be submitted towards the end of September. You would therefore need to query such an idea one to two months before this, around July. You need to bear these time lags in mind, so your planning is adequate and your phrasing is still relevant when the article appears. It is no good referring to something in your feature as happening 'last month'. You would need to specify that the event happened 'in September'.

Occasionally, and more often as you become more established as a feature writer, you may find yourself in the pleasant position of being asked to write a feature by an editor. In this case, the editor should provide you with a brief – a letter telling you what he or she expects, including details such as the topic, length, payment, and perhaps even mention of possible sources and a lead.

Researching a feature

Once you've decided on an idea, even before you try to sell your article, you need to begin researching it. The way in which you research an article will depend on its topic. You need to identify appropriate sources who will be authoritative in the context of your article and interview them, preferably in person, but also possibly on the telephone or via email. So if, for example, you are writing a feature entitled "How to Raise an Honest Child", you might interview child psychologists, parents, school principals and children themselves.

As with news writing, the feature writer has a range of sources at his or her disposal to interrogate, including websites, documents, books and photographs. But by far the most important source for feature writers is people. People like to read about other people and people's quotes always spice up writing. Taking them down and selecting them carefully requires hard work, but this will pay off. As a rule, punctuate your features liberally with quotes.

Don't be lazy about gathering a wide range of sources so that your feature is balanced and fair. It is better to have too many sources (who can then be edited out of an article if necessary) than too few.

All information that you include in your feature needs to be meticulously attributed. If you quote from a website, for example, you need to specify clearly which website it is; if you quote from a book, you need to provide the author, title, publisher, date of publication and even perhaps a current local price. You need to weave this information into your article seamlessly, so that a reader can absorb it quickly. So, for example, you may write something like:

"American author Mary Matthews made millions of women re-examine their attitudes to romance, sex and modern marriage in her 2005 bestseller, Five Steps to Finding Mr Right (Romance Press 2006), available for about R100 in local bookstores."

Structuring a feature

The structure of the article is its backbone, which the writer fleshes out with words. Essentially, the structure is the article's shape. Once the writer has conducted all the research, he or she can sit down and work out a rough structure for the article. It often helps to draw a mind map or "spider diagram", in which you draw yourself a graphic representation of the different parts to your article, before deciding on a structure.

Wall Street Journal or champagne glass structure

In this structure, made famous by the excellent feature writers on the *Wall Street Journal* in the USA, the writer starts with a strong lead, perhaps introducing an individual who the readers can identify with and who can personalise or symbolise an issue. Perhaps the article is about the bad working conditions in mines in a particular country. The lead could be something like this:

Feature Structures

1. Wall Street (Champagne Glass)
2. Stack of blocks
3. Circular structure

In the stifling heat one kilometre beneath the earth's surface, Patrick Gumede toils for eight hours a day. On the ride to the top in the wire lift cage each night, he struggles to stand up straight after bending over almost double all day. He suffers from bad backache but is afraid if he complains, he'll lose his job.

The next paragraph would then introduce the wider issue, using statistics and human sources to lend it credibility. The structure would then taper gently, and end with a 'kicker' conclusion – a strong quote or anecdote.

Stack of blocks structure

This structure is characterised by a series of blocks of ideas, around a central theme. If, for example, you were writing an article on the growth of cults, one block of ideas might focus on current members of cults, another on people who have escaped cults, another on family members of those who belong to cults, another on what local religious leaders think of the phenomenon, another on how the police are dealing with the issue, and so on. Each of these blocks would need to be linked to one another with strong transition sentences.

Circular structure

This is when the conclusion sews up the article by returning to the lead. For example, the writer may re-introduce a source or metaphor first introduced in the lead.

Writing a feature

What are the qualities of a good feature?

Once you've conducted your research and settled on a structure (which you will be able to refine as you go along), you'll be ready to write your piece.

So what makes a good feature? A good feature should be new and fresh in content, though it may revisit well-known issues. You could write a feature that's never been done before, for example, on a school that trains young jockeys, a newspaper for teachers. Or you could do a piece on 'How to find Mr Right' for a womens' magazine – something that's been done many times over. In this case, you would need to freshen it up with a new approach and new sources.

Be tailored for particular readers

This means that almost at the outset of your feature – as soon as you come up with an idea – you need to be thinking about the readers you are writing it for. Are they mostly men or women, young or old, wealthy or not well off, for example? Knowing exactly who you are writing for will determine your sources, tone and approach. For example, you would write the feature entitled 'How to find Mr Right' very differently for a women's magazine than you would for an international travel magazine – though both might be appropriate markets for your piece. If you are writing for the children's section of a family magazine, for example, you would need to use simple words and a sentence structure that your readers will understand. If you are writing for National Geographic, your writing would be far more complex in vocabulary, structure and content.

Start and end powerfully

As in news writing, the feature lead is the most important series of sentences in the article (in feature writing, the lead is often longer than a single sentence), because it is the line that hooks the reader and makes him or her decide to read on or not. Lead writing for feature articles is more creative than in news writing, and there are several types of feature leads to choose from.

The closing lines of a feature are as important as the opening lines, because they are what the reader is left with. Always try to end your piece on a high note. Save up a good quote or anecdote, or craft it so that it takes us back to the beginning of the piece. Don't let it fall 'flat' and make the reader feel that you really had nothing else to say. It is important to make your piece memorable, so spend as much time and effort on the ending as you do on your lead.

Be multi-sourced and meticulously researched

It is impossible to overstate the importance of sources. The quality of your piece will be defined largely by the quality of your sources (which include [most importantly] human sources, but also books, internet sites and others). Obtaining a variety of legitimate and authoritative sources forms the basis of news-gathering for all types of journalism, including feature writing. If you do not include any sources in your piece, it will lack credibility and punch. Never rely too heavily on one source. Ideally, every feature should include upwards of five sources. This will help your writing to be balanced and fair, as all journalism should be.

Check your work by reading it aloud.

Be free of grammatical, punctuation and spelling mistakes

For your work to come across as professional, it must be immaculate in terms of grammar, punctuation and spelling. You need to work at this. Be certain you know for sure why you used every comma and apostrophe (and other type of punctuation mark) in your piece. Check that there is nothing wrong with your spelling. Getting these details right takes a lot of concentration, checking, re-writing, and hard work – like looking up words in the dictionary and the rules of language when you're not 100% certain of things.

Be well-expressed, flow well and have a sense of rhythm

This means your language needs to be clear, concise and fresh. Vary your sentence and paragraph lengths to add interest for your readers. Reading your piece out loud to yourself should help with this. Always aim for clear expression. If a sentence doesn't read smoothly and easily, do it again. Say what you mean, and avoid imprecise, clumsy language. "Cosmopolitan writes for smart women" is incorrect because a magazine can't write, only writers can; "Cosmo caters for smart women" would be better.

As when writing news, avoid the passive voice

In cases where you are talking of examples in general, try to stick to the singular: "reward your child" (as though you are talking to a single reader only – this is more direct and personal for the reader), not "reward your children". Don't bounce between the two.

It's fine to not write full sentences once in a while, as long as you're aware that you're doing it and are careful not to overdo it - or it becomes tedious for the reader.

One of the ways to ensure your writing is fluid and readable is to practice your transition (linking) sentences. Transition sentences are sentences that link the ideas in one paragraph to the ideas in the next, and which may be positioned either at the end or beginning of paragraphs or which form a short paragraph on their own. Feature writers use transition sentences to create a smooth flow from one set of ideas to the next. They may introduce a new source or a different tack in the article. Take care that you use transition sentences when they're needed, so that your work is logically linked (or your rhythm will have an uncomfortable staccato [abrupt] feel to it).

Here are a few paragraphs from my feature about the lost meaning of South Africa's ancient rock art. The transition sentences – those that link ideas – are italicised.

> South Africa's San, or Bushmen, inhabitants created most of the country's rock art, but they are almost extinct, so working out what the paintings mean is a difficult and controversial process.
>
> One of the leading academics in this field in South Africa is David Lewis-Williams, professor of cognitive archaeology at Wits.
>
> *His colleague, Geoff Blundell, himself an expert on rock art, says, "From the work that Lewis-Williams has done, and subsequent work, the art has to do with the San's deepest religious beliefs.* It's highly symbolic. It symbolises religious belief.
>
> "We suspect many images are not representational and we think that the origins of art and religion are very closely tied to each other."
>
> Blundell says the San believed that rock art was a link to the spirit world.

He says that people used blood in paint.

"For San, blood was considered !Gi. It was one of the most central substances in the universe, and could live in animate and inanimate things. The substance was said to reside in the eland's blood, fat and sweat in particular."

"San say you have to harness the substance to go to the spirit world." (Turkington, 1999).

Convey an appropriate authorial voice

Each feature needs to convey a unique and appropriate authorial voice. The authorial voice is the tone and personality that you as the writer convey to the reader in a feature article. This may be muted or strong, depending on the article. As a feature writer, you need to adapt your authorial voice according to the readers you are writing for.

The authorial voice is largely dependent on which 'person' you choose to write in. There are three 'persons' to choose from in writing:

First person: 'I' is first person singular; 'we' is first person plural. All possessive forms of these – me, my, mine, we, our – are in the first person. You should seldom use the first person in feature writing – reserve it for those times when your personal experience forms an important component of the feature only. The first person is direct and can help to create a personal atmosphere. It is most often used in humour columns and opinion pieces. But bear in mind that the use of the word 'I' automatically conveys to your reader that you are expressing your opinion and that you deem yourself important in the piece. The use of the first person could convey arrogance or amateurishness if the reader is unable to clearly see why you are resorting to first person. Don't use the first person unconsciously and avoid it unless there is a good reason to use it.

1st person singular is...

1st person plural is...

Second person: 'You' is both the singular and plural of the second person, while 'your' is the possessive case of the second person. Like the first person, the second person is rarely used in feature writing, with the exception of the 'how-to' format, when it is often appropriate. An article entitled 'How to Position a Picture' for the magazine *Home & Garden* could use the second person:

2nd person singular is...

2nd person plural is...

"Be honest, when you moved into your home, did you place your furniture where it fitted best, then simply hung your pictures wherever the previous owners had left nails in the wall? Chances are then, you're not showing them off as best you could. Follow the five easy steps below to make the most of your pictures. ..."

3rd person singular is...

3rd person plural is...

Third person: 'He', 'she' or 'it' are the singular of third person (the possessive cases are his, her and its); 'they' is the plural (and 'their' the possessive form). This is the only voice that should be used in news writing, and is also the most common voice in feature writing because it is flexible, unobtrusive and not patently opinionated.

Generally, it is not a good idea to swap the 'persons' of your authorial voice in an article, though in some cases it may be necessary. Swapping 'persons' within a sentence or paragraph will usually lead to grammatical errors, apart from causing confusion for the reader.

While the choice of person is an important aspect of the authorial voice, an equally important contributor is tone. Tone refers to the personality and atmosphere of the piece. For example, the writer may choose to make it cheeky (if it's about sex – a favourite focus of features), serious (perhaps for an obituary about an influential bishop), or authoritative if it's an article on how the justice system in a country has changed in the past 10 years. The tone of a feature could also be humorous, tongue-in-cheek, witty, sophisticated or evocative. But above all, it shouldn't be boring.

A feature writer can vary tone in an article, but should always use it appropriately. Tone needs to complementary to the intention of the piece, and the tone of individual sentences or paragraphs should not jar with the tone of the overall article or publication.

> " It's not what you say but how you say it! "

10 MINUTE TASK

Read the excerpt by Dave Barry, columnist for the *Miami Herald Tribune*, written while covering the 2004 Olympic Games in Athens, below. With a partner, discuss:

1. The tone of the piece. What would you say the tone of this piece is? Can you identify sentences that convey this tone particularly well?
2. How does the use of first person, second person and third person vary in this piece? Can you identify three different lines using the first, second and third person?

Taking a taxi in Athens is taxing - Dave Barry

ATHENS - Without question, this city's most exciting mode of transportation - and I include, in this category, skydiving without a parachute - is to take a taxi.

> The thing is, Greek taxis are cheap. You can go a looonnnnng way, kilometre after kilometre, and the fare will be only a few euros centigrade. That's the good news. The bad news is, to make any money, the taxi drivers must cover a lot of distance, so they go very, very fast.
>
> Q: How fast do they go?
>
> A: Their taxis frequently burst into flames upon re-entering the atmosphere.
>
> You've probably been in some big, hectic city, like New York or Rome, where you thought the taxi drivers were crazy. I'm telling you that those drivers are deceased old ladies compared to the Athens taxi drivers. I have yet to take a taxi ride here in which I do not, at some point, decide that I needed to make my peace with my maker, except that all my maker would hear, if He tuned into my brain, would be "EEEEEEEEEEEEEE."

Feature leads

As with news writing, the lead is the most important line (or lines – it may extend over a whole paragraph, or even several paragraphs) of the article. It is this line that determines whether the reader reads on or doesn't. Unlike news leads, the feature lead is seldom formulaic. Avoid the summary lead containing the 5 W's and the H that you might see at the start of a typical inverted pyramid. Often statement leads are bland and boring. If you've written one, look at it critically – is it the best lead you can devise?

> **Styles of lead**
>
> 1. Statement
> 2. Anecdotal
> 3. Descriptive
> 4. Scenario
> 5. Quote
> 6. Question
> 7. Mixture

Statement lead

This is a simple statement and is the most common form of feature lead:

> Tough-guy rapper Sean 'Puffy' Combs suffers from a bizarre condition called claurophobia. But don't worry, it's not life-threatening. The 'illness' is a fear and hatred of – clowns. (People, 2002).

Anecdotal lead

This is a lead that includes a story, or anecdote.

Descriptive lead

This is a lead which relies heavily on description for effect. Here's one, from a story by John Parrish, entitled "What it's really like to be ... STRUCK BY LIGHTNING."

> A flash of blinding white light, an explosion of noise, it felt like someone was ripping my legs off. (Parrish, 1997).

Here's another, more extended one by Nigel Slater, for *The Observer*, a British newspaper renowned for its excellent feature writing, entitled "Summer serendipity":

> Sweet, light and nutty, a young Pecorino is just what I want with a plate of late-summer figs; the crunchy seeds and the pale, milky cheese have a gentle affinity, something to eat slowly in the shade of a tree. Barely three or four months old, this is a gentler, fresher-tasting sheep's cheese than the bolder stuff I grate over my fettucine. Thin, crumbly slices of Wensleydale do well with a fig, too, as they did last Sunday with a few very late cherries. An accidental marriage I shall do my best to remember next May and June, when the English cherries come into season. (Slater, 2003).

⑤ MINUTE **TASK**

Note the use of 'I' (the first person) in the lead, which is appropriate for an article reflecting personal experience. What type of readers do you think this lead would appeal to, in terms of class and age? How can you tell?

Scenario lead

This is where you start with a fictional scenario or scene which sets an atmosphere for your piece. Sue de Groot wrote this lead for a feature about being single entitled 'Home Alone' for a women's magazine:

> Wearing a tracksuit and eating mushy fish fingers in front of the TV, allowing your tears to mingle freely with the tomato sauce in your Tupperware dish as the pale heroine finally overcomes her misunderstandings with the dashing hero in the chick-flick video you've chosen... This is the pleasure of living alone. (De Groot, 2002).

Sometimes, a scenario lead can give you flexibility (and a sense of fun) that other leads simply couldn't.

What are the qualities of a good feature?

Quote lead

Yes, you've had it drummed into you that you should NEVER start a news story with a quote. You shouldn't – this is because a quote can rarely sum up what your article is about, which is important in a news story lead. You should also reserve starting features with quotes for those rare occasions when you have an unusual one that retains its power without needing exhaustive explanation. This lead started a story by Don Pinnock for a piece on the cichlids (a species of fish) of Lake Malawi:

"Their mouths are round like an O. They swim up to other fish and suck their eyes out. Pop! Just like that."

(Pinnock then explains these were the words of his lake guide.) (Pinnock, 2002).

Question lead

Question leads are rare and are more often mediocre than memorable, so you should use one only when an excellent opportunity presents itself. Here's a successful question lead, from an article in *Sports Afield* entitled "Skamania: Indiana's Super Steelhead":

> Which freshwater fish weighs an average of between 12 and 20 pounds, slams your lure with a hair-raising jolt, screams line off your reel with alarming speed, splits the air with slashing, leaping runs, and shucks free about three out of five times to leave you with nothing but a memory of it?

> The answer is Skamania, a very special steelhead found almost exclusively in Indiana. (Skamania, 1985).

Mixture leads

Here's an interesting mix of a statement lead and a descriptive lead:

> A sap-sucking bug that coats plants with wads of foamy spit has been crowned the insect world's greatest leaper. It has more jumping prowess than fleas, out hops the springiest grasshoppers, and clears the high bar more quickly than bush crickets.

And finally, a mixture between an anecdotal and quote lead.

> In his 15 years as a storm chaser, Tim Samaras had never seen a tornado this close.

> The thundering twister was heading straight for him. "It looked like a barrel," he said. "It was half a mile [0.8 kilometre] wide."

---

10 MINUTE TASK

Working in pairs, come up with an effective question, scenario, descriptive or anecdotal lead for a story on one of the following topics:

1. How to travel in an aeroplane with small children.
2. A survey of the most popular bars or restaurants in your town.
3. A profile of a sports coach (you choose the sport and the person).

4. The problem of men who say they'll "be home in an hour honey" and then disappear all night with their friends.

Packaging a feature

Editors think in packages – words plus pictures. While your writing may be top rate, it will be overlooked if illustrating it is going to take too much effort or resources. Therefore, try to provide – at the very least – multiple ideas for illustration, though actual pictures are even better. (As a feature writer, you should forever be trying to develop your photographic skills.) Ideas generate ideas, so if you come up with a few, this can be very helpful to an editor. Even better, you should arrange the illustration yourself, by taking your own pictures and gathering photographs from sources you interview, for example (offer to scan and return – and be reliable). Your pictures should be professionally presented – on a CD if they are in virtual format, or in a suitably protective envelope, if in print format. You should check first which format would be best for the publication you are writing for (many still do not accept digital images, unless taken with a high-end camera). You should clearly number your photographs and supply an accompanying sheet with suggested captions. Even if the editor does not specifically ask for pictures, you should be thinking of ideas to illustrate your piece. Good pictures could mean that the editor gives your piece more prominence in the publication, and might even mean you earn a photo byline and/or payment. Show initiative in this regard, and try to think laterally and creatively. Feature editors are looking for new ideas, not just old, rehashed ones. The more you (a) provide good, workable ideas and (b) reduce problems for your editors, the more they will use you.

Bear in mind, though, it is all very well to suggest, but you need to know that you can deliver on your suggestions. In other words, you must know that photographs exist (or could exist if you took them) before you can suggest them to an editor. This takes a lot of effort and attention to detail.

While it's a good idea to think about illustrations, it's not necessary (or desirable) for you to go into details about fonts and layout. Each publication has its own layout artists and specific set of style rules.

Packaging can also refer to the way you structure your article or articles. Perhaps you want to include a main feature, factbox and graphic, or a feature and related package, as long as it's appropriate.

> "Follow the brief!"

Delivering your feature

Deliver your feature in the form the editor requires it in (ask if you are uncertain). Most articles across the global media industry today are submitted as e-mail attachments. Find out which format is preferable, and ask the editor to confirm receipt of the article. You may need to courier photographs – plan this well ahead of time.

Deliver your feature when you say you will (or before – nothing impresses an editor more than submitting a piece before deadline) and deliver what you are asked to. If an editor asks you to write 300 words, don't deliver 3 000. Try to conceptualise how your feature will look in your mind's eye when it's laid out, and don't pass up an opportunity to sell an 'extra' component in your feature. If you need to provide illustrations, submit them. One of the most important things to learn in journalism is to follow the brief.

Some final tips for feature writers

Challenge yourself! While you need to 'think smart' about what sources to use and how to access information, don't always take the easy route. Trying to interview people who are in the public eye (and are therefore interesting to read about) is difficult, because they are often inaccessible. Don't adopt approaches to articles that have been done before. Think laterally. Work hard. It always pays off to extend yourself in the planning stages of an article. When you sit down to write, it will come that much easier to you, and what you write will be compelling for your readers. If writing an article was easy for you, the alarm bells should be ringing.

Don't break promises to your readers

Never disappoint your reader. Don't tease with promises, and then break them. If, for example, you write an enticing lead in which you summarise amazing events or facts, you need to go back and flesh these out.

Fill in the blanks

Your work needs to be perfect. That means, there should be no unnecessary spaces anywhere. L ike th is. They look ugly, make your work difficult to read, and some poor copy or sub-editor will have to delete them, making you unpopular. Don't leave a double space after full stops, either. This is an old-fashioned practice not used in the modern media anymore. It just means that sub has to sit and take all those out, too. And while on the subject, most magazines and newspapers don't leave blank lines between paragraphs (though websites often do). So replicate the publication's practice, and don't add in paragraph returns unless necessary.

Think of the future

You should be constantly thinking of future pieces, and possibly asking questions that you could use for secondary articles. For example, if you are interviewing a

teacher about HIV/Aids and she tells you about an amazing sex education programme that's happening in her school, ask her a couple of questions about it
and use it for a query to a different publication. This relates back to keeping an
'ideas' book or list of things that interest you, and to reading widely so that you
are aware of diverse potential markets for your work.

Give your piece a catchy title (or none at all)

Your title should be relevant to your piece. If you can't think of a clever, catchy
title (which is also in keeping with the tone of the publication it's intended for),
rather leave a title off. It is part of the copy or sub-editor's job to write the headline.

Respect your readers and always strive to be sensitive about class, culture, race
and gender. Be careful about coming across as patronising. Never talk down to
readers, who are intelligent. Bear in mind the feelings and dignity of both your
sources and your readers. Be sure to use sources of both genders and make sure
you interview people from various cultural, religious and linguistic backgrounds,
if you are writing for a local, national or international magazine with a general
readership.

Try to avoid words like 'businessmen' which apply only to one gender. There is
no point in being exclusive if you can rephrase to include everybody.

Similarly, if you're writing for a national publication on a general topic, avoid
gathering all your sources in one city. This will make your readers in other areas
feel excluded.

Be careful of sweeping generalisations like 'most black South Africans don't
have high-paying jobs'; 'most women have a deep desire to be mothers', and so
on. Generalisations are rarely true, and will only make you a target for criticism.
Beware too, of pandering to stereotypes. Don't assume that all homosexuals are
well dressed, or that women who stay at home aren't successful.

Extend your vocabulary

A good vocabulary adds colour. Every time you come across a word you don't
know, look it up in a dictionary and jot it down in a little book. Keep the book
somewhere handy (like in the bathroom) and revise your new-found words regularly.

Get it right, keep it tight & don't overwrite

Become more disciplined in meaning and understanding the impact of every word
you write. Frequently try to cut out every second word of a finished article – and
see how many are unnecessary. Extra words that aren't there for good reason
make your writing cumbersome and tedious. Writing tight is difficult. It requires

rereading your work and editing it yourself. Read your work over and over before submitting it, so that you can eliminate careless mistakes, which make your work appear sloppy and unprofessional. Have someone else read it for you – a fresh pair of eyes often picks up mistakes better.

" Work on leads "

At the end, go back to the beginning

Work, work, work on those leads. Your lead is the most important line of your entire article. Come back to it repeatedly until you know it's perfect. Think about the way you start a feature for a long time. Your lead may be descriptive or anecdotal; it may be a summary, a fictional scenario, or a stark statement. The way you start your piece will have enormous influence on the overall tone and structure of your article.

The feature writer's toolbox: figures of speech

The feature writer has the luxury of being able to paint a more descriptive picture for his or her readers than a hard news reporter may do. Some of the most important tools at a feature writer's disposal are figures of speech. To use these tools, you need to know what they are. While working through the list below, bear in mind that one expression can be more than one figure of speech at once – 'a giant of a man' is a metaphor, hyperbole and a cliché.

Figure of Speech	Explanation	Example	Notes
Simile	Direct comparison using the words 'like' or 'as'.	• She is as high as a skyscraper. • He laughs like a hyena with bronchitis. • He disappeared as fast as free chocolates in a student canteen.	
Metaphor	This is a comparison of one thing to another thing, without using the words 'like' or 'as'.	• The woman is a snake. • The boy was lion-hearted when he tried to save his sister from a fire.	When using metaphors and other figures of speech, be certain that the words you choose convey your intention and not something else.

Figure of Speech	Explanation	Example	Notes
		The old lady is in the autumn of her life.	You also need to choose metaphors carefully: for example, writing "shoppers rape the shelves for gifts before Mother's Day" is an inappropriately violent metaphor that does not fit well with the subject being discussed. Be careful, too, not to mix your metaphors. e.g. The novice reporter was already skating on thin ice when he suffered a baptism of fire.
Cliché	Clichés are overused figures of speech, which you should avoid repeating in your writing.	• as big as a house • as free as a bird • you are a star • barking up the wrong tree; • what goes around comes around • you can't teach an old dog new tricks	When using metaphors and similes in particular, it is easy to use clichés. Effective writing is writing that is fresh and original, so use figures of speech that are your own. All well-known idioms and even some catchy advertising slogans are clichés.

Figure of Speech	Explanation	Example	Notes
			As a general rule, if you've heard it before, it's a cliché.
Personification	When the writer gives an inanimate object or non-human animal human characteristics.	• the professorial pig • the sun smiles down on the world	
Alliteration	Repetition of consonants for effect.	• Peter Piper picked a peck of pickled peppers. • When we were young.	
Assonance	Repetition of vowel sounds.	• sailing away on a gay summer's day • how now, brown cow	
Onomatopoeia	Words that imitate sounds.	• He slurped his milkshake. • She landed splat in the mud.	
Hyperbole	This is extreme exaggeration.	• Cricket commentator on a big hit by Lance Klusener: "That's gone so far it'll earn frequent flyer miles". • I was so embarrassed, I could have died.	

Figure of Speech	Explanation	Example	Notes
Bathos/anti-climax	Almost the opposite of hyperbole, this is an anti-climax of some sort.	Britney Spears was due on next. The crowd was going wild, people were screaming, fans were hurling personal items onto the stage. She came out from the wings, her arms open, embracing the crowd - and fell flat on her face.	
Euphemism	Under-playing something.	The government referring to violent protests in which police kill people as 'unrest'.	
Non-sequitur	Something that simply does not follow logically.	It's a dog-eat-dog world. That's why I've always preferred cats, myself.	Sometimes used in humour writing. The trick is to use it intentionally, and not by mistake!
Synecdoche	Synecdoche is when the writer uses a part of the whole as a symbol to represent the whole.	Lend me your ears (give me your attention).	
Metonymy	When a word is substituted for another word closely associated with it.	• The courtier addressed the crown (as opposed to the king).	

Figure of Speech	Explanation	Example	Notes
		• The protestors emailed the Oval Office (as opposed to the American president).	
Oxymoron	An apparent contradiction contained within two words.	• an open secret • military intelligence • love-hate relationship	
Paradox	Also an apparent contradiction, but not contained to only two words.	"Fair is foul and foul is fair".	
Pun	This is when a word has a double meaning; it's a play on words that look or sound the same.	Headline for an article on hard-working dental technology students: "Students sink their teeth into their studies".	
Sarcasm	This has been called the lowest form of humour. Maybe that's because it is the easiest type of humour to create, is cynical and often has a nasty edge.	Wow, that lecturer is so great, I'd love to attend five of her classes in a row every day.	
Irony	This is a complex figure of speech. It involves a	A millionaire winning a jackpot would be ironic;	

Figure of Speech	Explanation	Example	Notes
	statement that has more meaning than first appears, or a twist.	it would similarly be ironic if a student failed basic arithmetic at school, then went on to become a billionaire businessperson.	
Satire	This is generally when prominent figures or social conventions are made fun of, often through exaggeration, sarcasm, irony or other figures of speech. While satire makes the reader laugh, its intention is serious, it's usually used to affect social change or at least provoke thought.		
Innuendo	This is when something is hinted at, not quite stated. It is often mean.	Have you ever noticed how the president walks with a wiggle? Likes to wear pink? And is said to have a Michael Jacksonesque passion for young boys? It makes one wonder...	Beware of being sued for defamation, though jest, fair comment and of course the truth are all defences for defamation.

16 Editing – getting it right!

Outcomes

At the end of this chapter, you will able to:

▶ Know what copy-editors or sub-editors do.

▶ Understand how to edit copy.

▶ Grasp the basics of writing headlines.

Introduction

There are many types of editors, and many types of editing. The editor is the head of a media organisation's staff and is the link between the board of directors of that newspaper, radio station, television channel or internet site, and the staff who produce the news. The editor must decide on the policy of the newspaper and make sure that staff respond accordingly. The editor is finally accountable for the success or failure (commercial and in terms of content) of the newspaper. Editors are therefore often autocratic [*dominating*] leaders who stamp their personality and will on their newspapers. Editors usually exert their influence by writing the editorial comment and controlling the editorial pages. Their influence is also applied during the frequent editors' conferences where the next issue or broadcast is planned. You as a reporter will have little or no contact with the editor unless you work for a small community newspaper or a small community radio station. You feel the editor's influence through other colleagues like the news editor and the assistant editors.

You will come into contact with the sub-editors who prepare a written story for publication, or the senior or executive producers who will assess electronic media before it is ready for airing. The sub-editors (also called copy-editors) apply the editorial policy of their own newspaper or media group when they edit stories. But they also use some more general principles of newspaper writing and editing which will be useful to consider.

House style

House style is the way publications choose to publish: single quotes or double, use of capitals and lower case, when to use italics and so on. Putting a piece into house style is the straightforward process of making it fit in with the rest of the publication. The main purpose is consistency.

The argument for consistency is very simple. Variation that has no purpose is distracting. By keeping a consistent style in matters of detail a publication encourages readers to concentrate on what the writers are saying. House style is for the benefit of the reader and the writer.

Style books are for the benefit of the sub. According to British freelance journalist and trainer Wynford Hicks and Nick Holmes of Cardiff University, who co-wrote such a book for the popular press, style books exist to save time and trouble, to make it possible to apply a consistent style without wasting time checking in back issues or discussing all over again what was settled last week. (Hicks and Holmes, 2002:19).

What is copy editing?

Copy editing or sub-editing (sometimes referred to as subbing or the subs' desk) is the assembling, preparing, modifying and condensing of written material for publication: putting the material together, correcting or altering it, making it shorter.

It is the copy-editor or sub-editor's duty to:

make the story readable;
keep the story brief and to the point;
guard against libel;
check the accuracy of the story; and
make sure the story fits the organisation's tone and style.

A copy-editor is allowed to alter your story, generally by decreasing the text. Here are some other interventions you can expect:

Rewording (this is where your thesaurus – print or online - comes in handy).

Correcting and updating information.

Changing the emphasis or angle of the story.

Checking verifiable facts [*things that can be proved correct or incorrect*], including the correct spelling of names and addresses.

Composing headlines.

Copy editing is one of the most important functions in a newsroom. The copy editor or sub-editor must make the story readable and ensure that it fits the requirements of journalistic writing. Phrases must not be ambiguous [*have more than one possible meaning*]. The writing must be clear, forceful and easy to understand at the first reading. This is difficult to achieve because newspaper readers represent a wide range of education from those who are newly literate to university graduates. The copy must be understood by all without offending any. The sub-editor must find the acceptable 'middle of the road' or average.

Efficient and accurate copy editing is taken for granted by readers. They don't notice it. But bad copy editing can make or break a newspaper's hard-earned reputation. Readers always remember the mistakes. You, the journalist, represent the first line of defence against inaccuracy and misinformation. Sub-editors are the publication's last line defence against errors.

What skills should a sub-editor possess? An important skill is a sound knowledge of the specific meaning of words. Moreover, sub-editors should be experienced reporters who are well-informed, confident and skilled in the use of all the common languages of that region or country. Sadly, modern newsrooms do not always observe all these requirements. Their publications lose quality as a result.

The sub-editor must enforce deadlines so that the newspaper is produced on time. Sub-editors often have to work extremely fast to make those deadlines. The job does not suit the inexperienced! As a reporter, you will have little contact with the sub-editors unless they wish to query aspects of your article. But it is a good strategic move to make yourself known to the sub-editors and hand out your contact numbers so that they may be able to consult with you if queries arise about your story.

Since most newspapers today are produced using desk top publishing with computer software, sub-editors and copy editors are also often responsible for the layout and design of the pages.

How to edit copy

First do nothing. The best way to start editing a story is to do nothing to the story except read through it at least twice. Only then, after reading the story for the second time and getting a sense of what the writer is trying to say, should you begin to edit.

A golden rule (which many sub-editors unfortunately ignore) is not to make any changes to the style and content of a story without consulting the writer. I paid dearly for ignoring this rule. When I was editor of a national sports publication, I employed a well known writer to write a column for me. The writer used to submit her articles to me on a stiffy disc, so when I received her article I put the article through a spell check without first reading the story. The very last word had been incorrectly spelt so I corrected it, still without reading the piece. The story was duly published and I soon had the writer on the phone shouting that the misspelt word was the punchline of the story.

Ask: does the story make sense? What point is the writer making? Is that point made clearly? Is there sufficient information to support that point of the story? Is the information arranged in a logical order? Are the arguments well balanced, and is opinion clearly distinguished from fact?

Ask: what, if anything, in the story could be cut? Some stories benefit from cutting because they are too long, with parts that reduce the strong thrust of the story. Others have to be cut simply because there is a shortage of space on the page. If you must cut, make sure that your cuts do not destroy the sense of the story.

Ask: is there any information that should be checked for accuracy? There may be information in the story that, if inaccurate, could involve your publication in great trouble and expense. Check this information with the writer if this has not already been clarified, or do the necessary reference and telephone work.

Ask: does the style of the story involve the reader and fit the publication? The story may make sense but this is not enough. It is important that the story involve the reader. The style of the writing should be appropriate for the intended medium and audience.

Check grammar and spelling. Is the story easy to read? Are sentences concise, clear, and written in the active voice? Has a grammar and spelling check been carried out?

Guard against libel. Eliminate or rewrite any statement that may libel the subject. Defence against libel is difficult so it is important that you take care when using words like liar, drunk, cheat, crook and fraud.

Cutting copy

Always be on the lookout for repetition, verbiage [*too many words*] and excessive detail.

If copy is too long, first cut large chunks before you start to fiddle with detail.

If the news story has been properly constructed, you can cut it from the end – but check first that this is so.

Always check that a cut doesn't destroy the logic and coherence of a piece (by removing the first stage of an argument or the first reference to something).

Adding length

First check that nothing has been cut (for space reasons) at an earlier stage.

Make an extra paragraph if this will gain a line.

Look for a long sentence at the end of a paragraph and add a word or two to turn the line into something lengthier.

Turn common abbreviations into the long form.

Replace short words and expressions by long ones – without making the piece seem padded.

⑩ MINUTE TASK

Find two or three news pages from any recent daily newspaper.

Select three or four stories from those pages.

Apply the guidelines for sub-editing to these stories and decide whether the sub-editors have done a good job in each case or not. Give your reasons for judging as you do.

Headlines

The term headline means the words above a story which show what it is about. Writing headlines is one of the most difficult sub-editing tasks. You could even say that headline writing is an art. You can follow certain rules but like all arts headline writing cannot be reduced to a simple formula.

The headline is the window to the story and convinces the reader to read on. An excellent story is useless if it is not read.

What does a headline do?

Summarise the story for the reader: Most readers scan a newspaper and only read articles which interest them. The headline therefore serves to summarise the story.

Attract the reader's attention: Many newspapers are sold and read because someone has been attracted by a headline. Headlines of feature stories can be humorous or thought-provoking. Headlines for straight news stories are mostly quite direct and conventional.

Show the story's importance: The larger the headline, the more important the reader will expect the story to be. The size of a headline should therefore be related to the importance of the story during copy editing. If a story has a large, bold headline – 'War Declared' or even simply 'War!' are the classic examples – the editor is expecting the story to be read thoroughly.

Give prominence to the newspaper. Well-written headlines improve the look of a newspaper and give it an edge in its competition with rival papers. Good headlines break the monotony of looking at columns and columns of grey type. It is for this reason that most newspapers try to adopt a distinctive [*special*] look and design for their headlines.

How to write headlines

Here are the basic general guidelines that you should use for writing headlines:

Summarise: can you condense the lead paragraph into three or four words? A good headline creates images: 'Romeo' for a lover or 'Cop' for police officer.

Readability: always ask yourself the question: Does this headline make sense? Develop a good command of vocabulary and be able to use words that create interest, summarise the story and arouse your readers' curiosity.

Use synonyms: substitute short words for long ones, job replaces career; work replaces employment; test or probe is preferred to examination; make or build works better than manufacture. It is essential to have a good thesaurus handy so that you can choose the correct synonym.

Use the active voice:
Poor: Students warned by President (passive voice)
Better: President warns students

Use specific language, if space permits:
Poor: Player hurt in soccer match
Better. Player breaks leg in soccer tackle

Avoid using ambiguous or confusing language:

Poor: Strikers ignore salary plans from management

Better: Strikers ignore management's salary plans

Feature stories should have appropriate headlines:

Poor: Fraudsters rob Children's Fund

Better: Children fund fraudsters

Include a strong verb:

Poor: Rain causes damage

Better: Rain damages roads

Attribute opinion in headlines:

Poor: Smokers at risk, given scolding

Better: Scientist scolds smokers: you're at risk

Designing headlines

When writing headlines, you also need to consider visual design and space requirements. The designer has to choose whether to use all caps or caps and lower case. All caps headlines are difficult to read and are not often used.

The standard style is to capitalise the first letter of each word. In the contemporary choice only the first word and proper names are capitalised.

Student Leaders Meet Mandela (Standard style)
Student leaders meet Mandela (Contemporary style)

Most headlines are simply one line long and set flush left, in other words right next to the left-hand column.

Student

leaders

meet

Mandela

---

⑩ MINUTE TASK

Find some recent daily or weekly newspapers. Work with a partner if possible.

▶ Cut out four stories (two from the news pages and two from the feature pages). Cut off their headlines and give the stories to your partner without the headlines. Your partner should do the same for you. (If you are working alone, try not to look at the headlines before you cut - you could try folding them back quickly.)

▶ Write down what time you start, and how long the next task takes you.

▶ Try to write headlines for the four stories. Apply all the guidelines for writing and designing headlines in this chapter.

> ▶ Now compare your headlines with the original headlines in the newspaper. Decide whether yours are more effective or less effective than the original headlines and why. If you are working with a partner, discuss this together.

Suggested Reading

Nel, Francois. (2005). *Writing for the Media in Southern Africa.* 3rd ed. OUP.

17 Development journalism

Outcomes

At the end of this chapter, you will able to:
- Explain development communication styles.
- Compare authoritarian and social responsibility models.
- Understand the developmental approach to journalism.
- Consider the advantages and disadvantages of the developmental approach to journalism.

Introduction

This chapter is about the amount of freedom the media should have. Should they (or we, as the case may be) be able to publish anything, at any time? Or should there be controls and limits on this? In particular, how should journalists treat the government of the country? And should there be any difference in how journalists should treat the government of a developing country, who may feel that they need the support of the media to tackle problems of poverty?

Several theories have influenced the way the press in the third world, sometimes described as the developing world, has responded to questions like these. In this chapter, we will look at three: authoritarianism, social responsibility and development. We will also look briefly at the libertarian theory and see how this has affected the other three.

In groups discuss the following:

Do you think that the media should be able to publish anything at all, or should there be controls over what can be published? Why? (Or why not?) If you think there should be control, what kind of controls do you think there should be? Who should exercise control?

Do you think that the media should be basically supportive of the government of a country or not? Why? Why not?

Influencing the third world press

The authoritarian theory

This theory argues that the media are in the service of the state and therefore subordinate to [*under*] the state. Journalists should do nothing which could undermine [*harm*] established authority. Television, print, the internet and radio must support the interests of the state at all costs.

The authoritarian theory of the press has always been popular with French, British, Belgian, Portuguese and German colonial governments in Africa (and of course in other parts of the world as well.) This was also true in South Africa, which became a British colony piece by piece, region by region, starting in 1805; it remained a colony until 1910. Many people might say that the old whites-only National Party government which governed from 1948 to 1994 did its best to put colonial-era authoritarian theory into practice. Why? What makes the authoritarian view so popular?

Because the authoritarian view holds that the state is more important than the individual, it also says that the individual can only achieve his or her goals if he or she is under state control. However, different individuals within an authoritarian state have different status [*importance*]. Some individuals are important. For example, the leader of an authoritarian state may be one person or an entire élite [*high-class, leading*] group who dominate the society. This kind of leadership uses the mass media to help them dominate the rest of the society, that is, the media are used as instruments of social control.

In an authoritarian society, truth is limited and not all individuals can access it. Most people have to accept the truth – whatever that may be - of the dominant person or group and must conform [*fit in*] with this so-called truth in their thoughts and actions.

Definitions

Authoritarian theory

Libertarian theory

Social responsibility theory

To stay in power, the leadership of the authoritarian state will use any means of persuading or force. At different times we have seen examples of this in Africa - in South Africa, in Zimbabwe under both Ian Smith and Robert Mugabe, and Kenya. In this kind of society, the ruling élite use the press as an educational outlet and propaganda tool for controlling the people. They tolerate little or no criticism of the government. They do not see objectivity and truth as the most important principles guiding the media. Their view is that the interests of the state must come first and they, the ruling élite, must decide what these interests are.

Libertarian theory

The libertarian theory states that the media is not just an instrument of the state. Libertarians believe we are rational beings, able to distinguish right from wrong, and that society should create a forum, a free market of ideas, so that people can assess different ideas and then choose freely. Libertarians object to formal controls over what can be published in the press or other media on the grounds that if all ideas have an equal chance, truth will stand out and win. This led to the acceptance of basic human rights such as freedom of speech and freedom of the press.

According to libertarianism anyone with enough money and interest could publish a newspaper. But what if the media could use information not to inform the public but just to increase the circulation of the newspapers or please the advertisers? A new point of view developed which proposed that the press could not function with total freedom.

Social responsibility theory

The social responsibility theory was born in the middle of the 20th century (in other words, the 1900's). The social responsibility theory encourages objectivity. After the Second World War (1939 - 1945), social responsibility swept the world as a standard to seek.

This viewpoint emphasises the media's responsibility to society more than it emphasises freedom. It says that the media should work within certain moral and ethical limitations that are like obligations [*duties, responsibilities*] they must accept. As the former South African journalist Gordon Jackson says:

> These obligations are mainly to be met by setting high or professional standards of informativeness, truth, accuracy, objectivity and balance. (Jackson, 1993:218).

During the apartheid (the word comes from the Afrikaans term for separation or 'apartness') era in South Africa, a few editors started to reject the strongly authoritarian control which the National Party exerted over print media and radio. (Remember, there was no internet, no mobile phones and no private radio stations

What is my role as a journalist?

for much of the era and until 1976, there was no television in South Africa at all, so it was possible to control a lot of information.) These editors began to feel that social responsibility could be a better guide for them. Their group included editors of English-language papers, and much later, editors of alternative papers which relied on international funding rather than advertising to survive, and so were able to be far more aggressive in their coverage. Social responsibility was also practiced by some editors of privately owned Afrikaans newspapers. Most English-language papers in South Africa in the early days of the 21st century (the 2000's) have taken social responsibility as their guiding theory and try to make sure that different attitudes and directions of thought are all fully and properly represented. The media must see to it that the public has enough information to make necessary decisions.

Freedom remains important in this theory. It says that the media must guard against possible interference by the state and by any other pressure groups which could threaten the media's freedom. Control of the media should not be the job of an élite group in government. Rather, the journalists themselves must exercise this social responsibility, while working for newspapers that are mostly privately owned. Journalists working with this theory generally try to reflect public opinion fully but they may also sometimes try to form or guide public opinion.

This theory rejects the way authoritarians made control lawful or legal, so that the media had no freedom of choice. On the other hand, it also rejects the idea of no limits to what the media can publish, that is, where they publish whatever they like and whatever will make the most money.

The social responsibility theory has not been without criticism. For example, according to the American professor and author Herbert Altschull:

> ...the painful reality is that the term social responsibility is a term devoid of [*without*] meaning. Put another way, it is a term whose content is so vague that almost any meaning can be placed upon it. As such it too, serves the ultimate end of social control... Perhaps this is the reason one cannot find the term 'social responsibility' in the Oxford English Dictionary. (Altschull, 1984:302-303).

Although Altschull sees problems and faults in the idea of social responsibility, he suggests that it still has value for the working journalist. First, it gives journalists a positive feeling that they are working in the public interest and doing a public service. Secondly, it frees journalists from writing only material that will sell well. They need not be slaves to whatever others say is in the interest of their readers.

The journalist as a change agent

In the poverty-stricken developing world, which ranges from Brazil to Nigeria to Pakistan to China, the mass media has been considered as a contributor to national development and as a relatively inexpensive means of speeding up the process. Richard Shafer, a former journalist and scholar who has worked in the Philippines, India and Malaysia, says:

> With the failure of most Third World nations to experience impressive development after over three decades of intensive efforts, the various methods applied to bringing about national development have come under harsh criticism. The role of the mass media in national development has been challenged. Mass media have not only been charged with failing as an agent of development, but in fact are said to primarily support the political and economic status quo, particularly the unequal distribution of national resources and the concentration of power in the hands of the oppressive few.

The Belgium-born, France-based researcher into cultural imperialism, Armand Mattelart argues that not only has the mass media proven inefficient as an agent of development but it has acted to sustain imperialism as well as a technocracy perpetuating a state of dependence. This state of dependence operates through images and obsessions intended to impersonalise, fragment and demobilise audiences. In this argument, the media reinforce the existing class structure. The ability of the masses to effectively organise is undermined by media promotion of competitive and individualistic behaviour, with press freedom strongly linked to freedom of property. Thus media primarily represents the political and economic interests of the wealthy and powerful.

Development journalism

A journalist's development goals might be specific ones mandated by the government or by company policy directives. Richard Schafer, now based at the University of North Dakota in the USA, employs a minimalist [*basic*] interpretation of development communication:

> the fundamental issue is the intent of the journalist to promote development goals, as opposed to the journalist's intent to remain objective and neutral. (Schafer, 1991:11).

I would also add that the development journalist forsakes being critical, a vital component of practising good journalism. One of the difficulties that proponents of development journalism fail to confront is how to prevent a development-oriented press from becoming a tool of government repression and corruption. If the press is supporting government's officially-announced development goals and projects, can the press change to being adversarial if the situation demands it?

Definitions

Development journalism

Development communication

The development theory became popular in parts of Africa, South America and Asia for obvious reasons. However, there are some problems with the idea. The three terms – 'third world', 'undeveloped nations', or 'developing nations' – seem to imply inferiority and something less than best. They seem to rate the industry, commerce and political life of many countries poorly against the industry, commerce and political life within the Group of Eight (G8) countries (France, the United States, Britain, Germany, Japan, Italy, Canada and Russia). American academic Herbert Altschull believes there can be no single definition on which most people will agree. Because of this, and because the term 'development' seems to imply inferiority, Altschull prefers the term 'advancing journalism'. (Altschull, 1984:202).

Development theory sees the press as an instrument of social justice and a tool for achieving positive, helpful social change. In other words, the media should accept and carry out positive development tasks in line with nationally established policy. There is an assumption that the press is seen as a two-way communication, with equal importance assigned to the writer and the reader, to the broadcaster and the listener.

Sadly, in reality, things have not worked out in line with the theory. In much of Africa generally there has been pressure on journalists to align themselves with the political forces but in doing so they have lost their independence.

The most problematic part of the theory is the principle that the state can interfere with the media and use methods like censorship, state subsidies or direct control and restriction if it does so in order to advance development. In this way journalists can be severely hampered from reporting fully, fairly and independently. Also, we cannot be certain that development does get advanced in such situations.

Obviously, a new government in a developing country may well wish to adopt the development model. It leaves control of the media in the hands of the government if required and yet the media must still take responsibility if the government decides that the media are not meeting its wishes or that they are challenging the state. The government can intervene and apply whatever censure or control it deems necessary.

Zimbabwe, in southern Africa, is a good example of a government seeking to use the press to advance government policies, especially on economic, racial or ethnic issues. In one scandal, *The Zimbabwe Independent* reported in 2005 that the government's spy body, the Central Intelligence Organisation, had forcibly taken over the *Daily Mirror* and *Sunday Mirror* newspapers from their founder, Ibbo Mandaza. Newspapers in Zimbabwe which report critically find themselves unable to renew their registration. Journalists who report critically find they are unable to receive a mandatory press card, effectively silencing them.

Editors who accept this approach from governments must give up some editorial autonomy or independent control to government officials. In doing so, they give up the constitutional right of freedom of the press. Journalists in South Africa have had a very unhappy experience with government authoritarianism in the past. Therefore, they might not trust any government uncritically or risk their independence in the way that the development approach requires. Their fears about doing so are based on what they have experienced and observed. Journalists feel that the developmental approach extracts too high a price.

(20) MINUTE TASK

In groups, discuss which theory has the most to offer in your society and why? Analyse your local newspapers to identify the theory that informs their approach to journalism.

Advantages of development journalism

How can a journalist best use this approach? According to Narinder Aggarwala, a former Indian journalist now with the United Nations' Development Programme, a reporter's duty is to:

> ...critically examine, evaluate and report the relevance of a development project to national and local needs, the difference between a planned scheme and its actual implementation, and the difference between its impact on people as claimed by government officials, and as it actually is.

The most important claim made by fans of development journalism is its ability to 'nation build'. Respected Kenyan independence leader Tom Mboya (1930 - 1969) once told a gathering of journalists that the African press had to serve the cause of nation building. Since the press served an informative, critical and educational function, it had to be permitted to operate in freedom and to join with African leaders in their nation building efforts. Mboya, who was later assassinated in what some saw as a political cover-up, charged that if editors and journalists did not act accordingly, they should be charged as traitors. Many were.

Pitfalls of development journalism

The pitfalls of the development approach are many. First, the press becomes less critical and eventually is forced to give up its 'watchdog' role in society. As it continually serves and tries to please the current government, the media loses its critical edge and becomes nothing more than another government mouthpiece.

When this happens it opens the way for a more hostile, fierce and aggressive underground or alternative press with a strong anti-government approach.

The most dangerous pitfall is the fact that the press gives up its right to question and demand accountability from the democratically-elected government of the day. As the press tries to promote the government and the common good, it can start to lose sight of the individual and the individual's human rights. In Richard Schafer's words:

> A developmental press has come to be equated with one in which the government exercises tight control and prevents freedom of expression, all in the name of noble ends.

Government censorship happens in many countries. In 1975, India's first female prime minister, Indira Gandhi, imposed strict censorship in the world's most populous democracy. But despite this censorship, Richard Schafer notes:

> ...many Indian journalists sneaked into their news columns words, phrases and even sentences and paragraphs that escaped the attention of the censors and that conveyed concealed meanings to knowledgeable readers.

There are many other examples of editors and journalists resisting censorship. The message for any government is that it will have to struggle to keep control of the media for very long because it will need huge resources to police this system. What starts out as an idea to promote economic, social and personal development seems to turn into a nightmare.

(10) MINUTE TASK

In groups, discuss the advantages and disadvantages of development journalism. Can you list examples of countries or media institutions which have supported developmental journalism, only to turn against it later? Can you list media organisations - perhaps government websites, municipal newsletters, state broadcasters or state-run news agencies - which would be considered examples of developmental journalism?

18 Investigative journalism

Outcomes

By the end of this chapter, you will able to:

▶ Explain why there is a need for investigative journalism.

▶ Summarise the obstacles and difficulties in obtaining information.

▶ Identify the need for follow-ups.

Introduction

There have been many famous examples of investigative journalism. The most famous one internationally is probably the investigative work done by *Washington Post* reporters Carl Bernstein and Bob Woodward, when they exposed the corruption of American president Richard Nixon and his administration in the Watergate affair in the USA in the 1970s. In South Africa there are a number of excellent examples of great investigative journalism: in the *Rand Daily Mail* newspaper, since shut down, there was Mervyn Rees and Chris Day's investigation of the Information Scandal, also in the 1970s, when the whites-only National Party secretly diverted public funds to start pro-government newspapers. Another example is the ex-SABC journalist Jacques Pauw, executive producer of the weekly television show *Special Assignment,* and his work on the apartheid-era Death Squads.

Most journalism students probably want to become investigative or political journalists. They feel that there is excitement and romance in this kind of journalism. People see investigative journalists as the 'cowboys' of the journalism world.

They seem to be the 'do-gooders' or heroes, who fight evil and put things right. Investigative journalism also seems to be the one area where a journalist can win awards and the admiration of the public.

Sadly, the real life of the investigative journalist is very different. Their work can be the most difficult and the loneliest form of journalism there is. Days, weeks and even years of tracking down leads and building up a story may prove fruitless. Investigative journalists may have to fight for editorial support. Also people often threaten them and try to pressure them not to continue or publish as the truth is not welcome to many powerful people. There are easier ways to make a living.

15 MINUTE TASK

In pairs, find an investigative story, a story that has dug up the truth about corruption or injustice in a newspaper known for its investigative journalism. Read the report carefully. Look for clues to any of the following:

Who did the reporter have to find and interview? How did this person or these people respond? What documents did the reporter have to find? What places did the reporter have to go to, and how? What threats or danger did the reporter have to face? How long do you think he or she (or the team of reporters) had to work on the story? What additional costs (outside their normal operating budget) must the newspaper have paid including legal advice?

What is investigative journalism?

Investigative journalism is the quest for truth. It is the job of bringing hidden facts to light and then finding out how they connect. The investigative journalist must spend more time on digging for facts and less time on looking for an interesting story angle. Investigative journalism gives the journalist a social responsibility. The public expects these journalists to examine people like government officials and important public issues critically [*very searchingly, evaluating them carefully*]. One kind of task for these journalists is to show where the achievements of government programmes do not match the claims and promises of government officials. For example, in South Africa, the claims of government officials on reducing crime or HIV/Aids generally do not correspond with what is observed and experienced by the average citizen.

Where do investigative journalists get their information? Information normally comes from sources within the organisation where the wrong or misdeed under investigation is being committed. Previously, we discussed such sources. There are a number of leakers [*sources*] of information such as someone who uses a leak to spite or embarrass another person or party. Perhaps you will remember the whistle-blower, who may be a civil servant who leaks information when he or she feels that something bad cannot be or is not being made right in the usual way. Such leakers are sometimes willing to make a public statement and be named, although they may risk losing their jobs.

The need for investigative journalism

Without investigative journalists, the world would be a far more corrupt place where truth and democracy would battle to exist. The influential German sociologist Ferdinand Tönnies (1855 - 1936) wrote:

> The press is the real instrument of public opinion, a weapon and a tool in the hands of those who know how to use it; it possesses universal power as the dreaded critic of events and changes in social conditions. It is comparable and in some respects, superior to the material power which the states possess through their armies, their treasuries and their bureaucratic civil service.

According to American author Ray Mungo, co-founder of the Liberation News Service, a leftist alternative news service which ran from 1967 to 1981:

> Facts are less important than truth and the two are far from equivalent... for cold facts are nearly always boring and may even distort the truth, but Truth is the highest achievement of human expression.

What is my social responsibility?

You could say that the investigative journalist has a social responsibility to dig up evidence of corruption and wrongdoing. He or she must publish such evidence so that the perpetrators can be brought to justice either in a court of law or in the court of public opinion. The investigative journalist must report the facts with complete accuracy and must therefore dig behind the facts to understand their context. In apartheid-era [*segregated*] South Africa, the Johannesburg-based *Rand Daily Mail* newspaper championed human rights – including the coverage of the 1976 Soweto uprising by high school studentsm which altered the country's history before the newspaper closed in 1985. *Vrye Weekblad*, edited by Max du Preez, the *New Nation* newspaper under Zwelakhe Sisulu and the *Weekly Mail* under Anton Harber were all weekly newspapers known for their investigative reporting – if not necessarily for their business acumen.

The influential South African columnist and journalist Percy Qoboza (1938 – 1988) edited *The World* newspaper (before it was banned in 1977 and he was thrown into jail without charges for six months). Qoboza, who returned from exile to edit the *City Press* weekly newspaper in the 1980s, said:

The Mail was not just another paper; it was an institution, a courageous crusader for justice and peace. Far ahead of white public opinion, it gave us the courage to go on.

Constraints on investigative journalism

Not all newspapers do investigative reporting. In South Africa and many other countries, investigative reporting is the exception rather than the rule. The weekly *Mail & Guardian* and to some extent *The Sunday Times* and some private radio stations stand out as organisations that are prepared to do what it takes to unearth wrong doing and corruption. The Independent Group, which controls many of the English-language dailies in Johannesburg, Cape Town and Durban, also have a small investigative unit. But a smart reporter will find ways to work investigative reporting into many of the stories assigned. You don't have to be defined as an investigative reporter in order to be doing investigative reporting!

You will find that even bold investigative journalists face many obstacles before their investigative story reaches the public. Even their own courage and convictions can weaken in the face of pressure and lack of support.

The cost of investigative journalism: This is the most costly form of journalism. It takes time and money and few newspapers can afford the expense. Can you imagine the cost to a newspaper (in salaries and other costs) of an investigation which takes more than a few days?

Manpower: Most newspapers are under-staffed and cannot afford to have one of their best journalists tied up on one story for a long time.

Failure of courage or the lack of will from the editor to publish the story: Editors may fear the legal and social repercussions [*results and responses*] that they will face once the story breaks. Investigative reporting upsets people and normally the people who get the most upset are important and powerful. It takes courage to stand up to such people and cope with the pressure they may apply. Quite often investigative reporters receive threats on their lives and even their families' lives. The government might use other forms of intimidation: during the 1970s Watergate affair, the US government threatened the *Washington Post's* lucrative [*profitable*] television licenses. The *Mail & Guardian* newspaper has had last-minute court applications trying to ban publication of the newspaper – which is distributed on a Friday – late on a Thursday.

Threat by advertisers to withdraw advertising: This usually only works where the newspaper is under severe financial difficulties and has strong competition. In the magazine world, however, it is another story. Women's magazines are threatened by cosmetic companies on a fairly regular basis.

Simply trying to convince your editor that the story deserves to be covered:
To do effective investigative journalism you need resources, time and money. Your editor must therefore be willing to support you and publish the story. Editors are unlikely to do this for a new journalist who has not yet proved reliable or accurate. And good investigative journalists often grow to realise that they will never move up the newspaper hierarchy because of their willingness to tackle powerful figures and forces.

Can you add any further constraints on investigative journalism?

The question of objectivity

Investigative reporting, among all the genres of journalism, poses questions about fact and value most decidedly, for it is the combination of righteous anger with the hardest of facts and the result of rigorous journalistic diligence.

The claim to objectivity in journalism depends on the belief that 'what is true' can be represented in story form. Journalists must reveal that violations of the law are 'not just technically wrong but terribly wrong' – a moral outrage. To do this they sometimes use the rhetorical device of irony [*a literary device in which there is a gap or incongruity between what a speaker or a writer says and and what has happened*]. Gordon Jackson resigned from South Africa's *To the Point* news magazine in 1979 after learning that it had been covertly [*secretly*] funded by the minority whites-only government in the information scandal discussed earlier. Now a respected professor, author and academic in the USA, Jackson says investigative reporting shows the violation of the law "to be not only illegal or unethical but an ironic turn of events in which any expectations of honesty or justice were bound to be cruelly betrayed. Irony transfigures the conventions of journalistic objectivity into a morally charged vocabulary for condemnation of the villains to whom we have foolishly entrusted our public affairs." (Jackson, 1993:71).

Investigative journalism reports the very hardest of hard facts. In addressing social problems, it does so by reporting specific instances of those problems: crime reports suppressed by the police department for example, or sexual assaults in the county jail. Verifying the facts in each and every one of these instances is the moment when investigative journalists most fully capitalise on the opportunity to go beyond the limits of daily reporting to confront reality more directly and completely. It is also the moment when journalists most vigorously insist that facts can and must be separated from values.

Investigative journalists point to the hard work of verification as the justification for accepting their published claims but often tussle [*wrestle*] with the question of whether their hard work has indeed produced a reason that is good enough. Does the evidence produced justify the credibility of their claims?

Occasionally, journalists suggest that the concept of objectivity is passé, or out of date and old-fashioned. The code of ethics adopted in 1996 by the US-based

Is this the truth?

Is this right?

Are the facts verified?

Society of Professional Journalists (www.spj.org) makes no mention of objectivity – a provocative departure from the previous code, revised only nine years earlier, which cited objectivity alongside accuracy as a professional standard. In its purest usage, the term suggested that journalism was so utterly disinterested [*neutral*] as to be transparent. The report was to be virtually the thing itself, unrefracted [*unaltered*] by the mind of the reporter. This, according to the book *Custodians of Culture: Investigative Journalism and Public Virtue*, involved a hopelessly naïve [*innocent*] notion from the beginning. (Ettema and Glasser, 1998:9).

⏱ **10** MINUTE **TASK**

In groups, discuss whether or not objectivity in journalism is a realistic goal? If you decide that it is not a realistic goal, is it still a goal worth pursuing anyhow?

Doing the investigation

Most investigations begin after a tip-off from a source, or because the journalist gets a hunch [*a strong suspicion or guess*]. There has to be some basis for beginning an investigation.

After receiving a tip-off or when following up on a hunch, it is best to do some preliminary investigations before forming a hypothesis. The hypothesis is a statement that you believe to be true. It will then be proved or disproved by your investigations. For example, your hypothesis could be: 'New houses are being allocated to the friends of government officials.' Making a hypothesis allows you to focus on the main point of what you want to investigate and removes any confusion about what is being investigated. At the same time, you should ask the question: Who cares? If you decide that no-one cares about the issue, you are probably wasting your time investigating it.

> "Keep an open mind"

Although you intend to prove your hypothesis, you must be open to the possibility that you may not be able to do so. Maintain an open mind and do not ignore evidence that may disprove your hypothesis.

The first part of the investigation, which should only take a day or two, is to determine whether or not you have a chance to prove your hypothesis. Are you able to obtain the information you need to prove your hypothesis?

Once you have decided that you can prove your hypothesis, you have to ask the question: Is there a story here? If your answer is yes you need to ask the question: Can I get this story?

Difficulties in obtaining information

Poor planning can lead to difficulties in your investigation. Good investigative journalism requires efficient planning and organisation. Sometimes you obtain so much information that you are unable to 'see the wood for the trees' [*the facts*]. It is important to keep asking: Does the information obtained help prove or disprove your suspicions? Draw up an action plan and carry it out. Do not get sidetracked on issues that are not relevant to the hypothesis. Remember, investigative journalism costs money.

Difficulties can arise if you risk the confidentiality of your sources. If this happens, and even if the source only suspects that it will happen, you may lose a valuable source as well as your own credibility. Remember to keep your source's names confidential so that you protect your sources even if your notes or files are subpoenaed by the courts as evidence.

Ethical difficulties can arise when you dig for information. Remember the International Federation of Journalists' code of conduct, which states: A journalist shall obtain information, photographs and illustrations only by straightforward means. The use of other means can be justified only by the overriding considerations of the public interest. The journalist is entitled to exercise a personal conscientious objection to the use of such means.

One of the biggest difficulties in obtaining information is in dealing with witnesses who are reluctant to talk. This reluctance often comes from their fear of losing their jobs. How can we get reluctant people to talk, bearing in mind that they have a right not to talk? You can use positive reinforcement statements such as: "It would be in the best interests of others if you could confirm this information..." or "Wouldn't you prefer it if something like this didn't happen to others...?" Sometimes this approach will encourage interviewee participation.

Checking facts

Accuracy is important in all reporting and it is absolutely essential to investigative reporting. Inaccurate reporting can lead to legal action and embarrassment which can detract from the good work the investigation has achieved. Those who are implicated in wrong-doing only require one small loophole to destroy the good work done.

Remember the golden rule: Check your facts, then check them again; because there is no excuse for error. During the Watergate investigations in the USA, the *Washington Post* newspaper checked information with two independent sources before they published any allegation. Many South African media have a similar policy.

Facts may indeed be a mixture of what can be discovered and what can be deduced [*worked out from the evidence available*]. But this must not become 'what can be invented.'

Following up

It is not always possible to know what reaction an investigative report will receive. Many people want to trust government and public figures, after all, that is why they voted them into power. But this is not something that is only an issue in politics. Unethical religious leaders, dubious business activities such as insider trading, shady sportsmen such as the late Hansie Cronjé, found after investigation to be taking bribes to swing international cricket matches, soccer officials found bribing referees and sexual harassment within non-governmental organisations have all been exposed in South Africa.

Even when there is overwhelming evidence against a public figure, the public may want to give the perpetrator the benefit of the doubt. For the investigative journalist, this can be a bitter pill to swallow. You may not be prepared for the overall public reaction to your exposé. If the response is negative you may not feel motivated to continue with your investigation. However, an important part of being a journalist who brings unwelcome news to the public is being able to handle the flak [*criticism*].

On the other hand, once a story has broken you are likely to receive new leads, particularly from people who were too scared to talk before. It is now important to keep up the pressure and also to sustain your motivation and your editor's motivation too. Editors often lose interest once the initial excitement of a story has died down, although there may be important follow-up stories, which pursue the story even when it has fallen from its key position on the front page, that can still be done.

⑤ MINUTE TASK

Look at the investigative story you chose earlier in this chapter. In pairs consider the following:
- Was this story closed by the end or did it need more follow-up? What aspects needed follow up? (Apply the above test to several other investigative stories too.)
- In your opinion, what obstacles might the reporter face in following up this particular story/stories?

Suggested Reading

Altschull, Herbert J. (1984). *Agents of Power*. Longman.

Ettema, James, and Glasser, Theodore. (1998). *Custodians of Conscience – Investigative Journalism and Public Virtue*. Columbia University Press.

Jackson, Gordon S. (1993). *Breaking story: The South African Press*. Westview Press.

Nel, Francois. (2005). *Writing for the Media in Southern Africa*. 3rd ed. OUP.

19 Online journalism

chapter

Outcomes

At the end of this chapter, you will able to:

▶ Define online journalism.

▶ Explain how online differs from other forms of journalism.

▶ Demonstrate what produces an online news story.

▶ Research how you can start publishing online.

▶ Use the internet to research stories for both online and offline media.

Introduction

A couple of decades ago the internet was nothing more than a military and academic network. Today, it influences society in a number of profound ways. Internet banking and e-commerce have changed the way products and services are purchased. E-mail (electronic mail) has meant that communication across the globe can occur in a matter of seconds and the world wide web has become an instant publishing platform for millions of individuals and companies.

This has changed how people access news. Researchers estimate that nearly one out of every three people in the USA use the internet regularly to get news. Internet usage is on the rise in China, India, Africa and Latin America. (Pew Reseach Center, 2007).

Yet news has traditionally been dominated by television, radio and print media. As internet access becomes more commonplace for people across the globe, more readers will be asking the question, "Why wait for the next newspaper edition or news bulletin when you can get the latest news online, instantly?"

Online journalism can offer both the immediacy of broadcast and the depth of print. Online journalism also provides opportunities for a new element that none of the traditional platforms for journalism can: interactivity. Now readers can 'choose the news' they want to access more than ever before. As a result, many traditional media are becoming far more interactive as well.

What is online journalism?

Is online journalism basically traditional journalism dressed in new 'digital' clothes?

This was the criticism of early news websites that copied or 'shoveled' a print publication's content onto the internet with little or no alteration. Today, news websites are producing more and more original content for the web as they discover the unique potential of the internet.

Online journalism is multimedia-driven, interactive journalism, uniquely produced for internet users. Multi-media means your online piece should be a combination of media (text plus sound, video, audio, photos and graphics). Your online piece should allow users to select the parts of the story they want to experience, and the story should be produced with the world wide web in mind.

Remember that online journalists cover the same areas and issues (known as 'beats') as normal reporters.

⑩ MINUTE TASK

In groups, consider which of the scenarios below is the best example of 'online journalism':

▶ A plain text article from the Reuters news agency at www.reuters.com.
▶ An investigative piece on the *Mail & Guardian Online* website on drug smuggling with linked video and sound clips and a discussion area where users can post their comments.
▶ A CNN video news broadcast that is streamed directly to your computer.

Online journalism as a primary news source

Often, people have regarded online news websites as more of a supplement to traditional media outlets rather than a primary source for news. As online journalism upstages traditional media forms in big news events more and more, people are seeing the value of news that is immediate, substantial and interactive.

The 1995-1996 sex scandal between then American President Bill Clinton and young White House intern Monica Lewinsky was one of the first examples of online journalism beating the mainstream media to a story. Controversial internet columnist Matt Drudge was the first to break news of an inquiry into Clinton's extramarital affair on his Drudge Report website (www.drudgereport.com) in 1998. The mainstream media followed suit soon afterwards. When the independent counsel Kenneth Starr's report investigating the affair was released in 1998 (Online journalism, nd), news websites again were ahead of the pack, putting the full document online hours before newspapers could print it. At one point www.CNN.com, the website of the Cable News Network television channel, was recording over 300 000 'hits' or page retrievals, per minute, although this isn't the best indicator of internet activity. About 20 million Americans, out of a population of more than 300 million, had seen the report online within 48 hours of its release.

Another example of the power of online journalism came after the capture of longterm Iraqi dictator Saddam Hussein by his former allies, the USA, in December 2003. The news of Hussein's capture after evading USA troops for nearly nine months broke early on a Sunday morning in America, the worst possible time for newspapers which had already printed and were distributing their Sunday editions. While television and radio broadcasters did not suffer as much from the timing of the event, major newspapers had to rely on their web presence to get the story out in text. They did more than this, offering video, timelines, essays, interactive graphics and multimedia biographies, all before the Monday papers hit the newsstands. (Online news, nd).

Producing an online package

Online journalists, like all journalists, first have to source material and then package it for publication. In previous chapters you have learned how to identify a story, find sources, conduct interviews and finally write a piece. Online journalists do exactly the same but at each of these stages they look for opportunities to capture multimedia and consider interactive [*a system or computer programme which is designed to involve the user in the exchange of information*] options for their piece.

Online journalists use digital cameras and digital voice recorders to capture video and audio clips for their stories, normally without the assistance of a crew. This practice has been referred to as 'backpack journalism', because the journalist needs to carry and use a few media devices in order to complete his or her story. Some critics say backpack journalism results in a journalist who is a 'jack of all trades and master of none' (a cliché meaning someone competent in many fields but not particularly brilliant at any). However, advances in technology have meant the job is getting easier.

Today, we don't really need backpacks because these devices have become small and multi-functional. Most digital cameras have a video function and some cellphones allow you to take photos, record sound bites and capture video clips. The journalist then downloads the information onto a computer using a data-transfer cable or wireless technology. The daily Afrikaans newspaper *Die Burger*, part of the News24 group, has been a leader in this regard.

After the material has been loaded onto the newsroom's computer system, it has to be packaged for the internet. Some newsrooms have specialist multimedia producers to help combine these elements for the internet. Others require journalists to package the work themselves.

Immediacy is one of online journalism's greatest assets and this should be exploited to maximum effect. The production of an online news story should be done at speed.

Definitions

Hyperlinks

Deep-linking

Hyperlinks

Online journalists use hyperlinks (sometimes simply called a link) to graft together their story into a multimedia, interactive form of story-telling. When a user clicks a hyperlink (normally visible as a blue, underlined word), he or she is taken to another part of the story on the website, or even to another relevant website.

In this way, a journalist can layer his or her story, providing the important information in the anchor piece and then allowing the user to access deeper layers through links to further reading and multimedia clips located on other pages.

Deep-linking is a term used to describe linking to a specific page within another website from within the story. It is a controversial method because deep-links allow the user to bypass the front page of a website (with its advertising) and link directly to content developed by another newsroom. You should check your website's policy before you deep-link to content off your site.

Multi-media

The internet is a powerful way to distribute information because computers can display different media elements on the same platform. Videos, sound clips, photos, animations and interactive graphics can all be played on a typical home or work or internet café computer, although people with dial-up modems can not download interactive news as easily as people with broadband access. Online journalists rely on these multimedia elements to enhance their stories.

Which multimedia elements are suitable for my story?

It is your job, as an online journalist, to harness these multimedia elements and use their strengths to make your piece more engaging and credible than one that is built out of only one media type.

It's important to consider the suitability of the media. You shouldn't link to a video of a rambling political speech when you can simply paraphrase it in the text. But sometimes your writing will be enhanced by a multi-media clip. If you describe how a politician left a meeting in a fury, it would probably add to the users' experience for them to see a video of the politician storming out and slamming the door. If you're describing the unusual call of an endangered bird, it might be a good idea to serve an audio clip of the way it sounds.

However, while using different types of media, you should always try to accommodate users whose computers might not have the facility to hear or watch certain elements. Important information should always be in the text, with multimedia enhancing the written version of events.

Different multimedia elements include:

Photos
Sound clips
Video clips
Flash presentations
A discussion area or voting poll
Source documents such as transcripts or court records
Simulations and games
Quizzes

Below are a few examples of common multimedia elements and how you can use them to liven up your story.

Photos: Photos are as vital in an online piece as they are in a newspaper. They bring colour and balance to a page full of text. Because space is limited on a computer screen, photos often have to be heavily cropped and resized, with a link to the full picture. Photos do not have to be high resolution on the internet, whereas they do have to be high-resolution for newspapers.

Sound clip: Nearly every story has sounds that can be captured and put online. You can record a speech or an interview and edit the key sound bites and upload them, or just provide clips of the subject you're writing about – like the sounds of war, a storm, or the chants of football fans.

Video clip: Video is visually powerful but it is also slow to download if you don't have a fast connection to the internet. Keep your video clips short (less than three minutes) and to the point. Video clips are suitable when they convey action and expression. They shouldn't be used when the subject matter is relatively dull or lacking in visual impact (here, your writing must energise the piece).

Interactive feature: Interactive features are usually developed for in-depth pieces on themes like the Soccer World Cup or the drug trade and encourage users to interact with the website. Photo galleries, user polls and forums are examples of interactive features. Timelines are also popular interactive features. After 2001 when commercial planes were hijacked by terrorists and flown into the World Trade Centre towers and the Pentagon military headquarters in the USA,

CNN.com ran an interactive timeline showing users when and where events of what is known as 9/11 (the ninth day of the eleventh month, September) took place. Normally interactive features are quite time-consuming to create but provide greater depth and interactivity to your story.

> ## 🔟 MINUTE TASK
>
> In pairs, select a substantial news story or investigative feature from a local newspaper. List possible multimedia options for that piece and underline the words you believe could be used as hyperlinks to background articles, research and further reading on the subject.

Blogging

Definitions

Blogging

Blogger

To publish online, all you need is an internet connection, your journalistic skill and preferably a digital camera with a movie function. It will be to your advantage to learn while employed in an online newsroom. But if you're itching [*longing or aching*] to get started there's no reason why you can't start publishing yourself, through a web log, better known as a blog. Blogs are online journals where people offer personal anecdotes and opinions and links to interesting material on the internet. The entries are stored in a chronological order, much like a diary.

Often the personal accounts of bloggers are more interesting than the links themselves, as in the case of the 'Baghdad Blogger' Salam Pax, a Baghdad local who gave a first-hand account of the build-up to the 2003 invasion and war in Iraq. His site, http://dear_raed.blogspot.com, soon recorded millions of hits as people found his work often more insightful than the mainstream media. In the words of New York Times writer, Peter Maass, Pax was "the Anne Frank of the war ... and its Elvis" (Maass, n.d).

While blogs aren't regarded as examples of true journalism because they remain unedited, many online journalists use them as live opinion columns that they update regularly and through which their readership can comment on their work.

Popular blogging sites include www.blogspot.com and www.xanga.com. After a simple, free registration process, you can begin writing anything from a personal journal to a campus news site.

Internet–aided reporting

The internet is not only a publishing platform, it is also a wonderful research tool. However, while the internet offers an incredible repository of information on a diverse range of issues, it is also a minefield of misinformation and what are known as 'red herrings', or misleading information. Journalists face the challenge of finding – quickly – information that is both accurate and relevant to their topic.

How to search

The easiest way to find information on the world wide web is to use a search engine. Search engines such as google.com and yahoo.com allow users to search millions of web pages in a matter of seconds through a keyword search. Users simply enter in a keyword or phrase, click search and then view the results of their search. Often searching can be frustrating because there are many websites that don't have the information they say they do.

Definitions

Search engine

It's important to limit your search range by using multiple keywords. If you're looking for information on the 2008 Olympics, don't just type the word 'Olympics'. Your results will contain every page on the internet containing the word Olympics, including any references to Olympic Games of the past, the history of the games and so on. Rather type: Olympics 2008 Beijing (or in some search engines: Olympics AND 2008 AND Beijing). You will narrow your search to pages that contain all three keywords. If you're looking for more specific information on an event in the Olympics – like tennis – then add this keyword to your search as well: Olympics 2008 Beijing tennis.

Sometimes searching for a specific phrase is more appropriate. If you want to know who wrote: "To be or not to be, that is the question," then enclose the whole sentence in quotation marks when you type it into the search window. Only pages containing the whole phrase will be returned in the results. (The same technique is used by editors to make sure you are not lifting (borrowing) someone else's quotes.) Quotation marks are also important when searching names. If you're conducting research on a newsmaker, make sure their full name is encased in quotation marks. A search for American pop singer Michael Jackson will return every page with these two words on it, even if they don't necessarily fall together. So if you search for Michael Jackson without inserting inverted commas around the name, you will receive pages which might contain something like "Michael Douglas and Jesse Jackson attended the function". A search for "Michael Jackson" – not Michael Jackson without quotation marks - will bring you pages containing the full name.

Sometimes, journalists use search engines to check the spelling of a word or name. The thinking is that if you type in the name in a variety of ways the number of returned pages will help you to decide which is the correct spelling. If you type in 'Michael Jackson', Google will return about two million hits, but if you type in 'Micheal Jackson', it will return only about 44 000 hits. Thus, you can conclude that 'Michael Jackson' is indeed the correct spelling.

However, you should beware this technique. Sometimes wrong spellings return the same number or even more results than correct ones – like milenium versus millennium or Barbara Streisand versus Barbra Streisand. Fortunately, there are also good dictionaries online.

Other tools

News websites:

Google's news search engine (news.google.com) is a great tool for journalists looking for a variety of perspectives on a certain issue. By reading and referencing old news stories, journalists can ensure that their current story has background and context and that it is sufficiently different from other stories on the same topic. The website allows a user to search for news items across thousands of news websites and the results are clustered into news themes. Thus, it's easy to compare three sources on the same news event.

Online dictionaries and thesauruses

Online dictionaries and thesauruses are broader and sometimes more accurate than your word-processor spell-check. Beware, however of Americanisms creeping into your results (unless of course you're writing for an American publication). Some online dictionaries offer results from multiple dictionaries. Make sure the one you're referring to agrees with your style guide.

E-mail

Online journalists use e-mail interviews to get a diverse range of sources in the shortest possible time. Mailing off your questions to sources and waiting for their response has its pros and cons. While some sources may prefer communicating by e-mail, their responses might not be the ones you were looking for – and the absence of an immediate follow-up question means it could take you longer to get the results you want.

After sending the e-mail, you should follow up with a phone call, if possible, to inform your source that you've sent it. The source is more likely to respond knowing there is a human behind the e-mail. You should also acknowledge that you've received e-mails. Once you've received an e-mail answering questions from a source, you may want to phone the source with a few follow-up questions.

Pick out a recent news event that has made international headlines. Using news.google.com or a similar news search engine, compare the coverage of the event by three different news providers. Did they report the facts in the same way? Can you detect differing biases in the content? Do any of them use multimedia and does this enhance or diminish the quality of their coverage?

Conclusion

Online journalism has a bright future because technology is on its side. Each year more people connect to the internet and spend longer on it than the previous year. Millions of people already log in to the internet to receive the news, and in coming years, this trend is likely to grow remarkably. While you might not see a career for yourself in online journalism now, you should be preparing for the journalism of tomorrow, today.

Sources and reading list

Adam, S. (1993). *Notes Towards a Definition of Journalism: Understanding an Old Craft as an Art Form*. St Petersburg: The Poynter Institute for Media Studies.

Altschull, H. J. (1984). *Agents of Power*. New York: Longmans.

Argyle (2000). In N. Lacey *Narrative and Genre: Key Concepts in Media Studies*. London: McMillan Press.

Bardwell and Thompson (2000). In N. Lacey *Narrative and Genre: Key Concepts in Media Studies*. London: McMillan Press.

Bignell, J. (2002). *Media Semiotics: an Introduction*. Manchester: Manchester University Press.

Blackman, L. and Walkerdine, V. (2001). *Mass Hysteria; Critical Psychology and Media Studies*. Basingstoke: Palgrave.

Branston, G and Stafford, R. (1999). *The Media Student's Book* 2nd ed. London: Routledge.

Brooks, Brian et al, The Missouri Group, (1992). *News Reporting and Writing* 4th ed. New York: St Martins Press.

Carey, J. (1997). The communications revolution and the professional communicator. In E.S. Munson and C.A. Warren (eds.), *James Carey: A critical reader*. Minneapolis: University of Minnesota Press.

Craig, A. P. et al. (1994). *Conceptual Dictionary*. Cape Town: Juta.

Croteau, D. and Hoynes, W. (2003). *Media Society: Industries, Images, and Audiences*. London: Sage Publications.

Ettema, J. S and Glasser, T, L. (1998). *Custodians of Conscience: Investigative Journalism and Public Virtue*, New York: Columbia University Press.

Femia, J.V. (1987). *Gramsci's Political Thought-Hegemony, Consciousness, and the Revolutionary Process*. Oxford: Clarendon Press.

Ferry, J. et al (1999). *Approaches to Media Literacy*, London: M.E.Sharp.

Garrison, B. (1999). *Professional Feature Writing* 3rd ed. New Jersey: Lawrence Erlbaum Associates.

Greer, Graham (1999). *A New Introduction to Journalism*. Cape Town: Juta.

Gudykunst, W.B. Mody, B. (eds), (2002). *Handbook of International and Intercultural Communication* 2nd ed, London: Sage Publications.

Habermas, J. (1993). *Justification and Application: Remarks on Discourse Ethics*. Cambridge, MA: MIT Press.

Hackett, R.A. and Zhao, Y. (1998). *Sustaining Democracy? Journalism and the Politics of Objectivity*. Toronto: Garamond Press.

Harris, G. (1993). *Journalism Media Manual: Practical Newspaper Reporting*, 2nd ed. Oxford, Focal Press.

Hay, V. (1990). *The Essential Feature*. New York: Columbia University Press.

Hicks, W. and Holmes, T. (2002). *Subediting for Journalists.* New York: Routledge.

Holsti, K.J. (1987). *The Dividing Discipline: Hegemony and Diversity in International Theory.* London: Allen & Unwin.

Hulteng, J. L. (1981). *Playing it Straight.* Connecticut: The Globe Pequot Press.

Hursthouse, Rosalind (1999). *On Virtue Ethics.* Oxford: Oxford University Press.

Kieran, Matthew (1997), Objectivity, Impartiality and Good Journalism. In Matthew Kieran (ed) *Media Ethics.* London: Routledge.

Jackson, G. S. (1993) *Breaking Story: the South African Press.* Boulder: Westview Press.

Klaidman, S. and Beauchamp, T. (1987) *The Virtuous Journalist.* New York: Oxford University Press.

Knowlton, S.R. and Parsons, P.R. (1994) *The Journalist's Moral Compass.* London: Praeger.

Kultgen, J. (1988) *Ethics and Professionalism: Parentalism in the Caring Life.* Pennsylvania: University of Pennsylvania Press.

Lacey, N. (2000). *Narrative and Genre: Key Concepts in Media Studies.* London: McMillan Press Ltd.

Lambeth, Edmund (1992). *Committed Journalism: An Ethic for the Profession.* Bloomington: Indiana University Press.

Lievrouw, L.A. and Livingstone, S. (2002). *Handbook of New Media.* London: Sage Publications.

Livingstone, S. (2002). *Young People and New Media,* London: Sage Publications.

Louw, E. (2001). *The Media and Cultural Production.* London: Sage Publications.

Lucas M. Oosthuizen (1996). *Introduction to Communication.* Cape Town: Juta.

McLuhan, M. in Lambeth, E. (1992) *Committed Journalism: An Ethic for the Profession.* Indiana: Indiana University Press.

MacIntyre, A. (1981). *After Virtue: A Study in Moral Theory.* London: Duckworth.

Martindale, C. (1993). *Pluralizing Journalism Education.* London: Greenwood Press,

McQuail, D. (1997). *Audience Analysis.* London: Sage Publications.

Medsger, B. (1996). *Winds of Change.* Washington: Freedom Forum.

Nel, F, (1994). *Writing for the Media.* Halfway House: Southern Book Publishers.

Nel, F, (2005). *Writing for the Media.* 3rd ed. Cape Town Oxford University Press.

Potter, W.J. (2001). *Media Literacy* 2nd ed. London: Sage Publications.

Ramsden, P. (1992). *Learning to Teach in Higher Education.* London: Routledge.

Rayner, P. et al (2001). *Media Studies: The Essential Introduction.* London: Routledge.

Rowlands, D. (1979). *Better Ways to Teach Journalism.* Cardiff: Thompson Foundation.

Ruddock, A. (2001). *Understanding Audiences,* London: Sage Publications.

Sawant, P. B. (1998). *Press as Leader of the Society.* New Delhi: Indian Institute of Mass Communication.

Schafer, R. (1991). *Journalists for Change: Development Communication for a Free Press.* Philippine: Philippine Press Institute.

Silverblatt, A. (2001). *Media Literacy.* London: Praeger.

Skamania: Indiana's Super Steelhead (1985). *Sports Afield,* January. Cited in Hay, V. (1990): *The Essential Feature.* New York: Columbia University Press.

Taylor, C. (1985). *Philosophy and the Human Sciences: Philosophical Papers 2.* New York: Cambridge University Press.

Taylor, C. (1989). *Sources of the Self: The Making of Modern Identity.* Cambridge, MA: Cambridge University Press.

Taylor, C. (1995). *Philosophical Arguments.* Cambridge, MA: Harvard University Press.

Watson, J. (1996). *Dictionary of Media Communication Studies.* London: Hodder Arnold.

Zelizer, B. (1997). Journalists as Interpretive Communities. In Dan Berkowitz (ed.). *Social Meanings of News.* Thousand Oaks: Sage.

Periodical articles and websites

Adam, S. (2001). The education of journalists. *Journalism,* 2(3): pp 315-339

Addley, E (2003). A girl's best friend? *Guardian* 10 March.

Benjamin, J. The 15 hottest spots for fast love. Published on. <http://www.magazines.ivillage.com/cosmopolitan>, accessed 4 August 2003 at 10h30.

Coldstream, P. (1997). No title to paper. In *Proceedings of the 5th UNESCO Consultation on Higher Education.* Paris, 1997.

De Beer, A.S. and Steyn, E. (2002). Sanef's 2002 South African national journalism skills audit: An introduction and the Sanef report regarding the media industry. *Ecquid Novi* 23(1): pp 11-86

De Groot, S. (2002). Home Alone. *Fair Lady,* 28 August .

Donegan, Lawrence, "J-Lo and Ben's £30m turkey is carved up", *The Observer,* Sunday August 3, 2003.

International Federation of Journalists *Principles on the Conduct of Journalists.* <http:/www.ifj.org>

Lovgren, Stefan, <http://www.nationalgeographic.com>, accessed 4 August 03 at 10h54.

Maass, P. <http://slate.msn.com/id/2083847>, accessed 6 July 2004.

Online Journalism and the Starr Investigation. Available at: <http://www.slate.msn.com>, accessed July 6 2004.

Online News Scores Coup on Hussein's Capture as Papers Are Caught Napping. <http://www.slate.msn.com>, accessed 6 July 2004.

Parrish, J (1997). What it's really like to be struck by lightning. *Maxim* magazine (South Africa), April.

People magazine (South Africa), (2002). Unbylined, no headline, June 14.

Pew Research Center Biennial News Consumption Survey. *Online News Audience Larger, More Diverse.* <http://www.people-press.org/reports/display.php3?PageID=835>, accessed 6 July 2004.

Pinnock, D. (2002). *Getaway* magazine, May.

Powell, M and Garcia, M (2004). *Washington Post,* Friday, May 14: C01.

Revill, J (2004). Killer virus hits past drug users. *Observer,* 4 July. <http://www.guardian.co.uk/medicine/story/0,11381,1253765,00.html>, accessed 4 July 2004.

Roach, John, <http://www.nationalgeographic.com>, accessed 4 August 2003 at 10h50.

Schaller, W. (1990). Are virtues no more than dispositions to obey moral rules? *Philosophy,* 20.

Schudson, M. (2001). The objectivity norm in American journalism. *Journalism* 2(2).

Schuller, T. Opinion – We seem unable to truly grasp the nettle of lifelong learning. *Guardian Education,* Tuesday April 22, 2003.

Singer, J. (2003). Who are these guys? The online challenge to the notion of journalistic professionalism? *Journalism* 4(2).

Slater, N. (2003). Summer Serendipity. *Observer,* August 3. <http://www.shopping.guardian.co.uk/food/story/0,1587,1011145,00.html>

Swanton, C. (2001). A Virtue Ethical Account of Right Action, *Ethics* 112, pp. 38.

Turkington, T. (1999) Meaning hidden in San rock art is still a mystery. *Sunday World,* 8 August.

Windschuttle, K. (1997). The poverty of media theory. *Equid Novi* 18(1).

Index

5 W's and 1H 74, 167, 171, 178

A

abbreviations 189
accuracy 104-6, 123-5
adverbs 187
advertising 16, 21, 40, 59, 87, 93
    corporate 91
age, referring to 143
alliteration 215
Althusser, Louis 49
ambiguity 60, 184, 187
analogy 12, 14
anchorage 64
anticlimax 216
anti-narrative 84
apostrophe 189
argument 2
    conclusion of 11
    evaluation of 7
    indirect 4
Aristotle 27
assonance 215
assumption 14
audience 88-100
    attitude 97
    background 96
    behaviour 36
    breakdown 93-4
    communications environment 97
    concern 97
    demographic profile 97
    ever-shifting 99
    identification 92-3
    interest level 97
    mass 90
    psychological profile 97
    /sender relationship, alternative
    models of 98
    stage of development 97
    theory 94-5
        alternative models 98-9
        expectancy-value 98
        hypodermic needle 98-9
        participant 98
        spectator 98

    transmission 98
    reception 96-7

B

background information 142
backpack journalism, *see* online journalism
Barthes, Roland 77-8
bathos 216
bias 107
Bill of Rights 32
blogging, *see* online journalism
body language, *see* non-verbal codes
bomb under the table method 83
Branzburg versus Hayes 30
byline 164

C

censorship 32, 51, 89, 232, 234
claims 9-11
clarity, establishment of 6
cliché 175, 214-5
cliff-hanger 83
code of conduct 22-3, 28, 113-4
    international 101, 113-4
codes 58, 65
    colour 65-6
    dress 65
    non-verbal 66-7
coercive strategies 16
colloquial language 176
commas 147, 178, 189
communication
    emotive appeal of 38
    interference, 41
    interpersonal 39, 43
    intrapersonal 39
    mass 39, 42
    model 43
        American mass 43, 91
        interpersonal 43
        mass 43
    process of 38
computer-assisted reporting 139
connotation 53, 37
conscience 25
content 57

copy
    adding length to 223
    cutting 223
copy-edit 220-2
    how to 222-3

D

dateline 164
dates 175
deduction 12
deep linking 246
demographics 94
denotation 53, 67
deontology 27
development journalism 227-34
advantages of 233
journalist as change agent 230-1
pitfalls 233-4
theory
    authoritarian 228-9
    libertarian 229
    social responsibility 229
docu-soap 85

E

editing 219-26
e-mail, *see* online journalism
emotion, removal of 7
enigma 77
ethical dilemma 28
ethics 18-33, 101-115
    code of, *see* code of conduct
    context 21
    definition of 24
    journalism and public life 20
    spin 20
    virtue 27-8
    work context 19
euphemism 216

F

fair comment 104
fairness, role of 103-4, 123-5
fallacy 14-5
    prejudice 15
    slippery slope 15
    straw man 15
feature

composite interview 194
how-to 192
human interest 195
humour column 196
interview 193-4
investigative 195
lead 207
news 191
obituary 193
packaging of 210
pro and con 194
profile 193
quiz 195
review 197
seasonal 194
structure of 201
    champagne glass structure 201-2
    circular 202
    stack of blocks 202
    Wall Street Journal 201-2
travel 196
trend 192
types of 191
writing 190-218
    process of 198-200, 202-18
    researching for 200-1
feedback 40, 91-2
Film and Publications Amendment Bill 32
First Amendment 30-1
flashbacks 83
foreign words 186
Foucault, Michel 50
freedom of the press 108-9

G

Gates, Bill 49
genre 81-7
    as a critical tool 82
    audience and 85
    narrative and, relationship between 83
geodemographics 94
geographics 93-4
Gramsci, Antonio 47-9, 95

H

headlines 223-6
    design of 225
    role of 224
    writing 224-5

hegemony 95-6
homage 86
house style 220
hyperbole 215
hyperlinks, *see* online journalism

I

iconography 82
ideology 44-51
idioms 175, 185-9
images
    analysis of 53
    angle 56
    depth of field 56
    dimension and shape 55
    distance 56
    form 55
    framing 55
    mobile frames 56
    reading 55
impartiality 107
induction 13
influence 109-10
information economy 91
innuendo 218
interference
    audience 41
    channel 41
    communicator 41
International Code of Conduct 101, 113-4
internet, *see* online journalism
interpretation of world 53
intertextuality 86
interviewing 149-62
    approaches to 156
    censoring 161
    conducting 155-6
    controlling 158-60
    establishing confidence 157
    formulating questions for 152-4
    importance of 149-50
    preparation and planning for 150-1, 155-6
    recording 161-2
    research for 151
    techniques 160
    time management 152
    whom 140
inverted pyramid 74-5, 167

investigative journalism 235-42
    checking facts 241
    constraints on 238-9
    following up 241-2
    information, difficulties in obtaining 240-1
    investigating 240
    need for 237-8
    objectivity in 239-40
irony 217-8

J

jargon 186

L

labels 145
lead 164, 166
    anecdotal 207
    delayed identification lead 173
    descriptive 207
    elements of 169
    feature 207
    guidelines for writing 169-70
    immediate identification lead 172
    mixture 209
    multiple elements lead 173
    question 209
    quote 208
    scenario 208
    sentence styles 167
    statement 207
    summary lead 167, 172, 174
        different types of 172
        with angle 171
libel 102-3, 114, 221, 223
linear presentation 83

M

manipulation 109-10
marketing 87
Marx, Karl 47
McLuhan, Marshall 42, 59
meaning
    contact 59
    context of message 58
    production of 58
media
    as change agent 110-11

influence 36

frequent messages and themes in 71

literacy 34-43

representation 52-71

text 60

medium as message 42, 59

message   60

metaphor 68, 213-4

metonymy 68, 216-7

mimicry 86

mise-en-scène 57

lighting 57

setting 58

subject 57

mode of address 78

modernism 79

moral fact 26

morality 24

multi-media 246

Murdoch, Rupert 49

N

names

first 141

spelling of 141

narrative 72-80

genre and, relationship between 83

construction 74

fairy tale 76

simplest 75

news

definition 117

sources 128-48

story 165

traditional tests of 118-21

value, assessment of 121-2

writing 163-81

basic rules 164, 174

newspaper language 182-9

newsworthiness 166

conflict 119

enjoyment 120

human interest 120

impact/consequence 118

novelty/curiosity 119

prominence 118

proximity/relevance 118

sex 120

timeliness 118

non-sequitur 216

notes 146

numbers   175

nut graph 173-4

O

objectivity 104-6, 123

in investigative journalism 239-40

off and on the record 141

online journalism 243-51

as a primary news source 244

backpack journalism 245-6

blogging 248

deep linking 246

e-mail 250

hyperlinks 246

multi-media 246

news websites   250

online dictionaries 250

producing an online package 245-6

searching the internet 249

onomatopoeia 215

oxymoron 217

P

paradox 217

parallel action 83

parody 86

pastiche   86

personification 215

persuasive strategies 16

Plato 27, 89, 105

postmodernism 79

power relations 16

preferred meaning   64

prejudice fallacy, see fallacy

premise 4-6

implied 5

pronouns 177

propaganda 51, 130, 229

Propp, Vladimir 76

psychographics 94

public

entitities 91

relations 1-2

trust   21, 108, 110

pun 217

punctuation 189

Q

qualifiers 177
quotes
    punctuation of 146-7
    recording of 146
    repetition of 146
    use of 145-7

R

reality 52
reception theory, *see* audience
representation 38
research 138
reviews 87

S

sarcasm 217
satire 218
Schiller, Herb 91
seductive strategies 17
semiotics 61
    criticism of 69
sentence length 184
signified 64-5
signifier 64-5
signs 37, 61
    arbitrary 63
    different types of 62
    iconic 63
    indexical 63-4
    polysemic 64
    symbolic 62
simile 213
slang 93, 176, 185-6
slippery slope fallacy, *see* fallacy
social class 94
sources
    acknowledging 143
    anonymous 135
    contact 132
    developing 131-7
    evaluating 136
    informant 132
    introducing 142
    leakers 136-7
        animus 137
        ego 137
        goodwill 137
        plant 136
        policy 137
        trial balloon 137
        true 136
        whistleblower 137
    protection of 148
    referring to 142
    respect for 147-8
    revealing 28-32
    talking to 140
    tipster 132
stereotyping 69-71
story and plot 73
straw man fallacy, *see* fallacy
structuralism 79
style, basic rules of 188-9
sub-edit, *see* copy-edit
subjectivity 123, 143-4
symbols 37
synecdoche 216

T

tautology 176
teleology 27
tenses 177
thirld-world press 228
Todorov, Tzvetan 76
tone 186
transition sentences 194, 202, 204
truth 104-6

U

utilitarianism 27

V

virtue ethics, *see* ethics
voice-over 78

W

Wall Street Journal method 75
women, media and 70, 111-3
word
    order 187
    use of right 184-5